Exploring metalworking

basic fundamentals

by
JOHN R. WALKER

Bel Air High School
Bel Air, Maryland

South Holland, Illinois
THE GOODHEART-WILLCOX CO., Inc.
Publishers

Library of Congress Cataloging in Publication Data

Walker, John R
  Exploring metalworking.

  Bibliography: p.
  Includes index.
  1. Metal-work.   I. Title.
TT205.W33   1976   684'.09   75—31808
ISBN 0—87006—199—2

INTRODUCTION

EXPLORING METALWORKING is a first course which teaches the fundamentals of working with metal, using both hand and power tools.

EXPLORING METALWORKING is written in easy-to-understand language. It contains an abundance of illustrations. Extra color is used to clarify details, and to illustrate major processes in steel making.

EXPLORING METALWORKING provides constructional details on carefully selected projects, also alternate designs and design variations which will help you design your own projects. The text tells and shows how to organize and operate a small manufacturing business in your school shop; how to mass produce items with proven student appeal.

Using selected material, EXPLORING METALWORKING may be used to present a six, nine, eighteen, or thirty six weeks metalworking program.

This text emphasizes the important place metals occupy in our everyday lives; it explores metalworking career opportunities.

John R. Walker

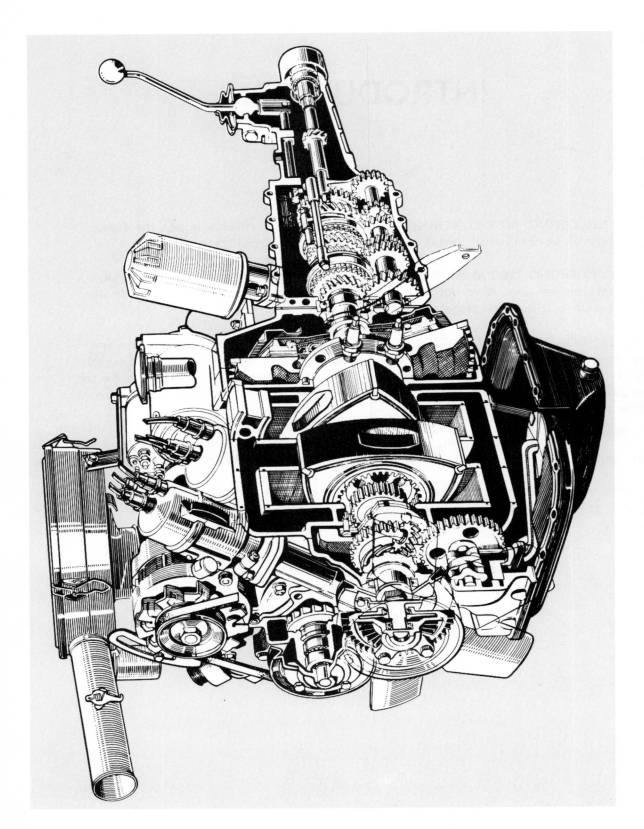

Industry illustration. This Wankel rotary engine was built using many different metals and metalworking techniques. Two triangular shaped rotors turn in a figure eight-shaped chamber and operate on the conventional four-stroke cycle of intake, compression, power, and exhaust. Conventional pistons, valves, and connecting rods are eliminated.

CONTENTS

Fig. 1-1. The metals used to construct aircraft must be light and strong.

Unit 1
THE METALS WE USE

The metals we use have many properties. Some of them, like aluminum, magnesium and titanium, are strong and light enough to be used to manufacture aircraft, Fig. 1-1.

Metals that withstand tremendous heat are needed for rocket and jet engines, Fig. 1-2. The fuel (uranium) that powers nuclear submarines, Fig. 1-3, is a metal. Only a few pounds are needed to power a submarine around the world.

Fig. 1-3. A metal fuel (uranium) powers this nuclear submarine. Only a few pounds are needed to propel it around the world. (General Dynamics Corp., Electric Boat Div.)

Fig. 1-2. The metal in the engines of this space vehicle must be able to withstand great heat without failing. (North American Aviation, Inc.)

Fig. 1-4. Many different kinds of metal must be used in high performance racing cars. (Champion Spark Plug Co.)

The racing car, Fig. 1-4, makes use of many kinds of metals. Each metal is selected for its special qualities - strength, lightness, ability to dissipate heat, rigidity, etc.

How many applications can YOU name that need metals with special qualities?

Hundreds of metals and alloys are used by industry. The small internal combustion engine, Fig. 1-5, that powers a model plane, car or boat, costs only a few dollars. However, its construction makes use of more than a dozen different metals.

How Metals are Classified

The metals you will use in your shop work are the same as those used by industry. They are available in a multitude of shapes and sizes, Fig. 1-6.

For identification purposes, metals fall into several categories:

BASE METALS are pure metals like gold, copper, lead, tin, etc. They contain no other metals.

ALLOYS are combinations of several metals fused (blended) together while the metals are in a molten state. For example, brass is an alloy of copper and zinc.

Fig. 1-5. Metals mined in all parts of the world (steel, aluminum, copper, brass, chrome, lead, tin, zinc, etc.) are needed to manufacture the various parts of the engine.

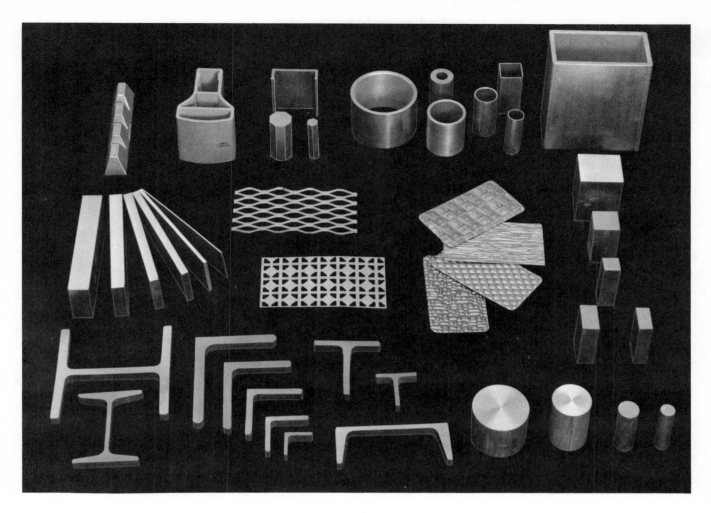

Fig. 1-6. A few of the hundreds of different metal shapes available to industry.

Metals are further classified as:

FERROUS METALS, alloys which contain iron as a major element in their composition. Steel is a ferrous metal.

NONFERROUS METALS are metals which contain no iron except in very small quantities as impurities. Metals like aluminum, brass and tin are nonferrous metals.

Metals Used in School Laboratories

The ferrous metals include carbon steels, tin plate and galvanized sheet. Carbon steels are classified according to the amount of carbon they contain. The carbon is measured in PERCENTAGE or in POINTS (100 points equal 1 percent).

A. LOW CARBON STEELS do not contain enough carbon to be hardened (less than 0.30 percent - 30 points). They are rela-

tively soft and are often called MILD STEEL.

As they are easy to machine, weld and form, they have many applications in bench metal work, Fig. 1-7. Mild steels

Fig. 1-7. This trivet is made from mild steel.

9

are available as rods, bars, strips and sheets.

B. MEDIUM CARBON STEELS contain 0.30 to 0.60 percent carbon (30 to 60 points). This type of steel is excellent for projects that require machining, Fig. 1-8.

Fig. 1-8. Medium carbon steel machines easily and was used to make this small lathe.

C. HIGH CARBON STEELS are sometimes called TOOL STEELS. They contain 0.60 to 1.00 percent carbon. These steels are used to make tools because they can be

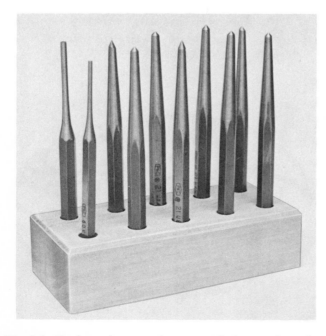

Fig. 1-9. Tools such as punches are made from tool steel.

heat treated (the controlled heating and cooling of the metal to bring about certain desirable characteristics such as hardness and toughness), Fig. 1-9.

Hot finished steel has a characteristic black coating (oxide). When cold finished, the steel has a surface that is smooth with no trace of the black scale, Fig. 1-10. TIN PLATE ("tin cans" are made from it) is a mild steel sheet to which a tin coating has been applied. GALVANIZED SHEET is a mild steel sheet on which a coating of zinc has been deposited.

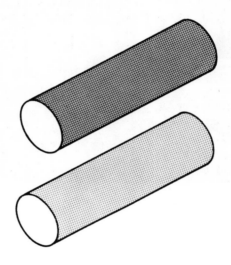

Fig. 1-10. Hot finish steel (above) has a characteristic black coating while cold finished steel (below) has a surface that is smooth with no trace of the black scale.

A recent addition is a mild steel sheet with a vinyl coating that can be cut, shaped, formed and joined like other steel sheets. Various colors and textured finishes are available.

Many nonferrous metals are also used in the school laboratory.

Aluminum

Aluminum is a term used to identify an entire family of metals (there are over 100 different aluminum alloys). They range from almost pure aluminum which is very soft, to an aluminum alloy tough enough to be used as armor plate, Fig. 1-11.

Fig. 1-11. Many kinds of aluminum were employed when this business jet was manufactured. (Pan American Airways)

Aluminum is similar to silver in color, but has a slight bluish tinge. It is lighter in weight than steel. Aluminum melts at approximately 1220 deg. F., and can be fabricated using regular metalworking techniques.

Aluminum can be purchased as foil, sheet, rod, bar, plate, wire and tubing.

Brass

Brass is an alloy of copper and zinc. The color varies from a reddish bronze to a yellowish gold depending upon the percentage of zinc it contains. Brass is easy to shape, cut, etch, solder, electroplate and color chemically. Brass is used extensively in art metal work, Fig. 1-12.

Brass is available in soft, half-hard, three-quarter and hard tempers.

*Fig. 1-12. This mug was made from brass. Note how the planished (hammered) surface enhances its appearance.
(H. J. Kauffman)*

Copper

Copper is an easily worked metal. It is reddish brown in color and melts at 1981 deg. F. The metal takes a brilliant polish, but like brass, it must be sprayed with a clear lacquer if the finish is to be retained. Copper is worked like brass.

Much copper is used in electric motors like those in the model car shown in Fig. 1-13.

Fig. 1-13. Much copper is used in the electric motors of these model racing cars.

Nickel Silver

Nickel silver or German silver is used as a substitute for silver in the manufacture of inexpensive jewelry, Fig. 1-15. It is a copper base alloy with varying quantities of nickel and zinc. It works much like brass but is a bit more brittle.

Fig. 1-14. Modern pewter contains NO lead and can be used, like this tankard, to serve food and drink. (Shirley Pewter Shop — Williamsburg)

Fig. 1-16. Sterling silver has outstanding working characteristics. It was used to make this porringer.

Pewter

Modern pewter or Britannia metal is an alloy of tin (91 percent), copper (1 1/2 percent) and antimony (7 1/2 percent). When polished, it has a fine silvery sheen. Modern pewter DOES NOT contain lead and can be used to serve food and drink, Fig. 1-14. Pewter is easy to work, but considerable skill is needed to join it properly.

Sterling Silver

Silver combined with a small amount of copper (7 1/2 percent) is known as sterling silver. When polished, it is shiny silvery-white in color. Sterling silver has outstanding working characteristics. It can be readily shaped and formed, and it hard solders well, Fig. 1-16.

Fig. 1-15. Inexpensive jewelry is made from German silver (nickel silver).

Shapes of Metals We Use

Metals are produced in many shapes and sizes. A few of the standard metal shapes are illustrated in Fig. 1-17.

The chart, Fig. 1-18, presents several sheet metals commonly found in the school laboratory; how they are measured and how they are purchased.

SHAPES		LENGTH	HOW MEASURED	*HOW PURCHASED	OTHER
	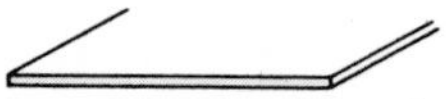 Sheet less than 1/4'' thick	to 144''	Thickness x width widths to 72''	Weight, foot or piece	Available in coils of much longer lengths
	Plate more than 1/4'' thick	to 20'	Thickness x width	Weight, foot or piece	
	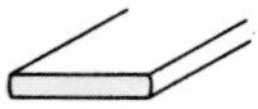 Band	to 20'	Thickness x width	Weight, or piece	Mild steel with oxide coating
	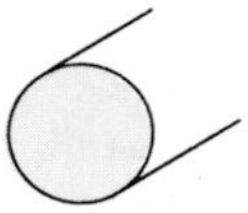 Rod	12 to 20'	Diameter	Weight, foot or piece	Hot rolled steel to 20' length – cold finished steel to 12' length – steel drill rod 36''
	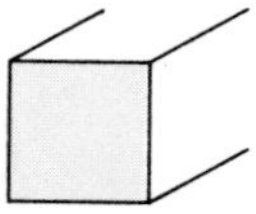 Square	12 to 20'	Width	Weight, foot or piece	
	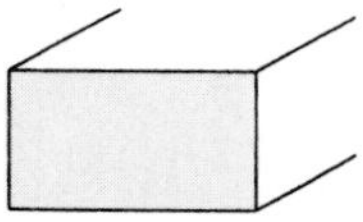 Flats	Hot rolled 20-22' Cold finished	Thickness x width	Weight, foot or piece	
	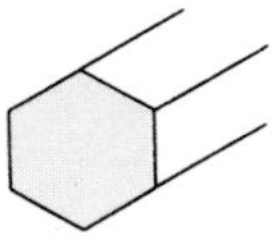 Hexagon	12 to 20'	Distance across flats	Weight, foot or piece	
	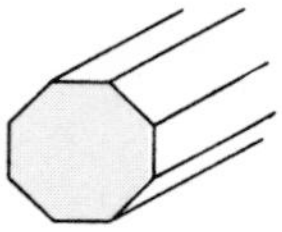 Octagon	12 to 20'	Distance across flats	Weight, foot or piece	
	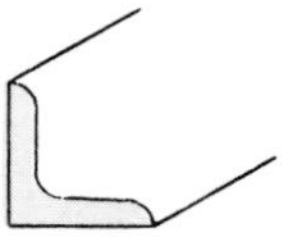 Angle	Lengths to 40'	Leg length x leg length x thickness of legs	Weight, foot or piece	
	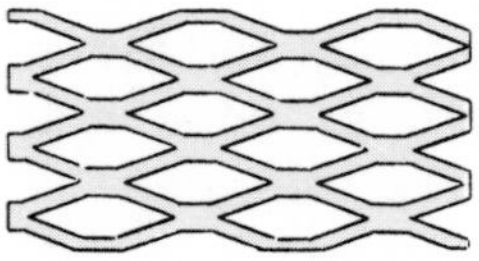 Expanded Sheet	to 96''	Gauge number (U. S. Standard)	36 x 96'' and size of openings	Metal is pierced and expanded (stretched) to diamond shape; also available rolled to thickness after it has been expanded
	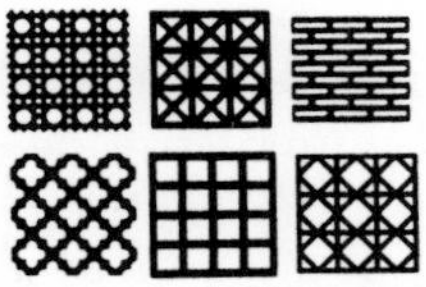 Perforated Sheet	to 96''	Gauge number (U. S. Standard)	30 x 36'' 36 x 48'' 36 x 96''	Design is cut in sheet. Many designs available.

* Charge made for cutting to other than standard lengths.

Fig. 1-17. Metals we use – the shapes available, how they are measured, purchased and some of their characteristics.

MATERIAL	HOW MEASURED	HOW PURCHASED	CHARACTERISTICS
Sheet (less than 1/4" thick)			
COPPER	Gauge number (Brown & Sharp & Amer. Std.)	24 x 96" sheet or 12 or 18" by lineal feet on roll	Pure metal
BRASS	Gauge number (B & S and Amer. Std.)	24 x 76" sheet or 12 or 18" by lineal feet on roll	Alloy of copper & zinc
ALUMINUM	Decimal	24 x 72" sheet or 12 or 18" by lineal feet on roll	Available as commercially pure metal or alloyed for strength, hardness, & ductility
GALVANIZED STEEL	Gauge number (U. S. Std.)	24 x 96" sheet	Mild steel sheet with zinc plating, also available with zinc coating that is part of sheet
BLACK ANNEALED STEEL SHEET	Gauge number (U. S. Std.)	24 x 96" sheet	Mild steel with oxide coating-hot rolled
COLD ROLLED STEEL SHEET	Gauge number (U. S. Std.)	24 x 96" sheet	Oxide removed and cold rolled to final thickness
TIN PLATE	Gauge number (U. S. Std.)	20 x 28" sheet 56 or 112 to pkg	Mild steel with tin coating
NICKEL SILVER	Gauge number (Brown & Sharp)	6 or 12" wide by lineal sheet	Copper 50%, zinc 30%, nickel 20%

Fig. 1-18. Metals we use — how they are measured, how they are purchased and some of their characteristics.

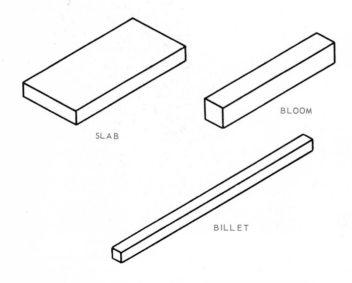

SLAB

BLOOM

BILLET

Have you ever wondered how metal is shaped? Many shapes start as ingots which are heated and passed through rolling mills where they are shaped into semifinished products called slabs, blooms or billets, Fig. 1-19. These pass on through other rolling mills, where rolls of different types and sizes fashion them into plates, sheets, rods and bars. The rolling process not only shapes the metal but also makes it tougher and stronger.

Sheet stock is made by passing a metal slab between rolls, Fig. 1-20, until the desired thickness is obtained. As the slab becomes thinner, its length increases. The slab can be made wider by passing it crosswise through the rolls.

Fig. 1-19. Most metal shapes start as slabs, blooms or billets.

The largest ship ever built in the United States, a 255,000-deadweight-ton tanker, is edged out of the building basin at Bethlehem Steel's Sparrows Point, Maryland shipyard. The 1,100-ft. vessel was taken in tow to an outfitting pier for completion.   (Bethlehem Steel Corp.)

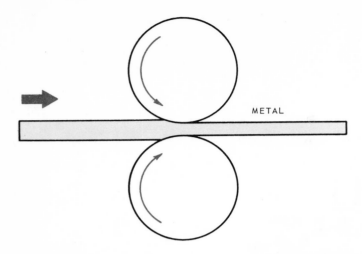

Fig. 1-20. *How sheet metal and plate is rolled to thickness.*

Bar, rod and other forms are also shaped by rolling. However, the process differs from the rolling of sheet in that the rolls are grooved to produce the specific shape desired. The rolling process starts with a billet which is gradually worked into the required shape. See Fig. 1-21.

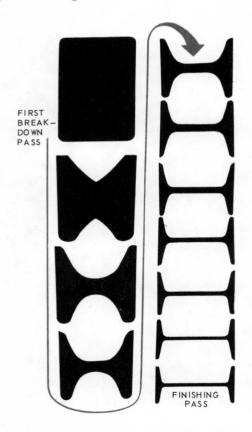

FIRST BREAK-DOWN PASS

FINISHING PASS

Fig. 1-21. *When rolling a structural shape the rolling process starts with a billet which is gradually worked into the required shape.*

Wire is made by a drawing process, Fig. 1-22. In wire drawing, the end of the rod is pointed and pulled through dies that reduce its diameter until the required wire diameter is reached.

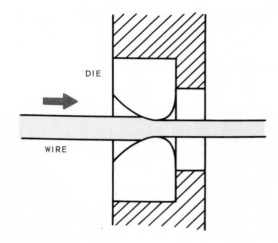

DIE

WIRE

Fig. 1-22. *Wire is made by pulling a rod through dies that reduce its diameter to the required size.*

Seamless tubing is produced as shown in Fig. 1-23. A cylinder is cupped at one end and drawn through well lubricated dies that reduces its diameter and increases its length.

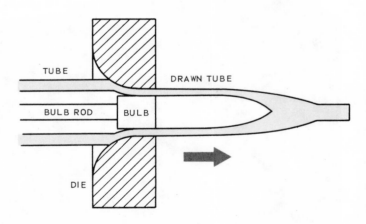

TUBE

DRAWN TUBE

BULB ROD

BULB

DIE

Fig. 1-23. *Seamless tubing is made by the drawing process.*

Seamless tubing can also be made by the extrusion process, Fig. 1-24. Pressure is employed to force the metal through a die of the required shape and size. The extrusion process is also employed to produce other complex metal shapes, Fig. 1-25.

MAJOR PROCESSES
IN THE STEEL INDUSTRY

It is hard to imagine a person who does not use many items made of steel every day of his life. Steel is a taken-for-granted material upon which people depend for such gigantic things as buildings and bridges and for such little things as safety pins and paper clips. Although steel is familiar in our daily lives, and is also found on the utmost frontiers of science, few people understand the full extent of human effort required to produce it. The following flow charts, courtesy of American Iron and Steel Institute, show some of the things that men must do to produce the metal steel in its first solid form.

The United States is the world's largest producer of raw steel. Markets in this country support some 200 companies operating steelmaking or finishing facilities in 38 states. More than half of these companies make raw steel and finish it themselves. Others buy semifinished steel from which they make bars, wire and wire products, hot and cold rolled sheets, plates, pipe and tubing and a wide variety of other products that the public seldom sees because they are further manufactured by the steel industry's customers.

The modern steel industry is concerned not only with producing huge tonnage of steel; it is also a partner with individuals, communities and government working for ecological (having to do with relations between living things and surrounding conditions) improvement. Each of the processes which follow has air and water quality control equipment designed into it.

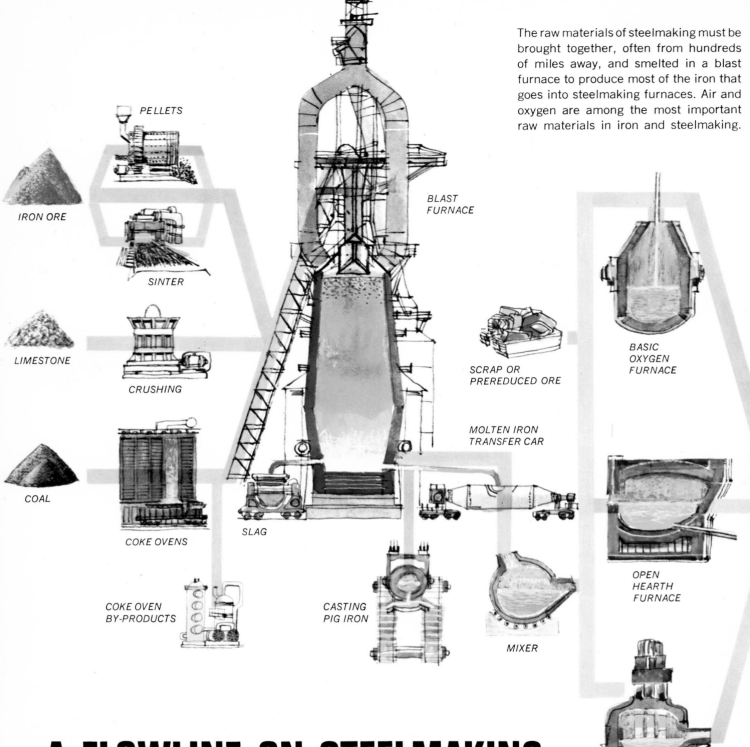

PELLETS

IRON ORE

SINTER

LIMESTONE

CRUSHING

COAL

COKE OVENS

COKE OVEN
BY-PRODUCTS

SLAG

CASTING
PIG IRON

BLAST
FURNACE

SCRAP OR
PREREDUCED ORE

MOLTEN IRON
TRANSFER CAR

MIXER

BASIC
OXYGEN
FURNACE

OPEN
HEARTH
FURNACE

ELECTRIC
FURNACE

The raw materials of steelmaking must be brought together, often from hundreds of miles away, and smelted in a blast furnace to produce most of the iron that goes into steelmaking furnaces. Air and oxygen are among the most important raw materials in iron and steelmaking.

A FLOWLINE ON STEELMAKING

This is a simplified road map through the complex world of steelmaking. Each stop along the routes from raw materials to mill products contained in this chart can itself be charted. From this overall view, one major point emerges: Many operations—involving much equipment and large numbers of men—are required to produce civilization's principal and least expensive metal.

Molten steel must solidify before it can be made into finished products by the industry's rolling mills and forging presses. The metal is usually formed first at high temperature, after which it may be cold-formed into additional products.

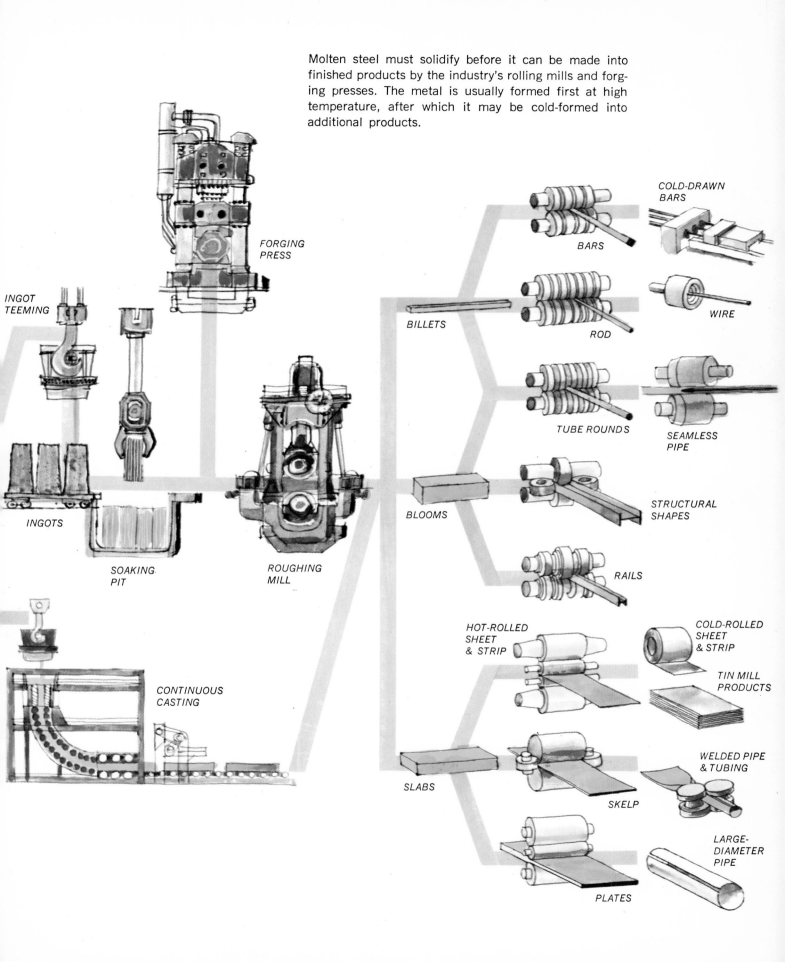

FORGING PRESS

INGOT TEEMING

INGOTS

SOAKING PIT

ROUGHING MILL

CONTINUOUS CASTING

BILLETS

BLOOMS

SLABS

BARS

COLD-DRAWN BARS

ROD

WIRE

TUBE ROUNDS

SEAMLESS PIPE

STRUCTURAL SHAPES

RAILS

HOT-ROLLED SHEET & STRIP

COLD-ROLLED SHEET & STRIP

TIN MILL PRODUCTS

SKELP

WELDED PIPE & TUBING

PLATES

LARGE-DIAMETER PIPE

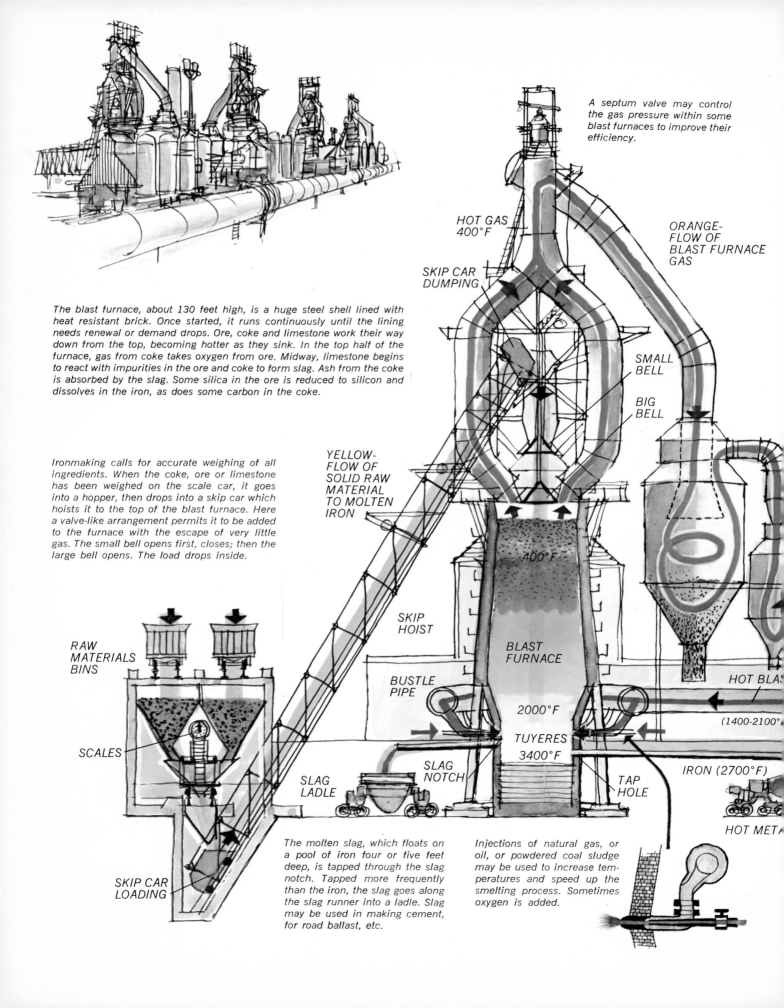

A septum valve may control the gas pressure within some blast furnaces to improve their efficiency.

The blast furnace, about 130 feet high, is a huge steel shell lined with heat resistant brick. Once started, it runs continuously until the lining needs renewal or demand drops. Ore, coke and limestone work their way down from the top, becoming hotter as they sink. In the top half of the furnace, gas from coke takes oxygen from ore. Midway, limestone begins to react with impurities in the ore and coke to form slag. Ash from the coke is absorbed by the slag. Some silica in the ore is reduced to silicon and dissolves in the iron, as does some carbon in the coke.

Ironmaking calls for accurate weighing of all ingredients. When the coke, ore or limestone has been weighed on the scale car, it goes into a hopper, then drops into a skip car which hoists it to the top of the blast furnace. Here a valve-like arrangement permits it to be added to the furnace with the escape of very little gas. The small bell opens first, closes; then the large bell opens. The load drops inside.

HOT GAS 400°F

SKIP CAR DUMPING

ORANGE-FLOW OF BLAST FURNACE GAS

SMALL BELL

BIG BELL

YELLOW-FLOW OF SOLID RAW MATERIAL TO MOLTEN IRON

400°F

SKIP HOIST

BLAST FURNACE

2000°F

RAW MATERIALS BINS

SCALES

BUSTLE PIPE

TUYERES 3400°F

HOT BLAST

(1400-2100°

IRON (2700°F)

SLAG LADLE

SLAG NOTCH

TAP HOLE

HOT META

SKIP CAR LOADING

The molten slag, which floats on a pool of iron four or five feet deep, is tapped through the slag notch. Tapped more frequently than the iron, the slag goes along the slag runner into a ladle. Slag may be used in making cement, for road ballast, etc.

Injections of natural gas, or oil, or powdered coal sludge may be used to increase temperatures and speed up the smelting process. Sometimes oxygen is added.

BLAST FURNACE IRONMAKING

Hot air is indispensable in a blast furnace. As much as four and one-half tons of it may be needed to make one ton of pig iron. It pours in at the bottom of the furnace and roars up through the charge of iron ore, coke, and limestone that has been dumped in from the top.

Fanned by the air, the coke burns. Its gases reduce the ore to metallic iron by removing oxygen from it while the limestone causes the earthy matter of the ore to flow. Freed, the heavy metal settles to the bottom. From there, 300 to 600 tons of pig iron are drawn off every three to five hours.

Air for the blast furnace is heated in huge stoves. At least two stoves are needed for each blast furnace. One stove heats while the other blows hot air into the bustle pipe and through tuyers to the bottom of the furnace. In a combustion chamber in the stove being heated, cleaned exhaust gases from the blast furnace are mixed with air and burned to raise the temperature of refractory brick.

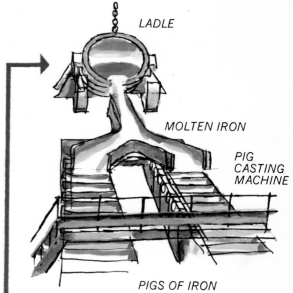

LADLE

MOLTEN IRON

PIG CASTING MACHINE

PIGS OF IRON

For convenience in shipping, liquid iron is ladled off into continuously moving molds, is then quenched and turned out in pig form. Each year, a small percentage of the pig iron output is shipped in solid pigs to thousands of foundries where it is made into a variety of castings. Solid pigs are also used by steel mills that do not have blast furnaces.

STOVES

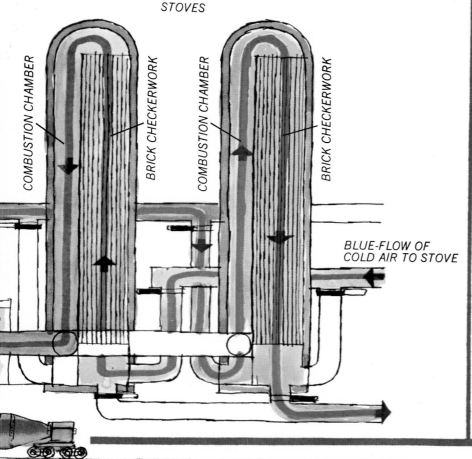

COMBUSTION CHAMBER

BRICK CHECKERWORK

COMBUSTION CHAMBER

BRICK CHECKERWORK

BLUE-FLOW OF COLD AIR TO STOVE

When the blast furnace is tapped for its store of iron, the molten metal is channeled into a hot metal car, a gigantic drum lined with refractory brick. A hot metal car holds about 160 tons of liquid iron, insulating it like a gigantic vacuum bottle. Most molten iron goes to open hearth or basic oxygen steelmaking facilities, but some goes to a casting machine where it is made into solid "pigs."

A ladle full of molten iron joins limestone, scrap steel and alloying materials in a basic oxygen furnace or in an open hearth to form a special heat of steel meeting rigid specifications.

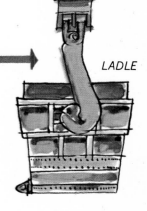

LADLE

This schematic drawing of a BOF facility shows the emphasis the steel industry places on air quality control. A hood over the furnace catches the dirty waste gases from the steelmaking process. The gases are conducted to air treatment facilities which occupy most of the space to the left of the crane-held ladle in the diagram.

GAS CLEANING EQUIPMENT

The principal material used in manufacturing steel by the basic oxygen process is molten iron. Therefore, most BOF facilities are built near blast furnaces. Some scrap steel is used in the process. Oxygen producing facilities are usually built in the same plant.

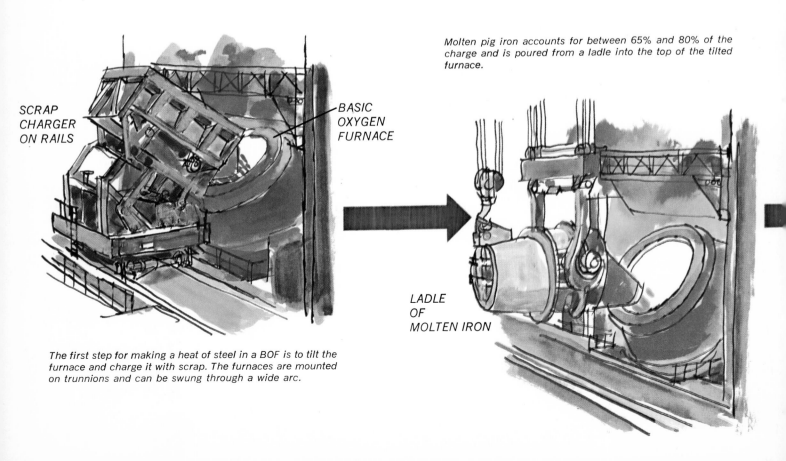

SCRAP CHARGER ON RAILS

BASIC OXYGEN FURNACE

Molten pig iron accounts for between 65% and 80% of the charge and is poured from a ladle into the top of the tilted furnace.

LADLE OF MOLTEN IRON

The first step for making a heat of steel in a BOF is to tilt the furnace and charge it with scrap. The furnaces are mounted on trunnions and can be swung through a wide arc.

BASIC OXYGEN STEELMAKING

America's capability to produce steel by the basic oxygen process has grown enormously from small beginnings during the middle 1950's. The high tonnage of steel now made in basic oxygen furnaces—commonly called BOF's—requires the consumption of large amounts of oxygen to provide operational heat and to promote the necessary chemical changes. No other gases or fuels are used.

The basic oxygen process produces steel very quickly compared with the other major methods now in use. For example, a BOF may produce up to 300-ton batches in 45 minutes as against 5 to 8 hours for the older open hearth process. Most grades of steel can be produced in the refractory-lined, pear-shaped furnaces.

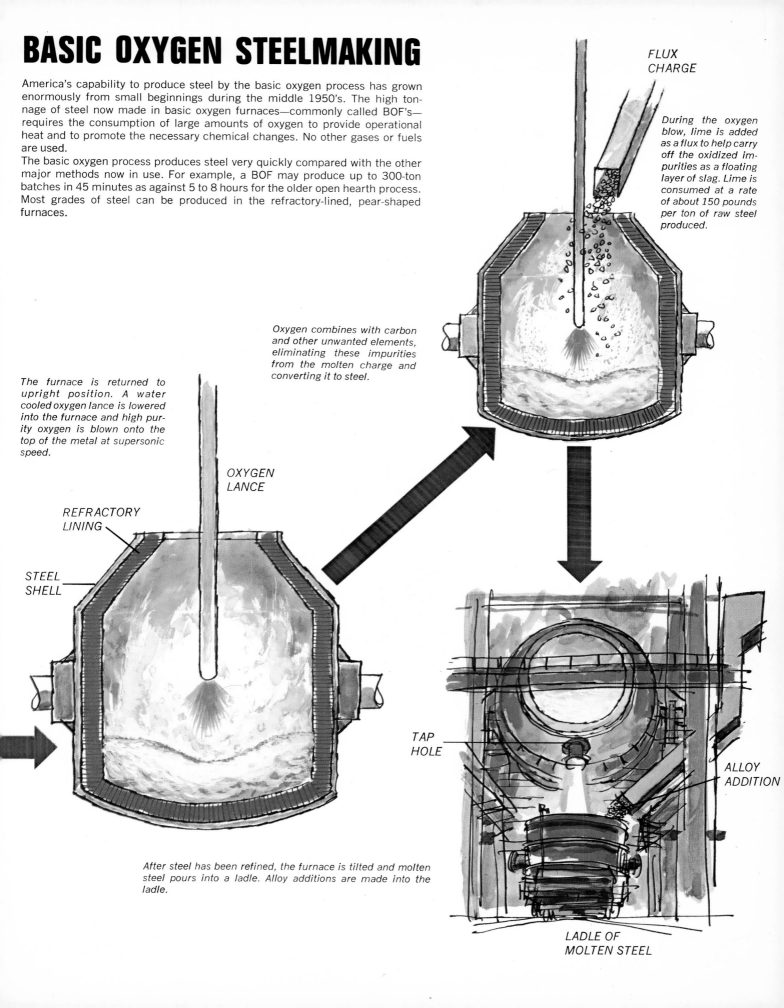

FLUX CHARGE

During the oxygen blow, lime is added as a flux to help carry off the oxidized impurities as a floating layer of slag. Lime is consumed at a rate of about 150 pounds per ton of raw steel produced.

Oxygen combines with carbon and other unwanted elements, eliminating these impurities from the molten charge and converting it to steel.

The furnace is returned to upright position. A water cooled oxygen lance is lowered into the furnace and high purity oxygen is blown onto the top of the metal at supersonic speed.

OXYGEN LANCE

REFRACTORY LINING

STEEL SHELL

TAP HOLE

ALLOY ADDITION

After steel has been refined, the furnace is tilted and molten steel pours into a ladle. Alloy additions are made into the ladle.

LADLE OF MOLTEN STEEL

OPEN HEARTH STEELMAKING

Open hearth furnaces are so named because the limestone, scrap steel and molten iron charged into the shallow steelmaking area (the hearth) are exposed (open) to the sweep of flames. A furnace that will produce a fairly typical 350 tons of steel in five to eight hours may be about 90 feet long and 30 feet wide.

The cutaway drawing below shows several steps simultaneously that would normally occur in sequence. First the long-armed charging machine picks up boxes of limestone and steel scrap, thrusts them through the furnace doors and dumps the contents. The flame of burning fuel oil, tar or gases partially melts the solid charge, after which molten iron (lower right) is poured into the furnace. High-temperature reactions cause several unwanted elements to combine with the limestone to form a slag.

When tests of samples show the steel to be of specified chemistry, the tap hole is opened by an explosive charge and the steel runs into a ladle. The slag, which is lighter than steel, floats on the metal and overflows into a slag thimble during pouring. Alloy additions are made to the steel in the ladle.

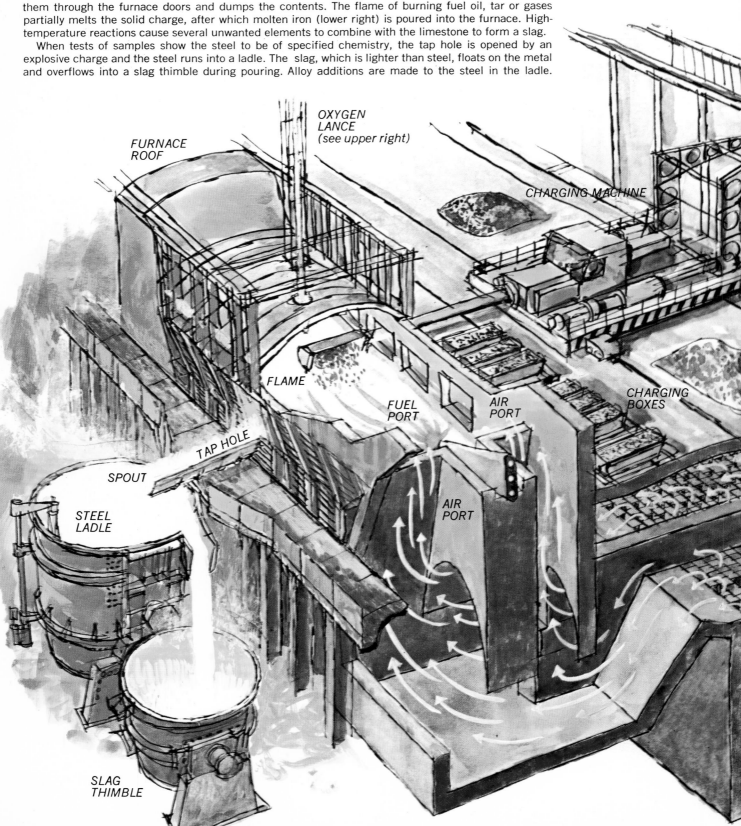

In recent years practically all open hearth furnaces have been converted to the use of oxygen. The gas is fed into the open hearth through the roof by means of retractable lances. The use of gaseous oxygen in the open hearth increases flame temperature, and thereby speeds the melting process.

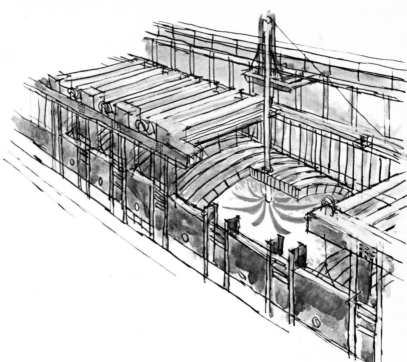

Molten iron from a blast furnace is a major raw material for the open hearth furnaces. A massive "funnel" is wheeled to an open hearth door and the contents of a ladle of iron are poured through it into the furnace hearth. The principal addition of molten metal is made after the original scrap charge has begun to melt.

CONTROL PANELS

BRICK CHECKER CHAMBERS

Brick checker chambers are located on both ends of the furnace. The bricks are arranged to leave a great number of passages through which the hot waste gases from the furnace pass and heat the brickwork prior to going through the cleaner and stack. Later on, the flow is reversed and the air for combustion passes through the heated bricks and is itself heated on its way to the hearth.

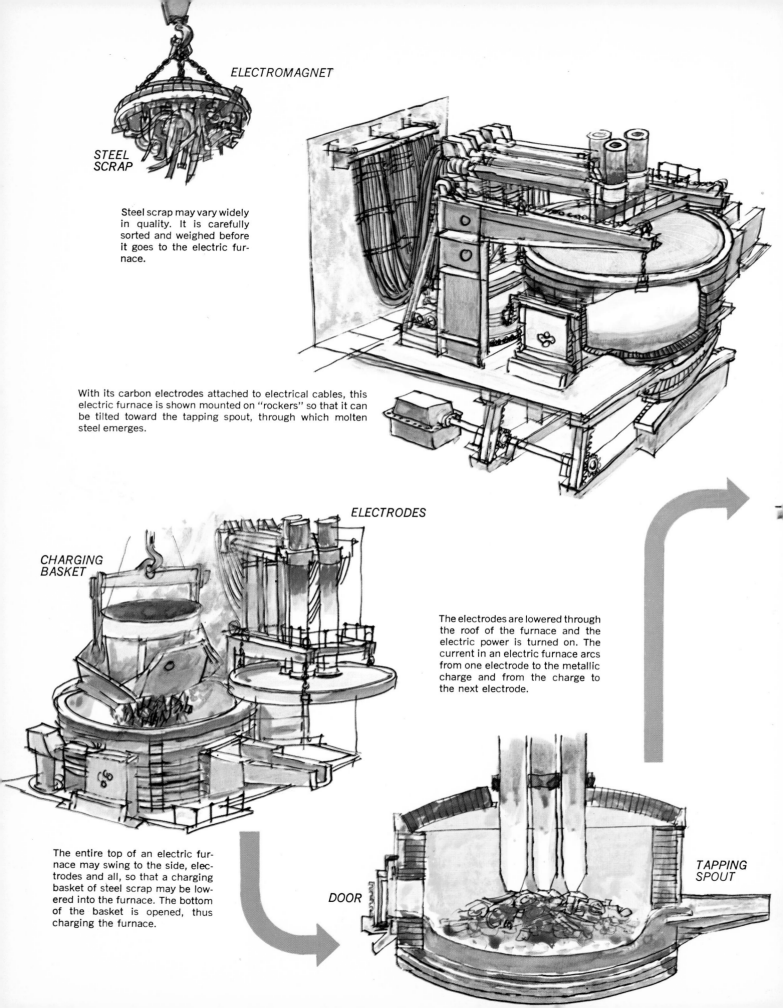

ELECTROMAGNET

STEEL
SCRAP

Steel scrap may vary widely
in quality. It is carefully
sorted and weighed before
it goes to the electric furnace.

With its carbon electrodes attached to electrical cables, this
electric furnace is shown mounted on "rockers" so that it can
be tilted toward the tapping spout, through which molten
steel emerges.

ELECTRODES

CHARGING
BASKET

The electrodes are lowered through
the roof of the furnace and the
electric power is turned on. The
current in an electric furnace arcs
from one electrode to the metallic
charge and from the charge to
the next electrode.

The entire top of an electric furnace may swing to the side, electrodes and all, so that a charging
basket of steel scrap may be lowered into the furnace. The bottom
of the basket is opened, thus
charging the furnace.

DOOR

TAPPING
SPOUT

ELECTRIC FURNACE STEELMAKING

A long-deserved reputation for producing alloy, stainless, tool, and other specialty steels belongs to America's electric furnaces. Operators have also learned to make larger heats of carbon steels in these furnaces; this development helps account for the record tonnage outputs of recent years.

The heat within the electric furnace is intense and rigidly controlled. Modern electric furnaces have top sections that can be moved away so that special containers can charge scrap into them from above. Sometimes pig iron is also charged and prereduced iron ore, in various forms, is rich enough in iron to be used as an electric furnace steelmaking charge.

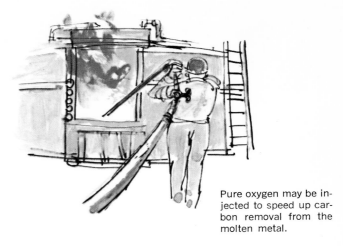

Pure oxygen may be injected to speed up carbon removal from the molten metal.

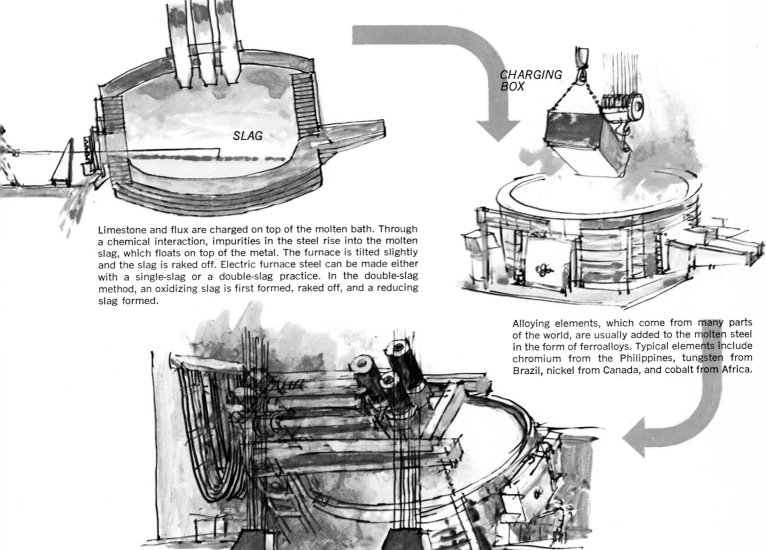

SLAG

CHARGING BOX

Limestone and flux are charged on top of the molten bath. Through a chemical interaction, impurities in the steel rise into the molten slag, which floats on top of the metal. The furnace is tilted slightly and the slag is raked off. Electric furnace steel can be made either with a single-slag or a double-slag practice. In the double-slag method, an oxidizing slag is first formed, raked off, and a reducing slag formed.

Alloying elements, which come from many parts of the world, are usually added to the molten steel in the form of ferroalloys. Typical elements include chromium from the Philippines, tungsten from Brazil, nickel from Canada, and cobalt from Africa.

When the chemical composition of the steel meets specifications, the furnace tilts forward so that molten metal may pour out through the spout. The slag comes after the steel and serves as an insulating blanket during tapping.

LADLE

FURNACE LADLE

VACUUM PROCESSING OF STEEL

Steels for special applications are often processed in a vacuum to give them properties not otherwise obtainable. The primary purpose of vacuum processing is to remove such gases as oxygen, nitrogen, and hydrogen from molten metal to make higher-purity steel.

Many grades of steel are degassed by processes similar to those shown on this page. Even greater purity and uniformity of steel chemistry than is available by degassing is obtained by subjecting the metal to vacuum melting processes like those shown on the facing page.

The Vacuum Degassers

In vacuum stream degassing (left), a ladle of molten steel from a conventional furnace is taken to a vacuum chamber. An ingot mold is shown within the chamber. Larger chambers designed to contain ladles are also used. The conventionally melted steel goes into a pony ladle and from there into the chamber. The stream of steel is broken up into droplets when it is exposed to vacuum within the chamber. During the droplet phase, undesirable gases escape from the steel and are drawn off before the metal solidifies in the mold.

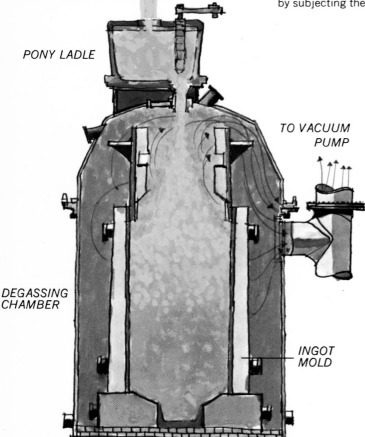

PONY LADLE

TO VACUUM PUMP

DEGASSING CHAMBER

INGOT MOLD

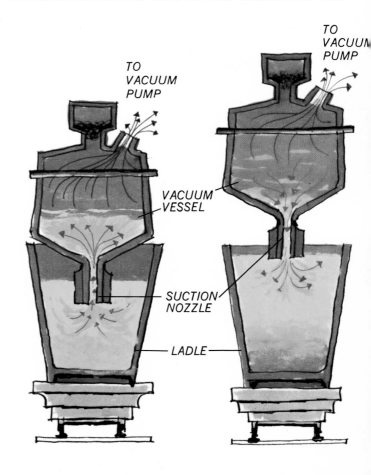

TO VACUUM PUMP

TO VACUUM PUMP

VACUUM VESSEL

SUCTION NOZZLE

LADLE

Ladle degassing facilities (right) of several kinds are in current use. In the left-hand facility, molten steel is forced by atmospheric pressure into the heated vacuum chamber. Gases are removed in this pressure chamber, which is then raised so that the molten steel returns by gravity into the ladle. Since not all of the steel enters the vacuum chamber at one time, this process is repeated until essentially all the steel in the ladle has been processed.

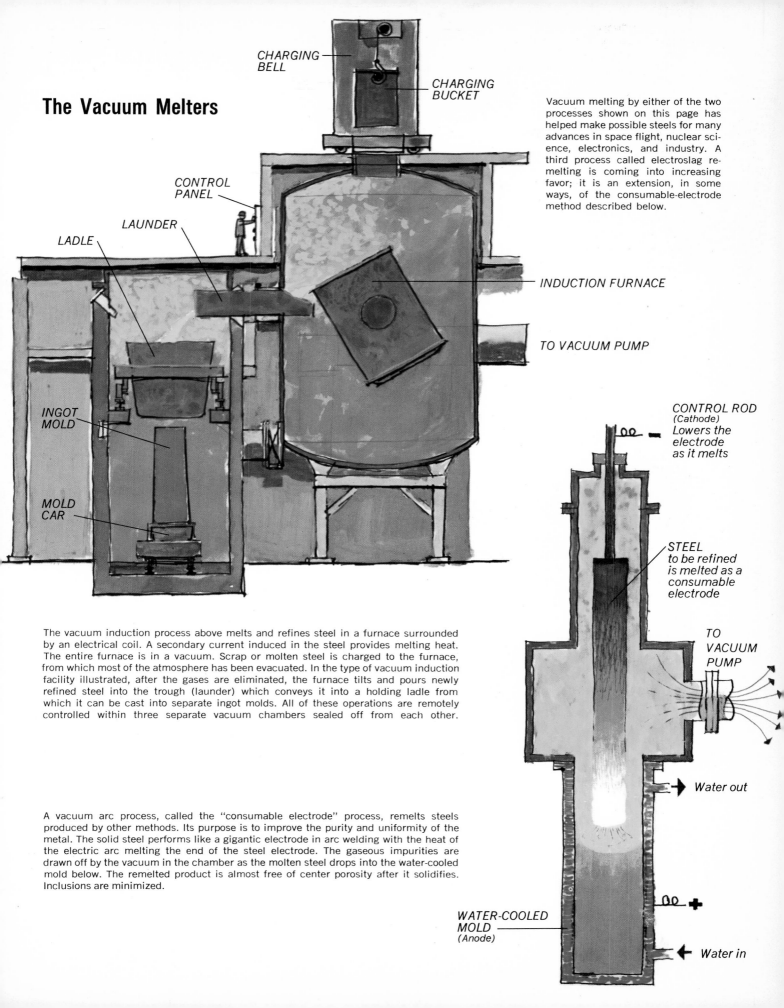

The Vacuum Melters

CHARGING BELL

CHARGING BUCKET

CONTROL PANEL

LAUNDER

LADLE

INGOT MOLD

MOLD CAR

INDUCTION FURNACE

TO VACUUM PUMP

CONTROL ROD
(Cathode)
Lowers the electrode as it melts

STEEL
to be refined is melted as a consumable electrode

TO VACUUM PUMP

Water out

Water in

WATER-COOLED MOLD
(Anode)

Vacuum melting by either of the two processes shown on this page has helped make possible steels for many advances in space flight, nuclear science, electronics, and industry. A third process called electroslag remelting is coming into increasing favor; it is an extension, in some ways, of the consumable-electrode method described below.

The vacuum induction process above melts and refines steel in a furnace surrounded by an electrical coil. A secondary current induced in the steel provides melting heat. The entire furnace is in a vacuum. Scrap or molten steel is charged to the furnace, from which most of the atmosphere has been evacuated. In the type of vacuum induction facility illustrated, after the gases are eliminated, the furnace tilts and pours newly refined steel into the trough (launder) which conveys it into a holding ladle from which it can be cast into separate ingot molds. All of these operations are remotely controlled within three separate vacuum chambers sealed off from each other.

A vacuum arc process, called the "consumable electrode" process, remelts steels produced by other methods. Its purpose is to improve the purity and uniformity of the metal. The solid steel performs like a gigantic electrode in arc welding with the heat of the electric arc melting the end of the steel electrode. The gaseous impurities are drawn off by the vacuum in the chamber as the molten steel drops into the water-cooled mold below. The remelted product is almost free of center porosity after it solidifies. Inclusions are minimized.

THE FIRST SOLID FORMS OF STEEL

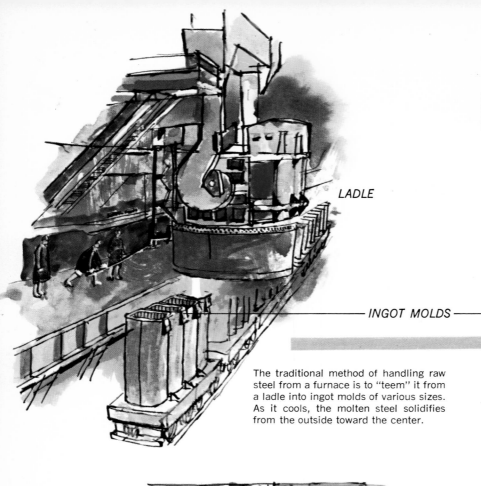

LADLE

INGOT MOLDS

The traditional method of handling raw steel from a furnace is to "teem" it from a ladle into ingot molds of various sizes. As it cools, the molten steel solidifies from the outside toward the center.

When an ingot has solidified on the outside, a stripper crane may remove the mold as shown here in cutaway. The tongs lift the mold while a "plunger" holds the ingot down on the ingot car.

INGOT

SOAKING PIT

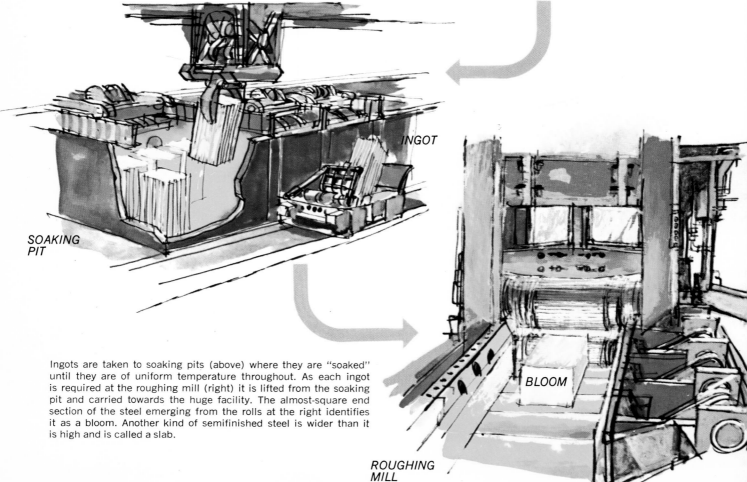

BLOOM

Ingots are taken to soaking pits (above) where they are "soaked" until they are of uniform temperature throughout. As each ingot is required at the roughing mill (right) it is lifted from the soaking pit and carried towards the huge facility. The almost-square end section of the steel emerging from the rolls at the right identifies it as a bloom. Another kind of semifinished steel is wider than it is high and is called a slab.

ROUGHING MILL

Molten steel from the nation's basic oxygen, open hearth, and electric furnaces flows into ladles and then follows either of two major routes towards the rolling mills that make most of the industry's finished products. Both processes shown on these pages provide solid, semifinished steel products to the finishing mills. The first step in the traditional method is shown at the left. A much newer method—strand casting—is diagrammed at the far right.

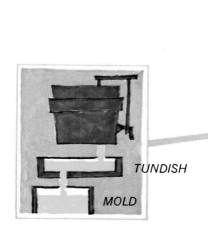

TUNDISH

MOLD

The transfer of molten steel from the ladle to a tundish is important. The tundish provides an even pool of molten metal to be fed into the casting machine. The tundish also allows an empty ladle to be removed and a full ladle to be positioned and to start pouring without interrupting the flow of metal to the casting machine.

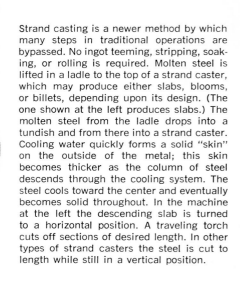

LADLE

MOLD OSCILLATOR

WATER SPRAY

PINCH ROLLS

Strand casting is a newer method by which many steps in traditional operations are bypassed. No ingot teeming, stripping, soaking, or rolling is required. Molten steel is lifted in a ladle to the top of a strand caster, which may produce either slabs, blooms, or billets, depending upon its design. (The one shown at the left produces slabs.) The molten steel from the ladle drops into a tundish and from there into a strand caster. Cooling water quickly forms a solid "skin" on the outside of the metal; this skin becomes thicker as the column of steel descends through the cooling system. The steel cools toward the center and eventually becomes solid throughout. In the machine at the left the descending slab is turned to a horizontal position. A traveling torch cuts off sections of desired length. In other types of strand casters the steel is cut to length while still in a vertical position.

SLAB STRAIGHTENER

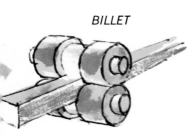

BILLET

Blooms (left) may go directly to finishing mills. Some are further reduced in cross section in special mills to make billets. These billets are a form of semifinished steel from which smaller finished products are made.

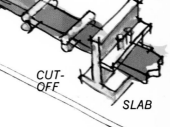

CUT-OFF

SLAB

SLAB

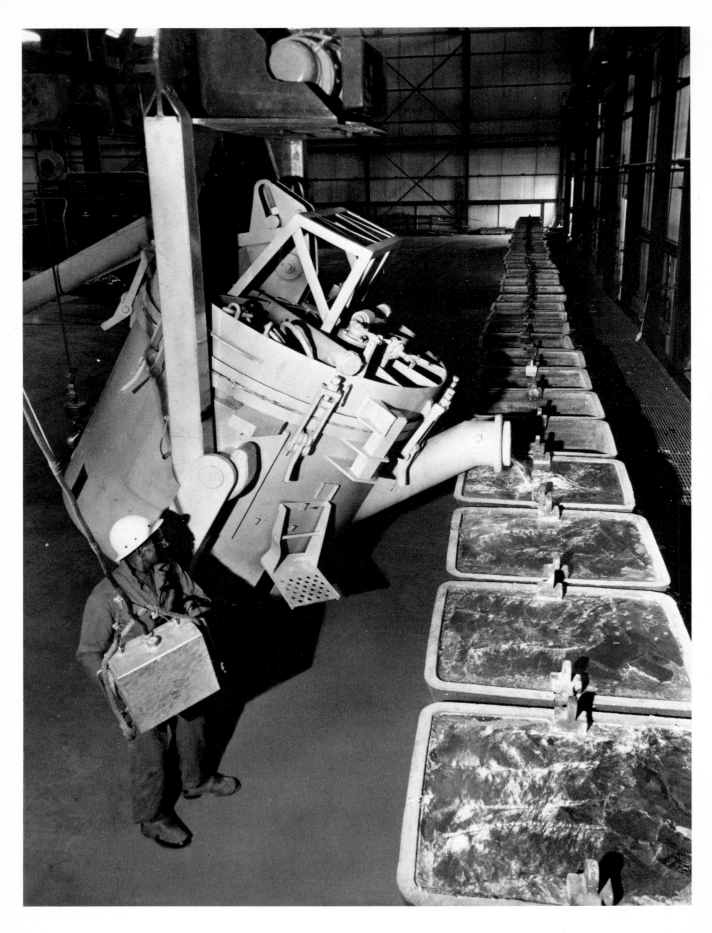

Pouring molten metal into molds that will form ingots. Note the electrical control panel that the operator uses to move and tilt the crucible.

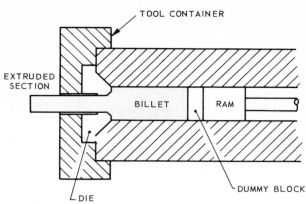

Fig. 1-24. The extrusion process. Metal is forced through a die of the required shape and size.

Fig. 1-25. A few of the many extruded shapes available. Almost any shape can be produced by this process.

Butt welded pipe is made from a heated strip called skelp which is formed and welded together, as shown in Fig. 1-26.

Metal is shaped by other techniques too. Many of the methods used will be described in this book.

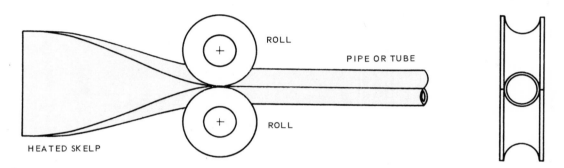

Fig. 1-26. How some pipe and tubing is made from flat metal sheet.

What Do You Know About Metals - Unit 1

Write your answers to these questions on a separate sheet of paper. Do not write in this book.

1. Aluminum, magnesium and titanium are used to manufacture airplanes because they are:
   a._____
   b._____
2. Base metals are _____.
3. Alloys are_____.
4. Ferrous metals are those metals which contain_____as the major element in their composition.
5. Nonferrous metals are_____.
6. Carbon steels are classified according to_____.
7. Hot finished steel has a_____. When cold finished it is _____.

NOTE: You may answer Questions 8, 9 and 10 by making a drawing of the process.

8. Metal in sheet or plate form is made by _____.
9. Wire is made by_____.
10. Seamless tubing is manufactured by___ _____.

Special Activities

1. How many applications can you name that need metals with special qualities? Classify them as Base Metals or Alloys.

2. Secure samples of as many metals as you can. Mount them on hardboard and label each of the samples.

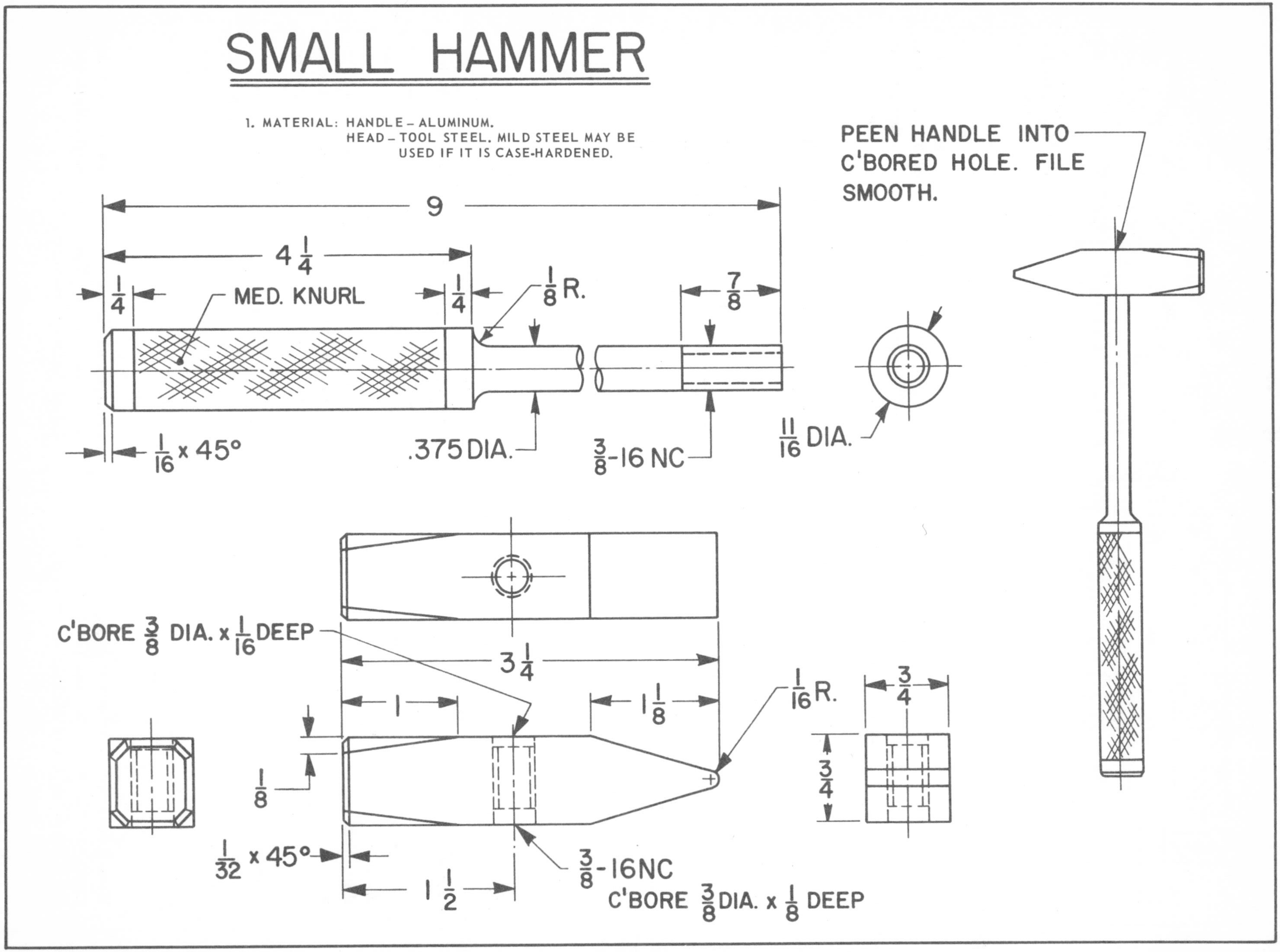

SMALL HAMMER

1. MATERIAL: HANDLE — ALUMINUM.
   HEAD — TOOL STEEL. MILD STEEL MAY BE
   USED IF IT IS CASE-HARDENED.

PEEN HANDLE INTO C'BORED HOLE. FILE SMOOTH.

$\frac{11}{16}$ DIA.

$\frac{7}{8}$

$\frac{3}{8}$-16 NC

$\frac{1}{8}$ R.

.375 DIA.

9

$4\frac{1}{4}$

MED. KNURL

$\frac{1}{4}$

$\frac{1}{4}$

$\frac{1}{16}$ x 45°

$\frac{3}{4}$

$\frac{3}{4}$

$\frac{1}{16}$ R.

$3\frac{1}{4}$

$1\frac{1}{8}$

1

$1\frac{1}{2}$

$\frac{1}{8}$

$\frac{1}{32}$ x 45°

C'BORE $\frac{3}{8}$ DIA. x $\frac{1}{16}$ DEEP

$\frac{3}{8}$-16NC
C'BORE $\frac{3}{8}$ DIA. x $\frac{1}{8}$ DEEP

Fig. 2-1. Working drawing of the project that will be described in this Unit.

Unit 2
PLANNING YOUR PROJECT

The experienced craftsman plans his job carefully before starting to work. You should plan your projects with the same concern. Planning will result in a saving of time, effort and material.

If plans are not available for the project you want to make, your first task will be to prepare working drawings. These drawings may be sketched or made with drafting instruments, Fig. 2-1. The plans should be drawn full size if possible.

During the preparation of the working drawings you will need to decide on methods of construction and fabrication you will use on your project.

The final steps in planning the project should be the preparation of a BILL OF MATERIAL and a PLAN OF PROCEDURE. A Bill of Material is a list of the materials needed to construct the project. A Plan of Procedure is a list of operations, in their sequential order, you propose to follow in the construction of your project. You may want to combine both of them on the same sheet, Fig. 2-2.

Fig. 2-2. Typical Project Plan Sheet.

ECK WYE ZEE SCHOOL
INDUSTRIAL ARTS DEPARTMENT
PROJECT PLAN SHEET

Name _____ Period _____

Name of Project _____

Date Started _____ Date Completed _____

Source of Idea or Project _____

BILL OF MATERIAL

Part Name	No. of Pieces	Material	Size (T x W x L)	Unit Cost	Total Cost
				Total Cost	

PLAN OF PROCEDURE

List the operations to be performed in their sequential order.
Indicate the tool(s) and equipment needed to accomplish the job.

No.	Operation	Tools and Equipment

ECK WYE ZEE SCHOOL
INDUSTRIAL ARTS DEPARTMENT
PROJECT PLAN SHEET

Name ___RICHARD J. WALKER_____ Period _3 MON, WED, & FRI.___

Name of Project __MACHINIST'S HAMMER_____

Date Started __SEPTEMBER 15_____ Date Completed __DECEMBER 10___

Source of Idea or Project __EXPLORING METALWORKING_____

BILL OF MATERIAL

Part Name	No. of Pieces	Material	Size (T x W x L)	Unit Cost	Total Cost
HAMMER HEAD	1	C. F. STEEL	¾ x ¾ x 3 ¼		
HANDLE	1	ALUMINUM	¾ DIA. x 9 ¼		
				Total Cost	

PLAN OF PROCEDURE

List the operations to be performed in their sequential order.
Indicate the tool(s) and equipment needed to accomplish the job.

No.	Operation	Tools and Equipment
	HAMMER HEAD	
1.	CUT STOCK TO LENGTH AND REMOVE BURRS.	RULE, SCRIBE, HACK SAW AND FILE
2.	FILE HEAD SQUARE.	FILE AND SQUARE
3.	LAYOUT AS PER PLANS.	SCRIBE, RULE AND SQUARE
4.	FILE CHAMFERS AND BEVELS ON HEAD.	FILE
5.	CUT WEDGE END.	HACK SAW
6.	FILE WEDGE END TO SIZE.	FILE AND SQUARE
7.	DRILL ⅜ DIA. HOLE ¼ DEEP.	DRILL PRESS, VISE, PARALLELS, CENTER FINDER, CENTER DRILL AND ⅜ DIA. DRILL
8.	DRILL "F" DRILL THROUGH.	SAME SET UP BUT FINISH DRILLING WITH "F" DRILL
9.	TURN HEAD OVER IN VISE AND C'BORE ⅜" DIA. BY ⅛ DEEP.	SAME SET UP. ⅜ DIA. DRILL
10.	TAP HOLE ⅜-16 NC.	⅜-16 NC TAP, TAP HANDLE AND SQUARE
11.	CLEAN AND POLISH.	ABRASIVE CLOTH AND OIL
12.	CASE HARDEN.	FURNACE AND CASE HARDENING COMPOUND
13.	FINAL POLISH.	ABRASIVE CLOTH AND OIL
	HANDLE	
1.	CUT STOCK TO LENGTH.	RULE, SCRIBE AND HACK SAW
2.	FACE ENDS AND CENTER DRILL.	LATHE, 3-JAW UNIVERSAL CHUCK, JACOBS CHUCK, CENTER DRILL AND R.H. TOOL HOLDER
3.	TURN A SECTION 5 IN. LONG BY ¹¹/₁₆ IN. DIAMETER.	L.H. TOOL HOLDER, CALIPER AND RULE OR MICROMETER
4.	MARK OFF SECTION TO BE KNURLED AND KNURL.	HERMAPHRODITE CALIPER, RULE AND KNURLING TOOL
5.	MOVE HANDLE CLOSE INTO CHUCK AND MACHINE CHAMFER.	R.H. TOOL HOLDER AND RULE
6.	REVERSE WORK IN CHUCK AND TURN SHANK SECTION TO .375 IN. DIAMETER.	L.H. TOOL HOLDER, RULE AND MICROMETER
7.	THREAD SHANK ⅜-16 NC.	⅜-16 NC DIE AND DIE STOCK
8.	ASSEMBLE.	
9.	PEEN HANDLE. FILE SMOOTH.	BALL PEEN HAMMER AND SINGLE CUT FILE

Fig. 2-3. Completed Project Plan Sheet for the hammer shown in Fig. 2-1.

Planning a Project

Using the project planning sheet from Fig. 2-2, let us plan the operations necessary to manufacture the hammer shown on page 18.

The completed planning sheet is shown in Fig. 2-3. See Figs. 2-4 and 2-5 for a pictorial presentation on making the hammer. The completed hammer is shown in Fig. 2-6.

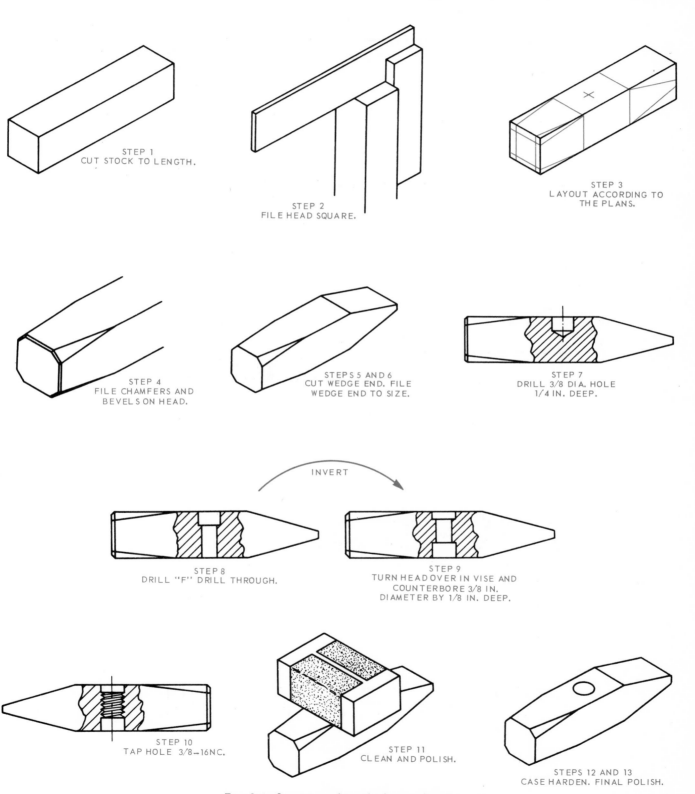

STEP 1
CUT STOCK TO LENGTH.

STEP 2
FILE HEAD SQUARE.

STEP 3
LAYOUT ACCORDING TO THE PLANS.

STEP 4
FILE CHAMFERS AND BEVELS ON HEAD.

STEPS 5 AND 6
CUT WEDGE END. FILE WEDGE END TO SIZE.

STEP 7
DRILL 3/8 DIA. HOLE 1/4 IN. DEEP.

INVERT

STEP 8
DRILL "F" DRILL THROUGH.

STEP 9
TURN HEAD OVER IN VISE AND COUNTERBORE 3/8 IN. DIAMETER BY 1/8 IN. DEEP.

STEP 10
TAP HOLE 3/8-16NC.

STEP 11
CLEAN AND POLISH.

STEPS 12 AND 13
CASE HARDEN. FINAL POLISH.

Fig. 2-4. Steps in making the hammer head.

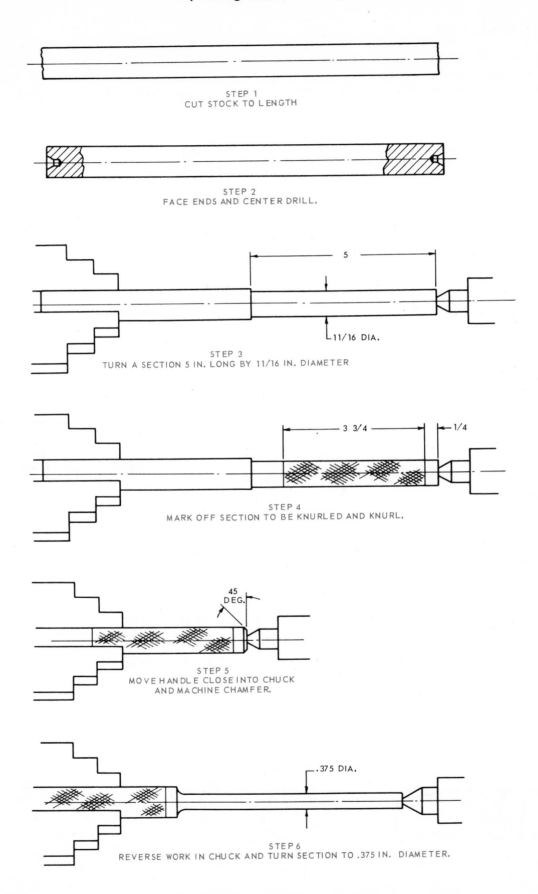

STEP 1
CUT STOCK TO LENGTH

STEP 2
FACE ENDS AND CENTER DRILL.

5

11/16 DIA.

STEP 3
TURN A SECTION 5 IN. LONG BY 11/16 IN. DIAMETER

3 3/4   1/4

STEP 4
MARK OFF SECTION TO BE KNURLED AND KNURL.

45 DEG.

STEP 5
MOVE HANDLE CLOSE INTO CHUCK
AND MACHINE CHAMFER.

.375 DIA.

STEP 6
REVERSE WORK IN CHUCK AND TURN SECTION TO .375 IN. DIAMETER.

Fig. 2-5. Steps in making the hammer handle.

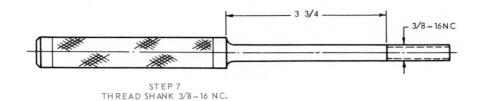

STEP 7
THREAD SHANK 3/8 – 16 NC.

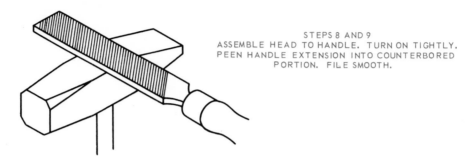

STEPS 8 AND 9
ASSEMBLE HEAD TO HANDLE. TURN ON TIGHTLY.
PEEN HANDLE EXTENSION INTO COUNTERBORED
PORTION. FILE SMOOTH.

Fig. 2-5. (Continued) Steps in making the hammer handle.

What Do You Know About Planning – Unit 2

1. Why should you plan your work carefully?
2. What is a BILL OF MATERIAL?
3. What is a PLAN OF PROCEDURE?
4. List the steps recommended for planning a project.

Special Activities

1. Design a PLAN OF PROCEDURE for your shop.
2. Secure samples of planning sheets used by other shops in your school and by the Industrial Arts Department in other schools.

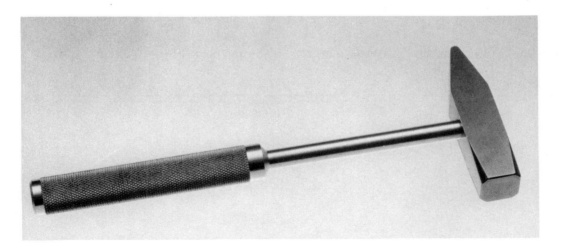

Fig. 2-6. Photo of completed hammer.

Unit 3
DESIGNING A PROJECT

Good design is hard to define. Like most things in life, it is relative. That is, it is related to the standards one sets for himself.

In many ways, good design may be considered a plan for a direct solution to a problem. It makes use of certain guide lines which point the way toward a well designed product.

Design Guide Lines

Good design is characterized by:

FUNCTION. How well does the design fit the purpose for which it was planned? Does it fulfill a need?

ORGANIZATION. Do the individual parts of the design create interest when they are brought together? Are the proportions in balance? Do the parts seem to belong together? Is there a flow of rhythm in the basic shape? Is the product pleasing in appearance?

CRAFTSMANSHIP. Good craftsmanship is an inherent part of good design. Quality must be built into the product.

Elements of Good Design

In the solution of a design problem, there are certain basic elements and principles that are common to good designs:

LINES. Lines are used to define and give shape to an object, Fig. 3-1.

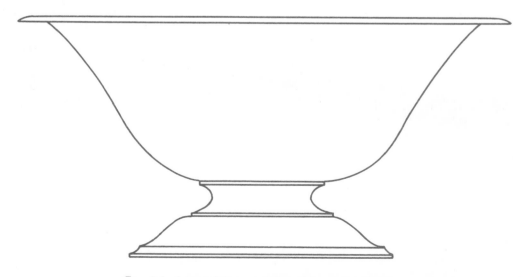

Fig. 3-1. Lines define and give shape to an object.

24

SHAPE. The shape of a useful object determines whether it is pleasing to the eye or touch, Fig. 3-2.

Fig. 3-2. The shape of the object helps determines whether it is pleasing to the eye. (Stieff Co.)

Fig. 3-3. Form is the three-dimensional shape of the object. These candle holders illustrate how several different geometric shapes may be used.

FORM. Form is the three-dimensional shape of the object. It may be round, square or some other geometric shape, Fig. 3-3.

PROPORTION. To a large extent, good proportion is a matter of balance between parts; each having the size best suited for its purpose.

BALANCE. An object has balance when its parts appear to be of equal weight, neither top heavy nor lopsided. SYMMETRICAL BALANCE is when the parts on each side of the center line are alike in shape and size, Fig. 3-4. INFORMAL BALANCE presents a design in such a manner that the balance cannot be measured and yet you get the feeling that it is balanced, Fig. 3-5.

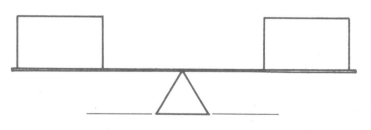

Fig. 3-4. Example of symmetrical balance.

Fig. 3-5. Example of informal balance. The front end of the car is long to counteract or balance the weight of the big engine located in the rear. (Champion Spark Plug Co.)

UNITY. A design that has unity seems to bring the various parts together as a whole. Each part of the object seems to have a relationship.

EMPHASIS. This is where the design is given a point of interest.

RHYTHM. Rhythm is achieved by the repetition of lines, curves, forms, colors and the textures within the design, Fig. 3-6. It gives an object a pleasing appearance.

TEXTURE. Texture is the condition of the surface of a material. Texture can be added by cutting, pressing, perforating, rolling or expanding.

COLOR. All metals have a color of their own. Colors may also be added using chemicals, paints, lacquers, or other finishing materials. Selection of color is important.

Fig. 3-6. Rhythm is achieved in this fruit bowl by the repetition of the curves around the perimeter of the piece. (Stieff Co.)

How Industry Designs a Product

Let's see how Industry, the Automotive Industry for example, goes about developing a new product.

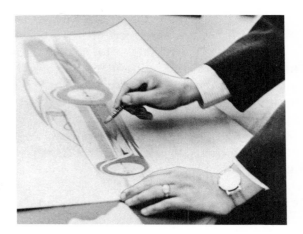

Fig. 3-7. *Drawings give inspiration to the final design of a new car. (General Motors Corp.)*

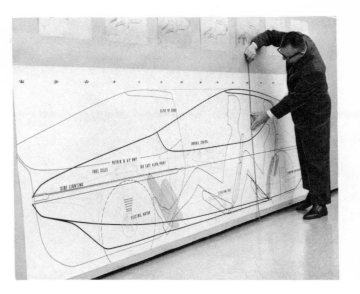

Fig. 3-9. *A full-scale outline of the proposed automobile design is laid out to aid planning of seating arrangement, placement of mechanical components, and the general "architecture" of the vehicle. This is typically done as a "tape-drawing," so that shapes and lines can be quickly changed as design modifications are suggested.*

New automobile designs are developed as a series of sketches around specifications established by management, Fig. 3-7. Large airbrush illustrations are made of promising sketches, Fig. 3-8.

A full size outline of the vehicle is prepared to show the location of mechanical components, Fig. 3-9. Line drawings and illustrations, while satisfactory for preliminary studies, do not provide the three-dimension qualities needed to test and prove design

Fig. 3-8. *A full size airbrush illustration of a design is made to enable designers to evaluate the shape as it would actually appear.*

ideas so a clay model must be constructed, Fig. 3-10. After further development, if the design is approved, a fiber glass prototype is fabricated, Fig. 3-11.

Fig. 3-10. Preliminary clay model of a proposed design.

Production planning utilizes accurate full size wood die models to serve as the primary source of information for preparing dies (to stamp out body panels), fabricating fixtures (devices to hold body panels while they are being welded together) and checking fixtures (measuring tools needed to maintain quality control). Finally, the new model is made available to the public.

Designing Your Project

When designing YOUR project, it will be much easier if you follow a pattern similar to that used by a professional designer. Think of the project as a DESIGN PROBLEM.

1. STATE THE PROBLEM. What is the purpose for which the project is to be used?
2. THINK THROUGH THE PROBLEM. What must the project do? How can it be done? What are the limitations that must be considered? How have others solved the problem?
3. DEVELOP YOUR IDEAS. Let's assume you want to develop a stand for plastic model planes. First, make sketches of your ideas. See Fig. 3-12. Develop the ideas and have them discussed by your teacher and fellow students. Determine which materials will be most suitable.
4. PREPARE THE WORKING DRAWINGS. When you are satisfied that you have developed a satisfactory design prepare working drawings, Figs. 3-13.
5. CONSTRUCT THE PROJECT. Make the project to the best of your ability. Do a job

Fig. 3-11. View of an advanced design studio in the General Motors Technical Center, Warren, Mich. In the foreground is a completed fiber glass prototype model of an experimental car. The model in the center of the room is a full-scale "seating mock-up" which is used to check interior dimensions, seating positions, steering wheel angle, location of controls, ease of entry and exit. On the rear wall is a full size engineering layout. Designers are at work at tables along the right hand side. (General Motors Corp.)

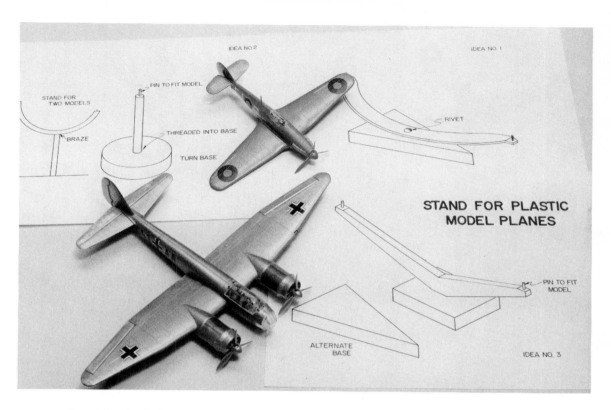

Fig. 3-12. *PROBLEM. Design a stand to display two model planes. The first step is to make sketches which show your ideas.*

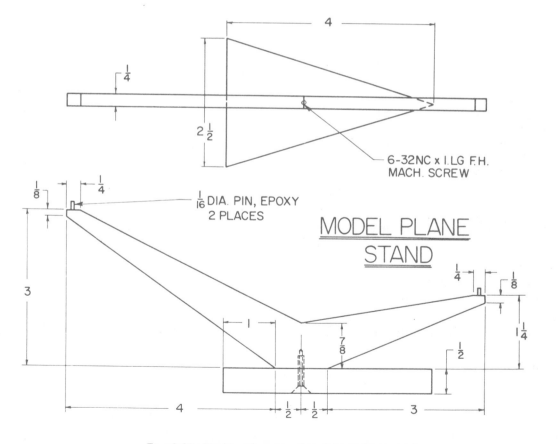

Fig. 3-13. *Working drawing of model airplane stand.*

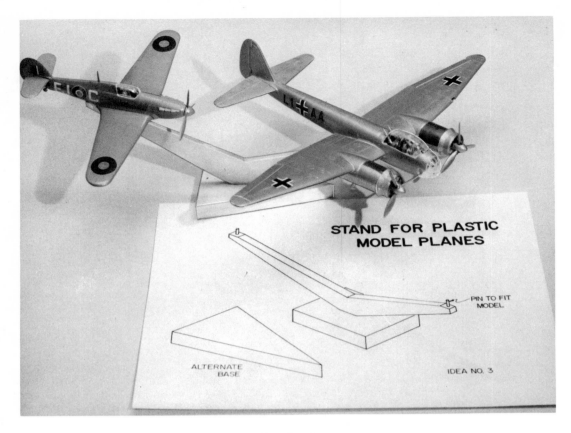

STAND FOR PLASTIC
MODEL PLANES

PIN TO FIT
MODEL

ALTERNATE
BASE

IDEA NO. 3

Fig. 3-14. Completed project.

that you will be proud to show others. See Fig. 3-14.

It takes time to acquire the ability to develop well designed projects. YOU LEARN BY DOING. Keep a notebook of your ideas. Include photos of the projects you have designed and constructed. By reviewing your notebook it will be easy to see how your design ability improves.

What Do You Know About Design? - Unit 3

1. Why is good design difficult to describe?
2. Good design is characterized by certain qualities or guide lines. Briefly describe each.
3. A series of steps are recommended to be followed to solve a design problem. List them and describe each briefly.

Special Activities

1. Design a table lamp.
2. Develop and make plans for a wall rack to display model cars. Your design should hold at least three cars.
3. Prepare sketches of your ideas for a coffee table that can be made from wrought metal.
4. Design a sheet metal tool box.
5. What are your ideas for book ends or a book rack? Prepare sketches of your ideas.
6. Design a model plane rack that is made from metal turned on the lathe.
7. Bird feeders that keep out squirrels are difficult to design. Prepare your ideas in sketch form. When you are satisfied that it will work, make a model of it.
8. Design a trivet (device used to prevent hot dishes and pots from scorching the table top) that can be made from band iron. You may want to use ceramic tile on the top.
9. Design an award that could be given for outstanding metal shop achievements.
10. Prepare sketches for a post lamp made from copper. Include in your design the electrical fixtures.

Unit 4
SAFETY IN
THE METAL SHOP

The nature of the work makes it necessary that YOU exercise extreme care when working in the metal shop.

Be sure all the machines are fitted with guards and are in good working condition. See Fig. 4-1.

Most accidents can be avoided. Develop safe work habits. BE ALERT ALWAYS. You are not a "sissy" if you wear goggles and follow safety rules. You're using good judgment. DON'T TAKE CHANCES.

Remember IT HURTS WHEN YOU GET HURT. Become familiar with the safety rules demonstrated by your teacher and those that are included in this text. OBSERVE THEM AT ALL TIMES.

General Safety Rules

The astronaut dresses for the hazards of space flight. The uniform the football player wears is designed to help protect him from bumps and jolts he will receive on the play-

Fig. 4-2. Dress properly when working in the shop. Wear an apron or shop coat, remove rings, watch and necktie. Above all, WEAR GOGGLES.

ing field. When YOU work in the shop, dress for the job. See Fig. 4-2.

Fig. 4-1. NEVER use a machine until ALL guards are in place. Left. Headstock interior of a modern lathe. Right. Headstock with gears covered and guards in place.

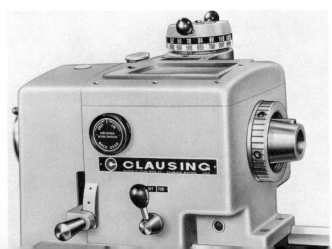

Fig. 4-3. Roll your sleeves above your elbows. There will then be no danger of them getting caught in moving parts of the machine.

1. Remove your tie. Tucking it into your shirt is NOT satisfactory. Wear a bow tie if you must wear a tie.

2. Roll your sleeves above your elbow, Fig. 4-3.

3. Wear approved safety goggles, Fig. 4-4. Wear special goggles or use a shield when welding, Fig. 4-5. This also applies to visitors.

4. Remove your wrist watch, rings and

Fig. 4-4. Approved safety goggles have lenses that will not shatter if struck by flying metal.
(Watchemoket Optical Co., Inc.)

other jewelry that might get caught in moving machinery.

5. Wear protective clothing when working in the foundry, forge and welding areas. See Fig. 4-6.

6. An apron or shop coat will protect your school clothing.

7. The shop is no place for practical jokes or "horseplay." All tricks and pranks are dangerous to YOU and your fellow students.

8. Vise jaws should be left open slightly so that the handle will be in a vertical position. There is less chance of an accident if the handle is left in this position.

9. Do not operate portable electric power tools in areas where thinners and solvents are used. A serious fire or explosion might result.

10. Always walk while you are in the shop. Running is dangerous. You might stumble or collide with a fellow student who is operating a machine or pouring molten metal.

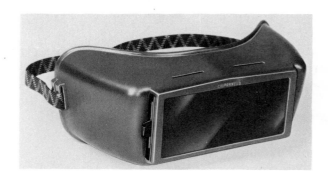

Fig. 4-5. Welding requires special goggles with tinted lenses.
DO NOT WEAR GOGGLES DESIGNED FOR GAS WELDING WHEN ARC WELDING.

11. Get immediate medical attention for cuts, burns, bruises and injuries no matter how minor they appear. Report any accident to your teacher.

12. It is recommended that you NOT wear canvas shoes in the metal shop.

13. Place scrap metal and shavings in containers furnished for them. Do not throw them on the floor.

14. Oil soaked and greasy cleaning rags should be discarded and placed in safety containers provided for them. Do not store them in your locker.

15. Use care when handling long pieces

Fig. 4-6. Wear special clothing when the job requires it. Note that these young welders are wearing face shields, leather jackets, gloves and fire resistant coveralls.

of metal so that you do not injure a fellow student or, when removing or replacing long pieces from a vertical storage rack, accidentally put them into a light fixture.

16. See your instructor before using fluids stored in poorly marked containers. Avoid trying to discover what is in the containers by breathing in the fumes, Fig. 2-7.

17. Clean machines with brushes provided for that purpose. Never use your fingers or hands to remove chips or shavings from your machine.

Safety When Using Hand Tools

Painful accidents can result through the incorrect use of hand tools or tools not in good repair.

1. Do not use a tool until you have received instruction in its proper use.

2. Keep tools sharp. Dull tools do not work properly and are dangerous.

3. Check each tool before use. Report defects like a loose or a split handle on a hammer. Grind mushroomed heads from chisels

TOO BIG A WHIFF—
AND YOU'RE STIFF!

Fig. 4-7. Student designed poster stressing the danger of testing the contents of a can by smelling.

and punches.

4. Files should NEVER be used without handles.

5. Use extreme care when carrying pointed hand tools or those with sharp edges. Do not carry them in your pockets.

6. When using dividers, scribes, etc., place them on the bench with the points and sharp edges directed away from you, Fig. 4-8.

7. One tool should not be improperly substituted for another. Avoid using a wrench for a hammer, a screwdriver for a chisel, pliers for wrenches, etc.

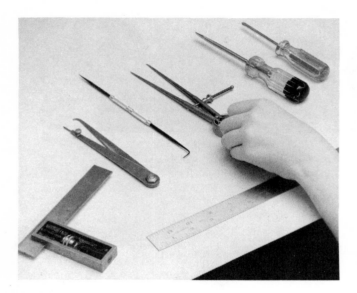

Fig. 4-8. Place sharp or pointed tools on the bench in such a manner that there will be no danger of being injured when you reach for them.

There is very little chance of you going wrong if you remember the A B C's of safety - - - ALWAYS BE CAREFUL.

What Do You Know About Safety in the Metal Shop? - Unit 4

1. Accidents can be avoided if _____.
2. Safety rules must be observed at all times because _____.
3. Describe the proper way to dress if you are going to work in the metal shop.
4. Only approved safety goggles should be worn in the shop because _____.
5. Painful injuries may be caused through _____.
6. Never clean a machine with your _____ use a _____ provided for that purpose.
7. What are the A B C's of shop safety?

Special Activities

1. Design safety posters using one or more of the following themes:
   IT HURTS WHEN YOU GET HURT
   BE ALERT ALWAYS
   WEAR YOUR GOGGLES
   ALWAYS BE CAREFUL
   AN IDEA OF YOUR OWN
   Sketch your ideas on scrap paper. Draw your final design(s) in color on 8 1/2 in. by 11 in. Poster Board.
2. Design a bulletin board display on eye safety.

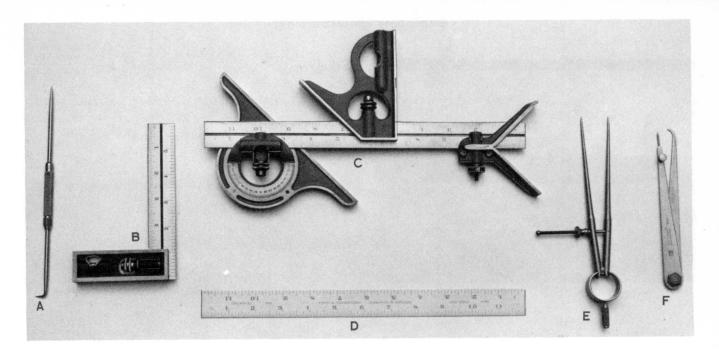

Fig. 5-1. Basic measuring and layout tools: A—Scriber. B—Adjustable square. C—Combination set. D—12 in. rule. E—Divider. F—Hermaphrodite caliper.

Unit 5
MEASUREMENT AND LAYOUT TOOLS

To do metalworking with any degree of accuracy, it is necessary to read and use correctly, basic measuring and layout tools. See Fig. 5-1.

Rule

The STEEL RULE is the simplest of the measuring tools. Various styles and lengths are used in school shops. See Fig. 5-2.

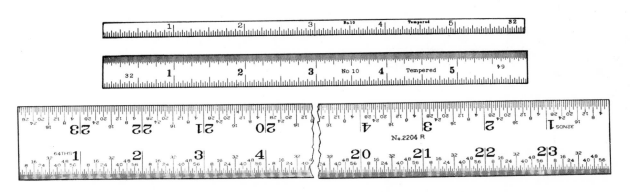

Fig. 5-2. A few of the many types of rules available to the metalworker.

35

Fig. 5-3. The fractional divisions of the standard No. 4 steel rule.

The rule usually has fractional divisions on all four edges of 1/8, 1/16, 1/32 and 1/64 in., Fig. 5-3. Lines representing the divisions are called GRADUATIONS.

The best way to learn to read a rule is to:

1. Practice making measurements with the 1/8 and 1/16 in. graduations until you are thoroughly familiar with them.
2. The same is then done with the 1/32 and 1/64 in. graduations.
3. Practice until the measurements can be made accurately and quickly.

Always reduce fractional measurements to their lowest terms. A measurement of 6/8 reduces to 3/4, 6/16 to 3/8, etc.

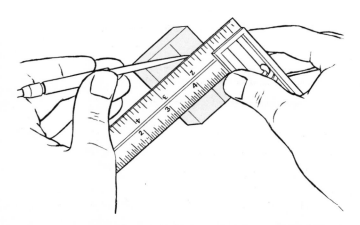

Fig. 5-4. In addition to being used to check squareness of stock, the machinist's square can also be used for layout work.

Squares

The accuracy of a 90 deg. angle can be checked with a SQUARE, Fig. 5-4. The tool is also used for layout work and simple machine setups.

Squares are manufactured in a variety of sizes and types.

Combination Set

Many different measuring and layout operations can be performed with the COMBINATION SET, Fig. 5-5. The tool is com-

Fig. 5-5. The combination set. Protractor head (left); square (center); center head (right); and 12 in. rule.

posed of four parts - - BLADE (rule), SQUARE HEAD, CENTER HEAD and BEVEL PROTRACTOR. The blade fits all three heads.

The SQUARE HEAD, when fitted with the blade, will serve as a try square and miter square, Fig. 5-6. The tool can be used as a depth gauge by projecting the blade the desired distance below the edge of the unit. Simple leveling operations can be performed utilizing the SPIRIT LEVEL built into one edge.

The center of round stock can be located quickly with the blade fitted in the CENTER HEAD, Fig. 5-7.

Various angles can be checked and laid out with the blade fitted in the BEVEL PROTRACTOR HEAD, Fig. 5-8.

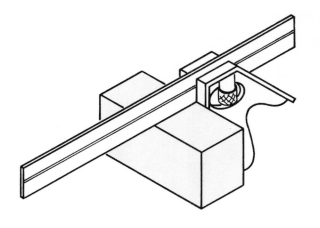

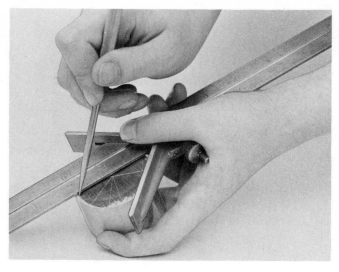

Fig. 5-7. Using *CENTER HEAD* to locate center of round stock.

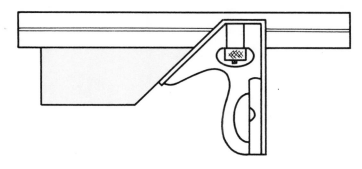

Fig. 5-6. In addition to being used for layout work, the *SQUARE HEAD* of the combination set can be used to check squareness and accuracy of 45 deg. angle machined surfaces.

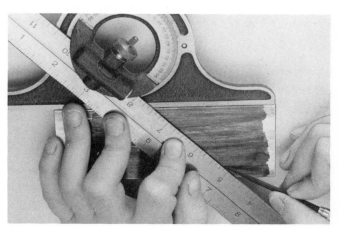

Fig. 5-8. Angular lines can be laid out using the *BEVEL PROTRACTOR HEAD* of the combination set.

Micrometer

The MICROMETER or "MIKE," is a precision measuring tool, Fig. 5-9. You should become acquainted with the major parts of the micrometer. A micrometer may be used to take measurements that are about one-

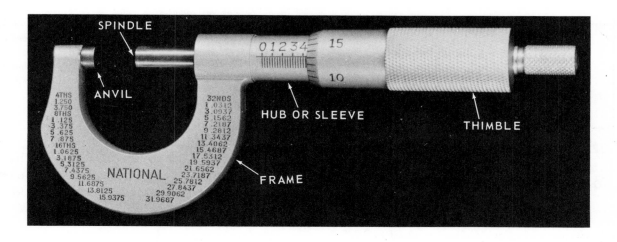

Fig. 5-9. The micrometer or "mike."

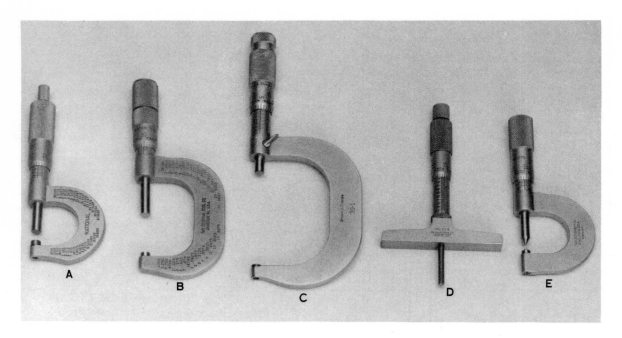

Fig. 5-10. A few of the many sizes and types of micrometers available: A—1 in. micrometer. B—2 in. micrometer. C—3 in. micrometer. D—Depth micrometer. E—Thread micrometer.

thirtieth the thickness of the paper on which this is printed. The "mike" is made in many different sizes and types. See Fig. 5-10.

How to Read the Micrometer

The operation of the micrometer is based on the 40 precision threads per inch on the SPINDLE. When the THIMBLE (which is attached to the spindle) is rotated one complete turn, the spindle will move 1/40 in. (0.025 in.).

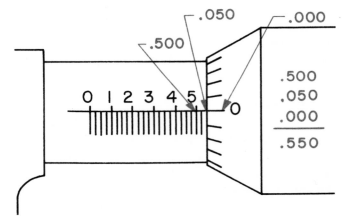

Fig. 5-12. The micrometer is read by recording the highest figure visible on the HUB --5 = 0.500. To this is added the the number of vertical lines visible between the number and the THIMBLE edge, 2 = 2 x 0.025 or 0.050. To this total is added the number of thousandths indicated by the line on the thimble that coincides with the horizontal line on the hub.

The line engraved on the SLEEVE is divided into 40 equal parts per inch, Fig. 5-11. This corresponds to the number of threads on the spindle. Every fourth division is numbered 1, 2, 3, etc., representing 0.100 in., 0.200 in., etc.

The THIMBLE has 25 equal graduations, each representing 1/1000 in. (0.001 in.). On

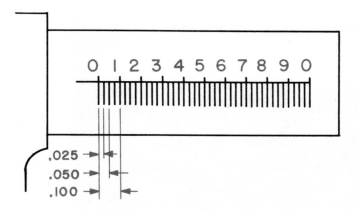

Fig. 5-11. The micrometer HUB or SLEEVE is divided into 40 equal parts per inch. Each division is equal to 0.025 in. Every fourth division is numbered 1, 2, 3, etc., representing 0.100 in., 0.200 in., etc.

some micrometers, each of the graduations is numbered. On others, every fifth graduation is numbered.

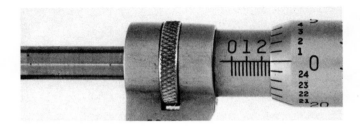

Fig. 5-13. *Can YOU read this micrometer measurement?*

Read the micrometer by recording the highest figure visible on the SLEEVE, such as 1 = 0.100, 2 = 0.200, etc. To this is added the number of vertical lines that can be seen between the number and the THIMBLE edge, 1 = 0.025, 2 = 0.050, and 3 = 0.075. Add to this total the number of thousandths indicated by the line on the THIMBLE that corresponds with the horizontal line on the SLEEVE.

Practice this sequence as indicated in Figs. 5-12, 5-13 and 5-14.

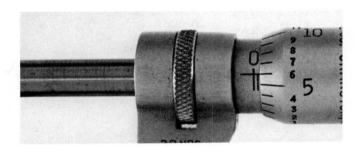

Fig. 5-14. *A section of sheet metal was measured with this micrometer. How thick is the metal?*

Metrication
(Using Metric System)

METRICATION: Pertaining to the use of the metric system as a basis for measurement.

There is a fast growing interest in the metric system in the United States. In 1968, Congress authorized a study to determine the advantages and disadvantages of increased usage of the metric system. The study, made by the National Bureau of Standards, has resulted in the recommendation to Congress that the U. S. change over to the metric system through a carefully planned program over a period of years.

The change over will be costly but it is thought necessary if the United States is to remain a leading nation in world trade. More nations use the metric system of measurement than the English based system we use and it is unlikely these nations will convert. Also, many corporations in the U. S. have manufacturing facilities all over the world, and parts they use in producing products in this country are made overseas.

FRACTIONAL INCH

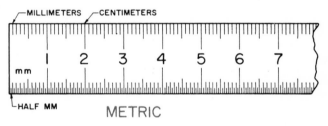

METRIC

DECIMAL INCH

Fig. 5-15. *A comparison of the metric (millimeter) rule with the familiar fractional and decimal inch rules.*

Metric Measuring Tools

The familiar rule and micrometer are available graduated in the metric system. Fig. 5-15 compares a metric (millimeter) rule with the conventional fractional and decimal inch rule.

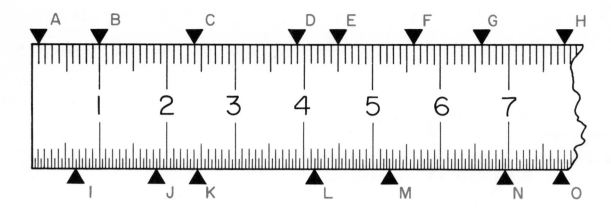

Fig. 5-16. *How many of the dimensions marked can you read correctly?*

How many of the dimensions marked on the metric rule, shown in Fig. 5-16, can you read? For example, measurement B would be read 10 mm. Measurement J would be read 18.5 mm.

The metric micrometer, Fig. 5-17, is used in the same manner as the English type, except the graduations are in the metric system and the readings are obtained as follows:

Since the pitch of the spindle screw in metric micrometers is 0.5 millimeters, one complete revolution of the thimble advances the spindle toward or away from the anvil exactly 0.5 millimeters.

Fig. 5-17. *Metric based micrometer.*

The longitudinal line on the sleeve is graduated in millimeters from 0 to 25 mm and each millimeter is subdivided in 0.5 mm. Therefore, it requires two revolutions of the thimble to advance the spindle a distance equal to 1 millimeter.

The beveled edge of the thimble is graduated in 50 divisions, every fifth line being

numbered from 0 to 50. Since a complete revolution of the thimble advances the spindle 0.5 mm, each graduation on the thimble is equal to 1/50 of 0.5 mm or 0.01 mm, two graduations equal 0.02 mm, etc.

To read a metric micrometer, see Fig. 5-18, add the total reading in millimeters visible on the sleeve to the reading in hun-

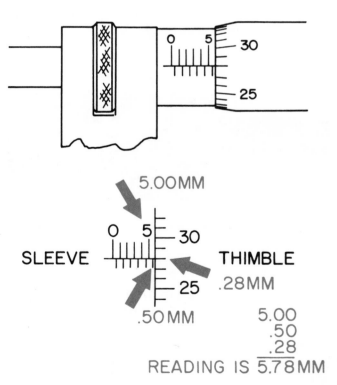

Fig. 5-18. *To read a metric micrometer, add the total reading in millimeters visible on the sleeve to the reading in hundredths of a millimeter indicated by the graduation on the thimble which coincides with the longitudinal line on the sleeve.*

dredths of a millimeter indicated by the graduation on the thimble which coincides with the longitudinal line on the sleeve.

Metric Dimensioned Drawings

You are familiar with drawings using the inch dimensioning system, Fig. 5-19. DUAL DIMENSIONING, Fig. 5-20, is the first step in the change over to metric dimensioning.

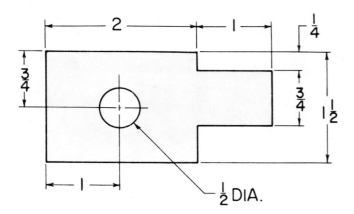

Fig. 5-19. A drawing dimensioned with the English base inch dimensioning system.

In dual dimensioning, both the inch dimensions and metric (millimeter) dimensions have equal status.

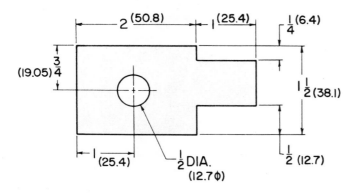

Fig. 5-20. A drawing using dual dimensioning. Both the inch dimensions and metric dimensions have equal status.

The final step will probably result in full metric dimensioning. See Fig. 5-21.

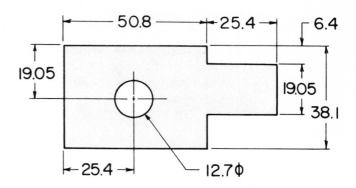

Fig. 5-21. A drawing with full metric dimensions.

A CONVERSION TABLE showing how to convert inches to the metric system and reverse is shown in Fig. 5-22.

CONVERSION FACTORS

LENGTH

Multiply	By	To Obtain
centimeters	0.3937	inches
centimeters	0.01	meters
decimeters	0.1	meters
feet	0.3048	meters
inches	25.40	millimeters
kilometers	3281	feet
kilometers	1000	meters
kilometers	0.6214	miles
kilometers	0.53996	nautical miles
meters	3.281	feet
meters	39.37	inches
miles	5280	feet
miles	1609	meters
miles	0.86898	nautical miles

AREA

Multiply	By	To Obtain
square centimeters	0.001076	square feet
square centimeters	0.1550	square inches
square feet	929.0	square centimeters
square feet	144	square inches
square feet	0.09290	square meters
square inches	6.452	square centimeters
square inches	0.006944	square feet
square inches	$6.452/10^4$	square meters
square inches	645.2	square millimeters
square meters	10.76	square feet
square meters	1.196	square yards
square millimeters	0.00155	square inches
square yards	9	square feet
square yards	1296	square inches

Fig. 5-22. Conversion table.

Helper Measuring Tools

A helper measuring tool is a tool which must be used with a steel rule or micrometer. The tool cannot be used to make a measurement without this aid.

Outside Caliper

External measurements can be made with an OUTSIDE CALIPER, Fig. 5-23, when a 1/64 in. tolerance or variance is permitted. The 1/64 in. tolerance means that the part can be 1/64 in. larger or 1/64 in. smaller than the size indicated on the plans and still be used.

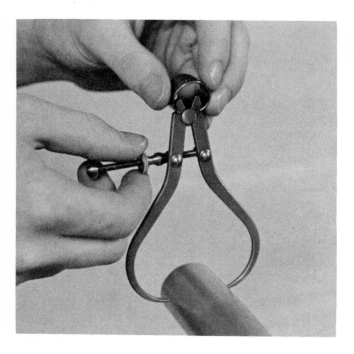

Fig. 5-23. Making a measurement with the outside caliper.

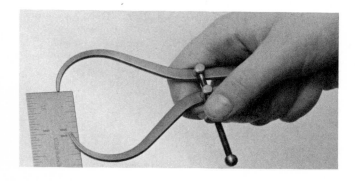

Fig. 5-24. Reading the measurement on an outside caliper.

Measurement of round stock is made by setting the caliper until the caliper leg bears lightly on the center line of the material. Hold the caliper to the rule to read the size, Fig. 5-24.

Never force a caliper over the work. This will "spring" the caliper legs and give an inaccurate measurement.

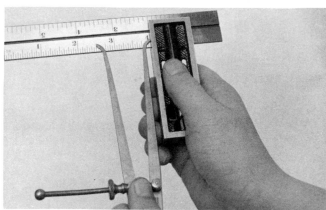

Fig. 5-25. Making a measurement with an inside caliper.

Inside Caliper

Inside dimensions are gaged with the INSIDE CALIPER, Fig. 5-25. Measurement is made by inserting the tool into the opening

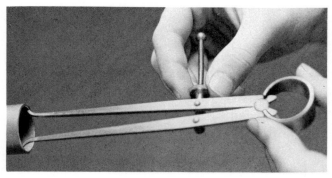

Fig. 5-26. Reading the measurement on an inside caliper.

and opening the legs until they "drag" slightly when moved in or out, or from side to side. To read the hole size, hold the caliper to a rule, Fig. 5-26.

Layout Tools

A LAYOUT is a series of reference points and lines that show the craftsman the shape to which the material is to be cut or machined, Fig. 5-27. It may also include the location of openings and holes that must be made in the job.

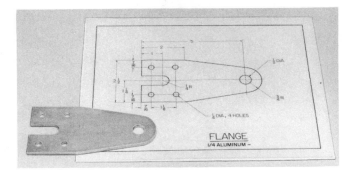

Fig. 5-27. A typical layout drawing and the part made using the drawing as a guide.

Accuracy depends, to a considerable extent, on YOUR skill in the proper use and care of the LAYOUT TOOLS.

Making Lines on Metal

It is not easy to see layout lines on shiny metal. A LAYOUT DYE, Fig. 5-28, is a coating that is applied to the metal to provide

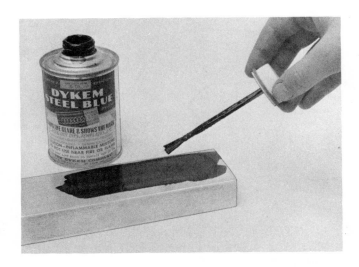

Fig. 5-28. Layout fluid is used to make scribed lines stand out on the metal surface.

contrast between the metal and the layout lines.

Chalk can be used on hot rolled metal as a layout background.

Scriber

Accurate layouts require scribing fine lines on the surface of the metal. The lines may be made with a SCRIBER, Fig. 5-29. The point is made of hardened steel and should be kept needle sharp by frequent honing on a fine oilstone. There are many styles of scribers.

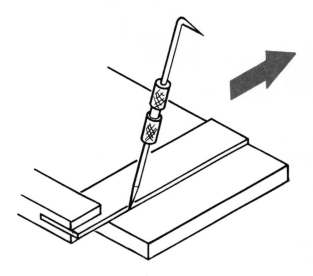

Fig. 5-29. Make sure the SCRIBER is held firmly against the straightedge before making the layout line.

A pencil should never be used to make layout lines. A pencil line is too wide and rubs off too easily.

CAUTION: NEVER CARRY OPEN SCRIBER IN YOUR POCKET.

Dividers

Circles and arcs are drawn on metal with the DIVIDER, Fig. 5-30. The tool may also be used to measure equal distances.

It may be set to the desired dimension by placing one point on an inch mark of a steel

Fig. 5-30. *Circles are drawn on metal with DIVIDERS.*

rule, and opening the divider until the other leg is set to the desired size, Fig. 5-31.

Hermaphrodite Caliper

The HERMAPHRODITE CALIPER, Fig. 5-32, is a layout tool which is a cross between an inside caliper and a divider.

Fig. 5-31. *Setting the divider to the required radius.*

It is used to lay out lines parallel to an edge or to locate the approximate center of irregular shaped stock.

Fig. 5-32. *Scribing a line parallel to the edge of the work with the HERMAPHRODITE CALIPER.*

Punches

Two types of PUNCHES are commonly employed in making layouts:

1. PRICK PUNCH, Fig. 5-33 (above). A hardened, pointed steel rod used to "spot" the point where the center lines intersect on a layout. The sharp point (30 - 60 deg.) makes it easy to locate points.

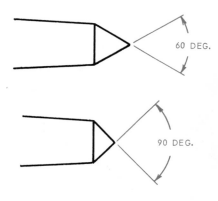

Fig. 5-33. *Above. Prick punch. Below. Center punch.*

2. CENTER PUNCH, Fig. 5-33 (below). Similar to a prick punch but with a more blunt point (90 deg.). It is used to enlarge the prick punch mark after it has been checked and found to be on center.

How to Make a Layout

Each layout job will have its particular problems and will require careful planning before starting. The following sequence (Figs. 5-34 and 5-35) is recommended:

1. Carefully study the plans.
2. Cut the stock to size and remove all burrs and sharp edges.
3. Clean the metal and apply layout dye.
4. Locate and scribe a BASE or REFERENCE LINE. All measurements are then made from this line. If the material has one true edge, it can serve as the reference or base line.
5. Locate all circle and arc center lines.
6. Locate and scribe angular lines.
7. Scribe all other internal openings.

If you make a mistake, apply another coat of dye and rescribe the line.

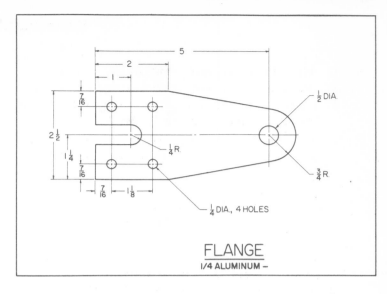

Fig. 5-34. Layout problem.

Layout Safety

1. Do not carry scribers, dividers or other pointed tools in your pocket.
2. Cover sharp pointed tools with a cork

CUT METAL TO APPROXIMATE SIZE

LOCATE AND SCRIBE BASE LINES

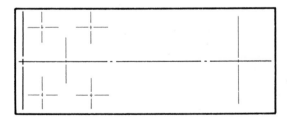

LOCATE CIRCLE AND ARC CENTER LINES

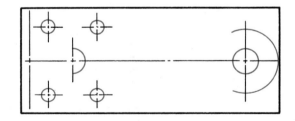

SCRIBE IN CIRCLES AND ARCS

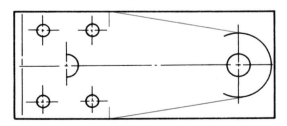

LOCATE AND SCRIBE ANGULAR LINES

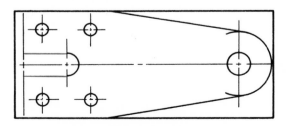

SCRIBE INTERNAL LINES

Fig. 5-35. Steps in laying out the job shown in Fig. 5-34.

when they are not being used.

3. Wear goggles when repointing layout tools.
4. Remove burrs and sharp edges from the stock before starting to work on it.
5. Get prompt medical attention for any cut, scratch or bruise, no matter how minor it may appear.

What Do You Know About Measurement And Layout Tools? - Unit 5

1. The _____ is the simplest and most widely used of the measuring tools.
2. How many of the measurements can YOU read on the sections of the rule shown in PART I, below.
3. Measure lines shown in Part II, page 47.
4. The accuracy of 90 deg. angles can be checked with a _____.
5. The combination set is composed of four (4) parts. Name them and briefly describe what each does.
6. _____ is another name for the micrometer.
7. Make the readings on the micrometer drawings in Part III, page 47.
8. What does the word metrication mean?
9. In 1968, Congress authorized a study of the advantages and disadvantages of using the metric system in the U. S. What did this group recommend?
10. Read the dimensions marked on the rule in Part IV, page 47.
11. What is meant by dual dimensioning?
12. Helper measuring tools cannot _____ _____.
13. A layout is used to _____ _____.
14. Straight layout lines are drawn with a _____.
15. Circles and arcs are drawn with a _____.
16. _____ is applied to provide contrast between the metal surface and the layout lines.

Special Activities

1. Secure a metric rule and micrometer from the Science Department at your school and instruct the class in their use.
2. Make a drawing of a project to be made in the school shop. Use metric dimensioning.
3. Discuss the metric system with your father. Find out whether the company where he works would find the system an advantage or a disadvantage.

PART I: PROBLEMS IN MEASURING.

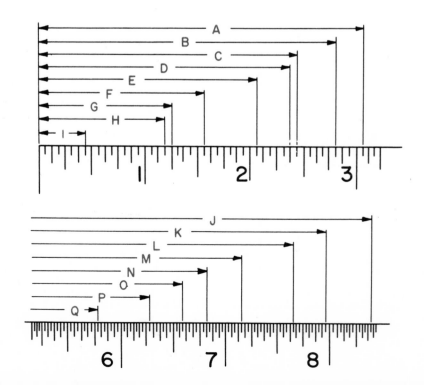

PART II: MEASURE EACH LINE TO THE NEAREST 1/32 IN.
REDUCE FRACTIONS TO THEIR LOWEST TERMS.

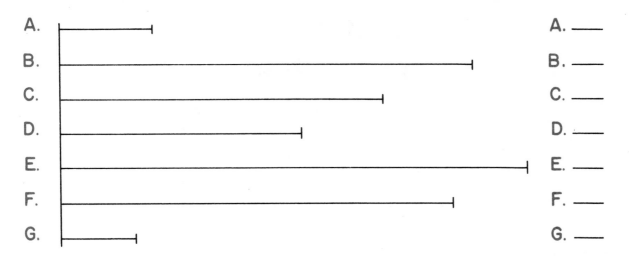

A. ——   A. ——
B. ——   B. ——
C. ——   C. ——
D. ——   D. ——
E. ——   E. ——
F. ——   F. ——
G. ——   G. ——

PART III: MICROMETER READING PROBLEMS.

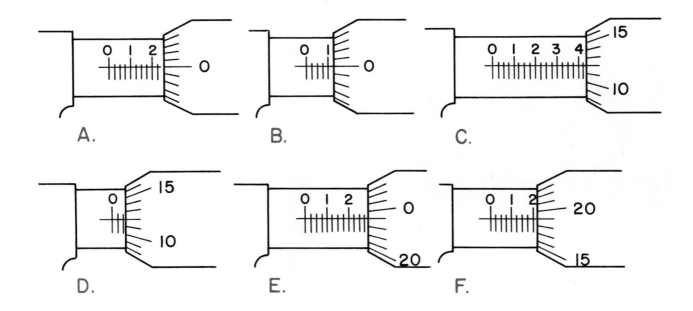

A.   B.   C.

D.   E.   F.

PART IV: PROBLEMS IN MEASURING.

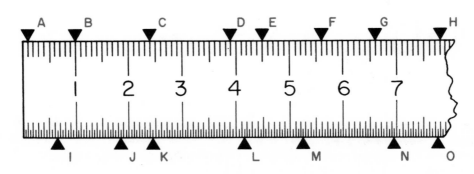

Unit 6
BASIC METALWORKING TOOLS AND EQUIPMENT

The proper and safe use of hand tools and machines is basic to all areas of metalworking.

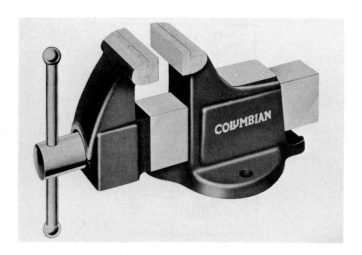

Fig. 6-1. Vise used in metalworking.

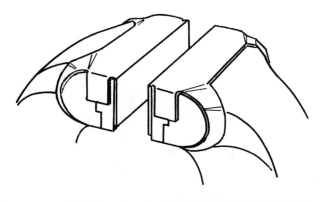

Fig. 6-2. Caps protect the material from being marred by the serrations on the vise jaws. The caps are made of soft metal.

Vise

Metal is normally held in a VISE while it is being worked, Fig. 6-1. There are many sizes and types of vises.

CAPS made of soft metal, Fig. 6-2, should be fitted over the vise jaws to protect the work from being damaged or marred by the jaw serrations (teeth).

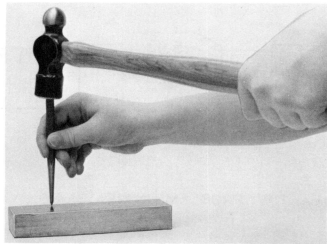

Fig. 6-3. Ball peen hammer.

Hammers

The BALL PEEN HAMMER, Fig. 6-3, is the hammer usually used in metalworking. Its size is usually described by the weight of the head, 4 oz., 8 oz., etc.

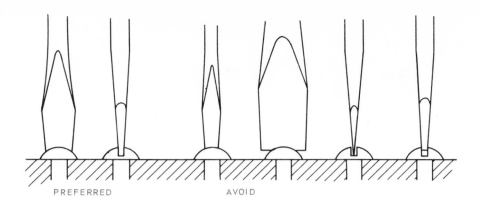

PREFERRED AVOID

Fig. 6-4. Use the correct size screwdriver for the job to be done.

Ordinarily, the lightest hammer that will do the job easily and safely should be used.

Screwdrivers

Select the screwdriver that fits the screw being driven, Fig. 6-4. Two types of SCREW-DRIVERS commonly used in the school shop are the STANDARD TYPE for slotted heads, and the PHILLIPS TYPE for X-shaped recessed heads, Fig. 6-5.

Pliers

Many holding, bending and cutting jobs can be done with PLIERS, Fig. 6-6. Pliers

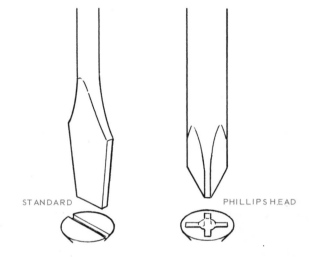

STANDARD PHILLIPS HEAD

Fig. 6-5. Two of the more widely used screwdriver types.

Fig. 6-6. A few of the many types and sizes of pliers available to the craftsman. A—Linemen's side cutting pliers. B—Long nose cutting pliers. C—Needle nose pliers. D—Diagonal cutting pliers. E—Short reach needle nose pliers. F—Groove joint pliers. G—Slip-joint or combination pliers.

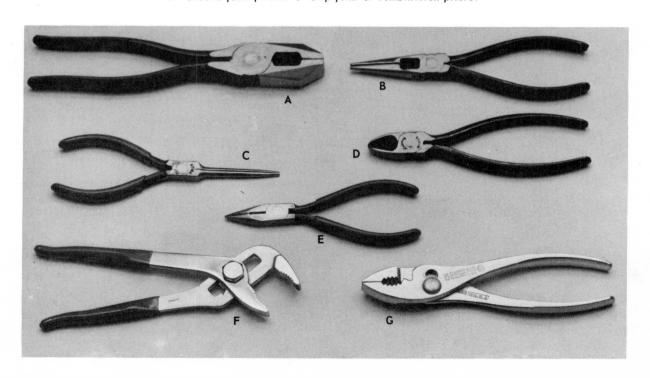

are made in many sizes and styles to handle a variety of jobs. PLIERS SHOULD NEVER BE USED AS A SUBSTITUTE FOR A HAMMER OR A WRENCH.

Pliers commonly found in the school shop include:

COMBINATION PLIERS (also known as SLIP-JOINT PLIERS) have many uses. The slip joint makes it possible to adjust the jaws and grip both large and small work. The jaws have serrations or teeth. On some slip-joint pliers, a short cutting edge for severing wire is located near the hinge.

The cutting edges of DIAGONAL PLIERS are at an angle so they will cut flush with the work surface.

Heavier wire and pins can be cut with SIDE-CUTTING PLIERS.

Wire and light metal can be bent and formed with ROUND NOSE PLIERS. The smooth jaws will not mar the work.

LONG or NEEDLE NOSE PLIERS are useful when space is limited, or where small work is to be held.

When using pliers keep your fingers clear of the cutting edges. When doing electrical work be sure to insulate the handles with rubber tape, or use specially manufactured rubber grips.

Fig. 6-7. Adjustable wrench.
(Diamond Tool Co.)

Wrenches

Many types of wrenches are available to the metalworking craftsman. Each type is designed for a specific use.

While many wrenches are adjustable to fit different sizes of nuts and bolts, the type wrench shown in Fig. 6-7, is the wrench usually classified as an ADJUSTABLE WRENCH. It is manufactured in a range of sizes. Use the smallest adjustable wrench that will fit the nut or bolt being worked on.

The PIPE WRENCH, Fig. 6-8, is also adjustable. The movable jaw has a small amount of play built in so that it can take a "bite" on round stock. A pipe wrench will leave marks on the stock. This type wrench should not be used on nuts and bolts unless the corners have been damaged so a regular wrench cannot be used.

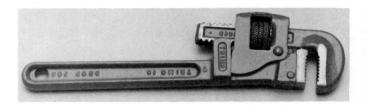

Fig. 6-8. Pipe wrench.

The size of the space between the jaws of the OPEN-END WRENCH, Fig. 6-9, determines its size. Open-end wrenches are made in many different sizes and styles.

Fig. 6-9. Open-end wrench.

The BOX-WRENCH, Fig. 6-10, completely surrounds the bolt head or nut. It is usually preferred over other wrenches because it

Fig. 6-10. Box-wrench.

will not slip. These wrenches are available in sizes to fit standard nuts and bolts.

The COMBINATION OPEN AND BOX WRENCH, Fig. 6-11, has one open end and a box wrench at the other end.

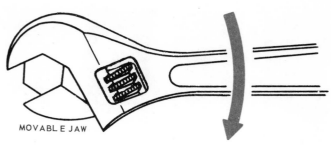

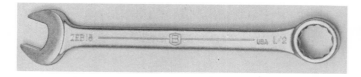

Fig. 6-11. Combination open and box wrench.

SOCKET WRENCHES, Fig. 6-12, are box like and are made as a detachable tool that fits many different types of handles. A typical socket wrench set contains various types of handles and a wide range of socket sizes and styles.

PULL - - NEVER PUSH on any wrench. Pushing is considered dangerous. If the nut loosens suddenly, you may strike your knuckles on the work (this is known as "knuckle dusting"). The movable jaw of a wrench should ALWAYS face the direction the fastener is being turned, Fig. 6-13.

Files and Filing

FILES are frequently used to remove surplus metal.

MOVABLE JAW

Fig. 6-13. The movable jaw of the wrench should ALWAYS face the direction the fastener is being turned.

How Files are Classified

Files are classified by their shape, Fig. 6-14, by the cut of their teeth, Fig. 6-15,

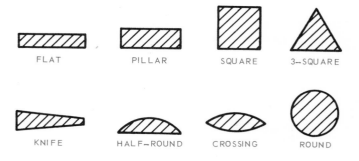

FLAT   PILLAR   SQUARE   3-SQUARE

KNIFE   HALF-ROUND   CROSSING   ROUND

Fig. 6-14. File shapes.

and by the coarseness of the teeth (rough, coarse, bastard, second-cut, smooth and dead smooth).

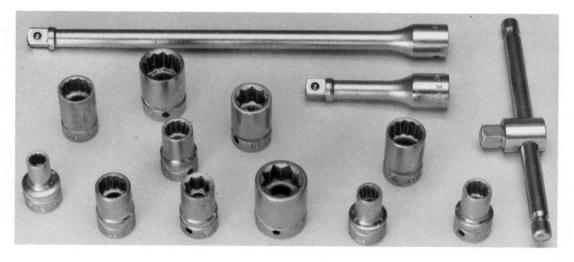

Fig. 6-12. Socket wrench set with extensions.

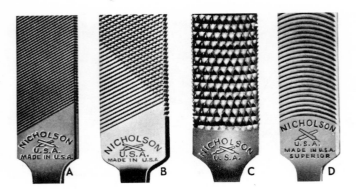

Fig. 6-15. Single-cut, double-cut, rasp and curved-tooth files.

File Care

Your file should be cleaned frequently using a FILE CARD, Fig. 6-16. This will prevent PINNING (small slivers of metal that clog the file and cause scratches on the work). DO NOT try to clean a file by striking it against the bench top or vise.

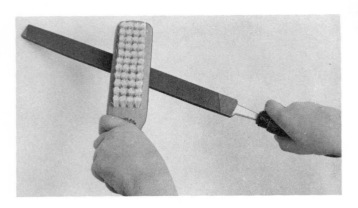

Fig. 6-16. Clean a file with a file card.

File Selection

The nature of the work will determine the size, shape and cut of the file that should be used.

A SINGLE-CUT file is generally used to produce a smooth surface finish. DOUBLE-CUT files remove metal rapidly but produce a rougher surface finish. RASPS are used on wood and some plastics, while flat surfaces of steel and aluminum are worked with a CURVED-TOOTH file.

How to Use the File

Most filing is done while the work is held in a vise. Mount the work at about elbow height for general filing. STRAIGHT or CROSS FILING is done by pushing the file lengthwise, straight ahead or at a slight angle across the work, Fig. 6-17. DRAW FILING, Fig. 6-18, usually produces a finer finish than straight filing.

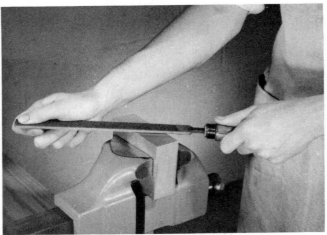

Fig. 6-17. The proper way to hold the file for straight or cross filing.

For safety sake, NEVER USE A FILE WITHOUT A HANDLE. Avoid running your fingers over a newly filed surface. You might cut yourself on the sharp burr formed by the file.

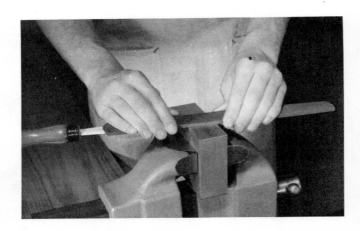

Fig. 6-18. Draw filing improves the surface finish when done properly.

Cutting Metal by Hand

Some metal cutting can be done easily and safely by hand using a chisel or hacksaw.

Chisels

CHISELS are used to cut or shear metal. The four types shown in Fig. 6-19 are widely used. These are usually referred to as COLD CHISELS.

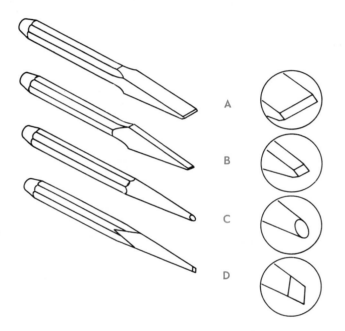

Fig. 6-19. *COLD CHISELS. A—Flat Chisel is used for general cutting. B—Cape Chisel has a narrower cutting edge and is used to cut grooves. C—Round Nose Chisel is used to cut round grooves and radii. D—Diamond Point Chisel is used to square corners.*

NEVER USE A CHISEL WITH A MUSH-ROOMED HEAD, Fig. 6-20. Correct this dangerous condition by grinding.

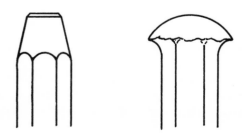

Fig. 6-20. *NEVER USE A CHISEL WITH A MUSHROOMED HEAD.*

Shearing is done with the stock held in a vise, Fig. 6-21. Flat stock should be cut on a soft steel backing plate; NEVER on the vise slide or on top of the anvil.

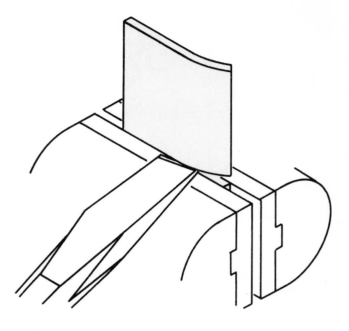

Fig. 6-21. *Shearing work held in a vise with a chisel.*

Hacksaws

Most HACKSAWS are adjustable to fit various blade lengths, Fig. 6-22. Some are

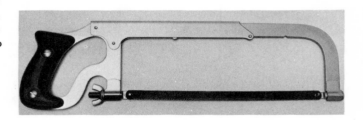

Fig. 6-22. *The adjustable hacksaw.*

made so the blade can be installed in either a vertical or horizontal position, Fig. 6-23.

A fine-tooth blade should be used to cut thin stock. Heavier work is cut with a coarse-tooth blade. Keep in mind the THREE TOOTH RULE (at least three teeth of the blade should be in contact with the work) when selecting the blade to be used.

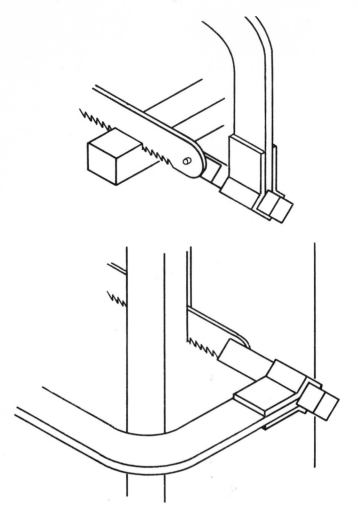

Fig. 6-23. The blade can be installed in either a vertical or horizontal position.

Install the blade with the teeth pointing AWAY from the handle, Fig. 6-24. Tighten until the blade "pings" when snapped with your finger.

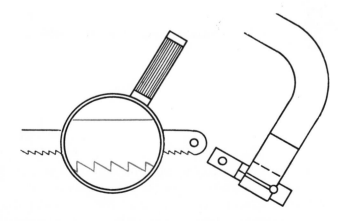

Fig. 6-24. Install the blade with the teeth pointing AWAY from the handle.

Holding Work for Sawing

Clamp the work close to the vise, Fig. 6-25. This will eliminate "chatter" (vibra-

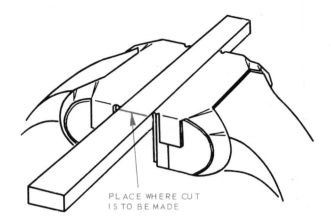

PLACE WHERE CUT IS TO BE MADE

Fig. 6-25. Make cut as close to vise as possible to prevent chatter (vibration) that can ruin the saw blade.

tion that dulls the teeth). Mount it so the cut is started on a flat edge rather than on a corner or edge, Fig. 6-26. Start the cut using

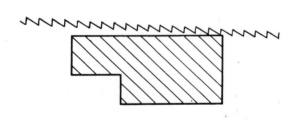

Fig. 6-26. Start the cut on a flat edge of the work rather than on a sharp corner.

the thumb of your free hand to guide the blade. Holding different shapes of metal for cutting is shown in Fig. 6-27.

Cutting Metal

Hold the saw firmly (but comfortably) by the handle and the front of the frame. Apply pressure on the cutting (forward) stroke. Lift the saw slightly on the return stroke. Make about 40 strokes per minute using the full length of the blade.

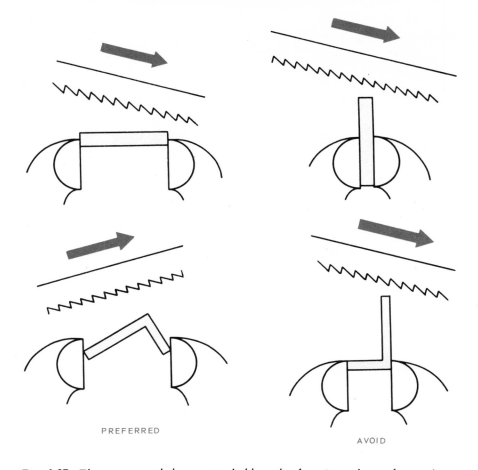

PREFERRED   AVOID

Fig. 6-27. The recommended ways to hold work of various shapes for sawing.

Saw slower when the blade has cut almost through the metal. Support the material so it will not drop when the cut is completed.

Where practical, reposition the work so a new cut can be made after you replace the blade. The new blade will be pinched in the old cut and dull rapidly.

DO NOT TEST SAW BLADE SHARPNESS BY RUNNING YOUR FINGER ACROSS THE TEETH.

Cutting Metal with Machines

Large metal sections can be cut more quickly with the POWER HACKSAW. See Fig. 6-28.

As in hand sawing, the THREE TOOTH RULE applies. In general, large pieces and soft material require saws with coarse teeth.

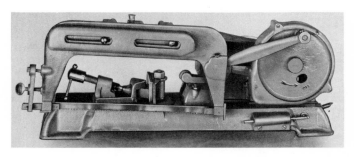

Fig. 6-28. Above. Reciprocating type power hacksaw. Below. Band type power hacksaw.

*Light, strong metals were used in the construction of this soaring plane.
(Schweizer Aircraft Corp.)*

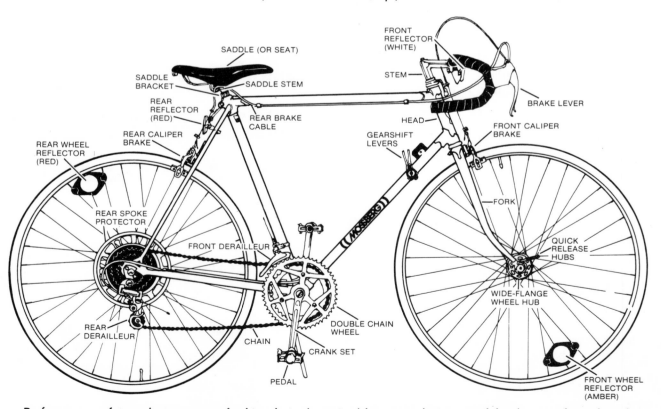

Performance, safety and appearance of a bicycle is determined by proper design, careful selection of metals and by the craftsmanship of those who make it. (O. F. Mossberg & Sons, Inc.)

Small or thin work and hard materials require a fine tooth blade.

Mount the blade so it cuts on the power stroke. This is the back stroke on most reciprocating (back and forth) power saws.

Be sure the work is mounted solidly before starting the cut.

KEEP YOUR HANDS CLEAR OF THE MOVING BLADE AND STOP THE MACHINE BEFORE ATTEMPTING TO MAKE ADJUSTMENTS. PULL THE PLUG WHEN CHANGING BLADES OR MAKING ADJUSTMENTS.

Thin material can be cut with a SABRE SAW, Fig. 6-29. The metal and its thickness will determine the type of blade to use. If a cutting chart came with the saw use this as a guide.

Fig. 6-29. Sabre saw.

Drilling

The DRILL PRESS, Fig. 6-30, is primarily used to cut round holes in metal. It operates by rotating a cutting tool (the DRILL)

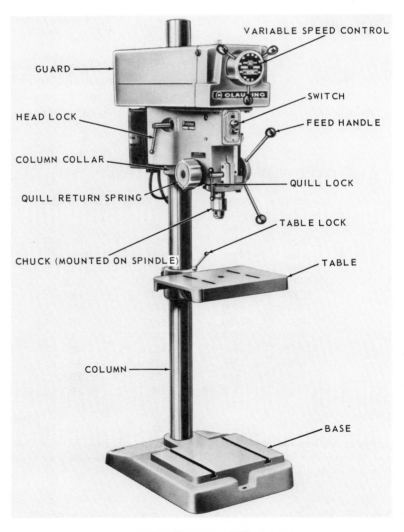

Fig. 6-30. Floor type drill press.

Fig. 6-31. Portable electric drill.

against the material with enough pressure to cause the drill to cut into the material. The PORTABLE ELECTRIC DRILL, Fig. 6-31, and the HAND DRILL, Fig. 6-32, are

Fig. 6-32. Hand drill.

also used to drill holes in all kinds of material.

Drills are made of HIGH SPEED STEEL (HSS) or CARBON STEEL. High Speed drills are more costly when first purchased. However, if used properly, they will cut faster and last longer than carbon steel drills. Recommended cutting speeds (how fast the drill should rotate) for several metals are given in Fig. 6-33.

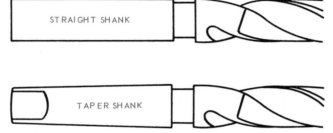

Fig. 6-34. Types of drill shanks.

STRAIGHT SHANK drills, shown in Fig. 6-34, above, must be held in a chuck. TAPER SHANK drills, Fig. 6-34, below, mount directly in the drill press spindle.

CUTTING SPEEDS FOR HIGH SPEED DRILLS

DRILL DIAMETER	ALUMINUM	BRASS	CAST IRON	MILD STEEL	TOOL STEEL
1/16	4500	4500	4500	4000	3500
1/8	2000	3000	1800	1800	1500
3/16	1800	2900	1500	1400	1200
1/4	1700	2300	1200	1100	1000
5/16	1500	1900	950	850	725
3/8	1200	1500	750	700	600
7/16	1100	1300	650	600	525
1/2	1000	1150	575	525	375
9/16	850	1000	500	525	350
5/8	750	900	450	425	300
3/4	600	750	375	350	250
7/8	550	650	325	300	225
1.000	450	575	280	265	185

PLEASE NOTE:

These cutting speeds are recommended. It may be necessary because of the characteristics of the material to increase or decrease the drill speed to do a satisfactory cutting job.
Use a cutting fluid on all metals EXCEPT cast iron.

Fig. 6-33. Suggested cutting speeds for drilling various types of metal.

Drill Sizes

Drill sizes are shown in one of the following series:

NUMBER DRILLS - No. 80 to No. 1 (0.0135 in. to 0.2280 in. diameter).
LETTER DRILLS - A to Z (0.234 in. to 0.413 in. diameter).
FRACTIONAL DRILLS - 1/64 in. to 3 1/2 in. diameter.

Number drills and letter drills are often needed for drilling holes that are to be tapped (threaded) or reamed.

The drill size, except on very small drills, is stamped on the drill shank. Should the size wear away, the drill diameter can be checked using a DRILL GAUGE, Fig. 6-35.

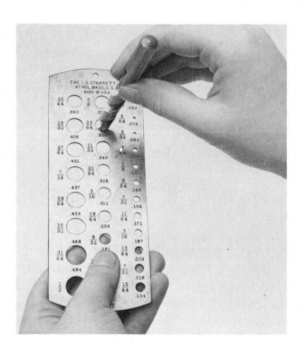

Fig. 6-35. Drill size can be checked quickly with a drill gauge.

Drilling

1. LAY OUT WORK TO BE DRILLED.
2. MOUNT THE WORK SOLIDLY ON THE DRILL PRESS. Where practical use a vise, Fig. 6-36, or clamp the stock to the drill press table. Be careful not to drill into the vise or the table.

Fig. 6-36. Work mounted for drilling.

When drilling, do not hold short pieces or thin stock by hand. A "merry-go-round" may result and cause a painful injury.
3. CENTER THE WORK USING A "WIGGLER" (center finder) OR A CENTER. See Fig. 6-37.
4. SELECT THE DRILL. Check the drill for size and sharpness. Mount it in the chuck. BE SURE TO REMOVE THE CHUCK KEY FROM THE CHUCK.
5. SET THE DRILL PRESS TO THE CORRECT SPEED. In general, use slow speeds for large drills and hard materials; faster speeds for small drills and soft materials. Check a drill speed chart to determine the correct speed for the drill and material being used. See Fig. 6-33.
6. TURN ON THE MACHINE AND BRING THE DRILL INTO CONTACT WITH THE WORK. A few drops of cutting fluid (machine or lard oil) applied to the drill point from time to time will improve the cutting action. Reduce pressure as the drill starts through the work.

Fig. 6-37. Two techniques for locating the hole center when drilling. A—Wiggler or center finder. B—Small center.

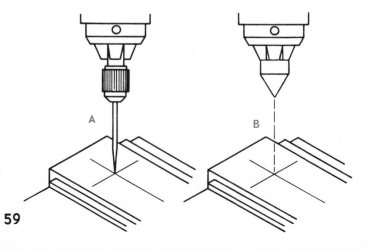

7. TURN OFF THE MACHINE. Clean away chips WITH A BRUSH -- NOT WITH YOUR HANDS. Unclamp the work and remove all burrs.

8. CLEAN THE DRILL PRESS AND THE DRILL. Return the drill to its proper place.

When drilling holes larger than 1/2 in. diameter, it is usually advisable to first drill a smaller PILOT HOLE, Fig. 6-38.

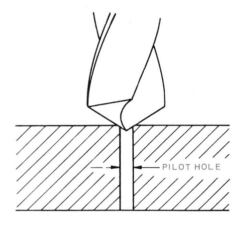

Fig. 6-38. A pilot hole makes drilling large diameter holes easier.

Holes to take flat head fasteners should be COUNTERSUNK. This is done with a COUNTERSINK, Fig. 6-39. Countersink the

Fig. 6-39. Countersink.

hole deep enough so that the head of the fastener is flush with the work surface. See Fig. 6-40.

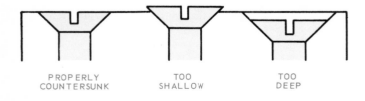

Fig. 6-40. Countersink deeply enough so that the screw head is flush with the work surface.

Hand Threading

Spiral grooves found on nuts, bolts and screws are called THREADS. The operation that cuts this groove is called THREADING.

Threads are cut by hand with a TAP and DIE, Fig. 6-41. INTERNAL THREADS (like those in a nut) are cut with a TAP. Threads on rods (EXTERNAL THREADS) are cut with a DIE.

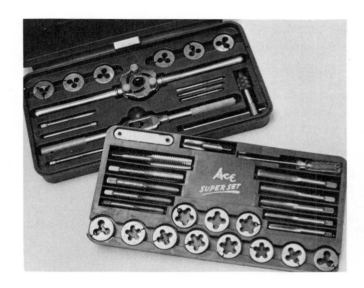

Fig. 6-41. Tap and die size.

Thread Series

There are two common thread series. The NATIONAL FINE SERIES (NF), Fig. 6-42, left, is often found in precision assemblies. The NATIONAL COARSE SERIES (NC), Fig. 6-42, right, is used for general purpose work. Both series are part of the standardized AMERICAN NATIONAL THREAD SYSTEM.

Cutting Internal Threads

A hole must be drilled before an internal thread can be cut. The hole diameter which must be smaller than the tap size, is made with a TAP DRILL. A tap drill is a conventional number, letter or fractional drill used to drill the hole to be tapped small enough to permit the tap to cut threads. A TAP

Fig. 6-42. Left. National Fine Thread (NF). Right. National Coarse Thread (NC).

DRILL CHART SHOULD BE USED TO DETERMINE THE CORRECT SIZE DRILL TO BE USED WITH A SPECIFIED TAP. You will find such a chart on page 244 of this text.

Taps

Taps are made in sets of three, Fig. 6-43, TAPER, PLUG and BOTTOM TAPS.

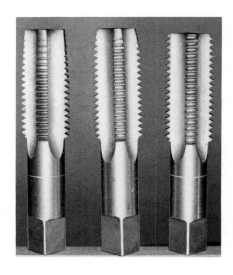

Fig. 6-43. Tap set. Left, taper tap. Center, plug tap. Right, bottoming tap.

The TAPER TAP (the point has a pronounced taper) permits easy starting and is used for tapping through holes (the threads are cut all of the way through the work).

The PLUG TAP is used to thread blind holes (holes not all of the way through the material) if the holes are drilled deeper than the threads are to be cut.

The BOTTOM TAP is used when the thread must be cut to the bottom of a blind hole. Start the thread with a taper tap, cut with a plug tap, and complete with the bottom tap.

Fig. 6-44. T-handle tap wrench is used with small taps.

Tap Holders

Taps are turned into the work with a TAP HOLDER or TAP WRENCH. See Figs. 6-44 and 6-45. Tap size will determine which is to be used.

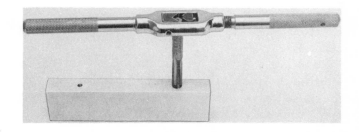

Fig. 6-45. Hand tap wrench.

The T-HANDLE TAP WRENCH is used with small taps (under 1/4 in.). It allows a sensitive "feel" when tapping and reduces the danger of tap breakage.

As more leverage is required with larger taps, the HAND TAP WRENCH should be used.

How to Tap a Hole

To keep tap breakage to a minimum, this procedure is suggested:

1. Drill the required size hole.
2. Start the taper tap square, Fig. 6-46. A drop of cutting oil will improve cutting efficiency.

Fig. 6-46. The tap must be started square.

3. Turn the tap into the work a partial turn. Back it off (turn it counterclockwise) until you feel the chips break loose. Do not force the tap.
Continue the sequence until the hole is tapped.
4. Use cutting oil for tap lubrication. If a blind hole (a hole that does not go through the stock) is being threaded, back the tap out frequently to remove chips.
5. Use care. Broken taps are difficult to remove from the work.

Fig. 6-47. Two types of adjustable dies.

Cutting External Threads

External threads are cut with a DIE, Fig. 6-47. A DIE STOCK, Fig. 6-48, holds the die and serves as a wrench for turning it.

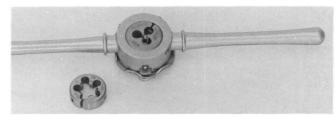

Fig. 6-48. Die stock.

When cutting external threads, remember the following:

1. Stock diameter is the same size as the desired threads. That is, 3/8 - 16NC and 3/8 - 24NF threads would be cut on a 3/8 in. diameter rod.

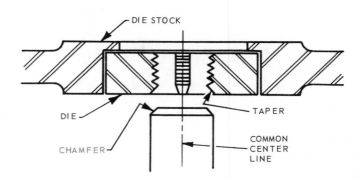

Fig. 6-49. A small chamfer ground or turned on the end of the stock will permit the die to be started easier.

2. Grind a small chamfer on the end of the stock, Fig. 6-49, to make it easier to start the die.

3. Start the cut with the tapered end of the die.

4. Mount the work solidly in a vise.

5. If an adjustable die is used, make trial cuts on scrap stock to see whether the die is properly adjusted.

6. Back off the die every turn or two to break the chips and allow them to fall free.

7. Use liberal quantities of cutting fluid. Be careful not to spill oil on the floor. Do not remove chips from newly cut threads with your fingers.

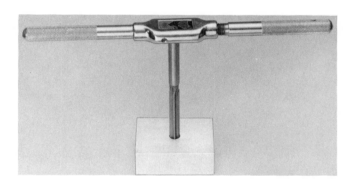

Fig. 6-50. Hand reamer mounted in tap wrench.

Reamers

Drilled holes may be accurately enlarged to the desired size with a REAMER. The HAND REAMER, Fig. 6-50, is used with a tap wrench. Like the MACHINE REAMER which is used with the drill press, it is available with STRAIGHT or SPIRAL FLUTES, Fig. 6-51.

Fig. 6-51. Cutting portion of machine reamers.

EXPANSION REAMERS, Fig. 6-52, permit slight size adjustment.

Fig. 6-52. Adjustable reamer.

After drilling the hole to the correct size for reaming (see Fig. 6-53 for recom-

These allowances (how much smaller the hole must be drilled) are recommended for reaming:

   a. To 1/4 in. diameter allow 0.010 in.
   b. 1/4 to 1/2 in. diameter allow 0.015 in.
   c. 1/2 to 1.0 in. diameter allow 0.020 in.
   d. 1.0 to 1 1/2 in. diameter allow 0.025 in.

   Use sharp reamers.

Fig. 6-53. Reaming table.

mended allowances), use the following sequence to hand ream a hole:

1. Mount the work solidly in a vise.

2. Position the reamer in the hole. The end of the tool is tapered slightly so it will easily fit into the hole. If proper alignment is a problem, use a square.

3. Slowly turn the reamer CLOCKWISE until it is centered in the hole.

4. After the reamer is centered, continue turning the wrench clockwise with a firm, steady pressure until the reamer is through the work. Use cutting oil or machine oil to lubricate the reamer. Remove the tool from the finished hole by turning the wrench clockwise and raising the reamer simultaneously.

CAUTION: DO NOT TURN THE REAMER COUNTERCLOCKWISE AT ANY TIME. THIS WILL DULL THE REAMER.

What Do You Know About Metalworking Tools and Equipment? – Unit 6

MATCHING QUESTIONS. Match the words listed below with the sentences below. Place the letter of the word in the appropriate blank.

1. ____ The soft metal covers used to protect work held in a vise.
2. ____ The screwdriver used to drive slotted screws.
3. ____ The screwdriver used to drive "X" slotted screws.
4. ____ The file cut used to produce a smooth surface finish.
5. ____ The file cut that removes metal rapidly but produces a rougher surface finish.
6. ____ Used to clean files.
7. ____ Tool used to saw metal.
8. ____ Cuts holes in metal.
9. ____ The drill that is held in a drill chuck.
10. ____ Cuts internal threads.
11. ____ Cuts external threads.
12. ____ Tool used to permit flat head screws to be mounted flush.
13. ____ Used to indicate the NATIONAL COARSE THREAD SERIES.
14. ____ Used to indicate the NATIONAL FINE THREAD SERIES.

a. hacksaw
b. double cut
c. standard
d. vise caps
e. file card
f. single cut
g. Phillips head
h. die
i. countersink
j. NC
k. tap
l. straight shank
m. NF
n. washer
o. nut
p. bolt
q. machine screw
r. cap screw
s. twist drill
t. rivet

15. Identify the following file shapes.

A B C D

E F G H

16. Make a sketch showing the hacksaw blade properly installed.
17. Name the three commonly used drill series.
   a. _____
   b. _____
   c. _____
18. What are the correct names of the taps shown?
   a. _____
   b. _____
   c. _____

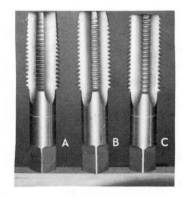

19. The _____ tap is used to start the thread.
20. The _____ tap is used to cut threads to the bottom of a hole.
21. What taps should be used to cut threads in the jobs shown on the top of page 65? List them in the order they would be used.

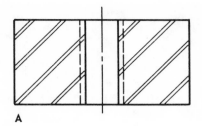
A

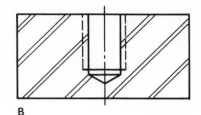
B

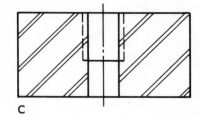
C

Special Activities

1. Examine the tools in your shop and repair those that are damaged.
2. Prepare a series of safety posters on the proper way to use tools.
3. Make special tool holders to mount tools safely and properly on tool panel.
4. Inventory the hand tools in your shop. Using tool catalogs, determine how much it would cost if they had to be replaced.
5. Paint the tools in each work area. Example: Use red for sheet metal tools, yellow for layout tools, etc.
6. Design a new tool panel and storage facility for your shop.
7. Devise a method for quickly checking whether all tools were returned to their proper place at the end of the work period.
8. Find out how a local industry dispenses tools to workers and report to your class.

Fig. 7-1. In Colonial America the blacksmith hammered and worked metal into useful shapes.
(Colonial Williamsburg)

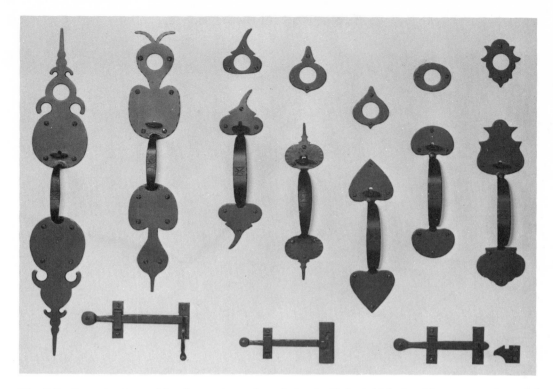

Fig. 7-2. Reproductions of hand wrought work made by the Colonial blacksmith are not only useful, but also decorative. (Old Guilford Forge)

Unit 7

WROUGHT METAL

In Colonial America the wrought metalwork was hammered and worked into shape by BLACKSMITHS, Fig. 7-1. Their products were not only useful, but were also decorative, Fig. 7-2.

Today wrought metalwork is also known as ornamental ironwork and bench metal.

The metal most commonly used is wrought iron. It is almost pure iron and contains very little carbon (carbon makes iron harder and tougher). Wrought iron is easy to bend (either hot or cold) and may be readily welded. However, wrought iron is expensive and standard hot rolled steel shapes are often used as substitutes.

Fig. 7-3. Bar and rod stock can be sheared to length on a ROD PARTER. (Di-Acro)

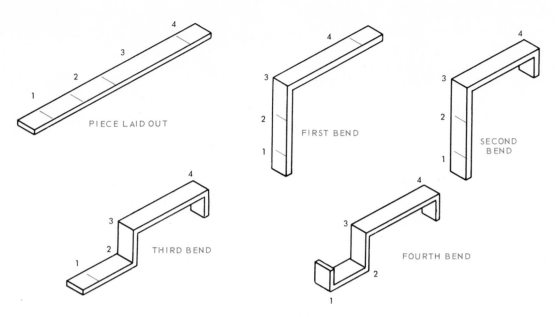

Fig. 7-4. Recommended bending sequence.

Bending with Hand Tools

Metal up to 1/4 in. thickness can be bent cold. Heavier metal bends easier if it is heated.

Cut the metal to length. This can be done with a hacksaw or a ROD PARTER, Fig. 7-3.

In working with wrought iron, the length of the metal is reduced slightly by each bend.

To make up for this reduction, add one-half the metal thickness to the length of the piece for each bend.

Some projects require that several bends be made in the same piece of metal. The bending sequence must be planned carefully or it may be difficult to make all of the bends with accuracy, Fig. 7-4.

Fig. 7-6. Many bends can be made in a vise with a hammer.

Many bends in wrought ironwork can be made using a heavy vise and a ball peen hammer. Make the necessary layout. Place the metal in the vise with the extra material allowed for the bend projecting above the jaws,

Fig. 7-5. Add one-half the thickness of the metal to the total length of the piece, for each bend. Place the section with this extra metal above the vise.

Fig. 7-5. Start the bend by striking the metal with the flat of the hammer near the vise, Fig. 7-6.

Right angle bends are squared by using one corner of the vise jaw as a form, Fig. 7-7. Strike the metal near the bend.

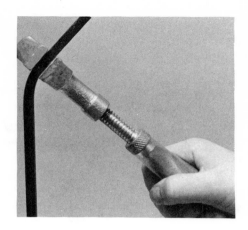

Fig. 7-9. Making an obtuse angle bend with the monkey wrench.

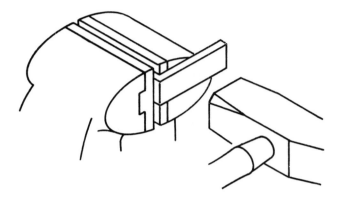

Fig. 7-7. Making a right angle bend using the vise.

ACUTE ANGLES (angles less than 90 deg.) can be made in the vise after an initial bend has been made, Fig. 7-8.

Fig. 7-10. Thin stock can be bent by placing it between two pieces of angle iron and making the bend with a mallet.

Twisting Metal

Wrought metal may be twisted for additional strength and rigidity, for decorative purposes, or to break the monotony of long flat sections, Fig. 7-11.

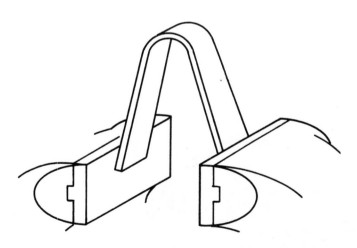

Fig. 7-8. Making an acute angle bend in the vise.

OBTUSE ANGLES (angles more than 90 deg.) may be made using a MONKEY WRENCH as a bending tool, Fig. 7-9.

Thin stock can be bent in a vise using two pieces of angle iron or wood to position the metal. Make the bend with a mallet, Fig. 7-10.

Fig. 7-11. Twisted sections add extra strength and rigidity, and are also used for decorative purposes.

Lay out the section to be twisted. Allow extra material because twisting shortens the metal slightly.

Short sections may be twisted in a vise. Place the metal in the vise with the bottom layout mark flush with the jaws. Place a monkey wrench at the top mark and make the required number of turns, Fig. 7-12.

Long sections have a tendency to bend out of line when twisted. This problem can be re-

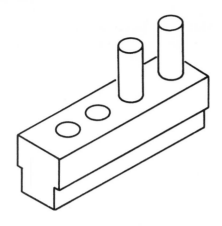

Fig. 7-14. One type of bending jig.

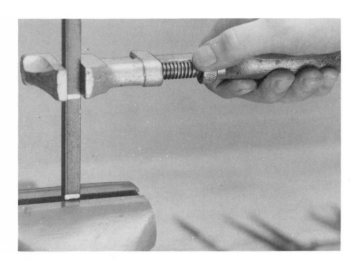

Fig. 7-12. To make a twisted section, place a monkey wrench at the top mark and make the required number of turns.

duced by sliding a section of snug fitting pipe over the portion to be twisted. Minor bends can be straightened with a mallet.

Bending Circular Shapes

Some wrought ironwork makes use of curved sections for decorative purposes, Fig. 7-13. The curves can be made over the anvil horn or with a BENDING JIG, Fig. 7-14. For best results, it is advisable to make a full size pattern of the proposed curve.

Stock length can be determined by forming a piece of wire over the pattern. Straighten the wire and measure its length.

Fig. 7-13. A wrought iron trivet that makes use of curved sections.

The SCROLL, Fig. 7-15, is frequently used. It is a curved section with a constantly expanding radius that resembles a loose clock spring.

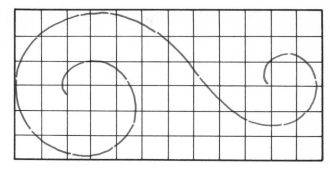

Fig. 7-17. A pattern for a double end scroll.

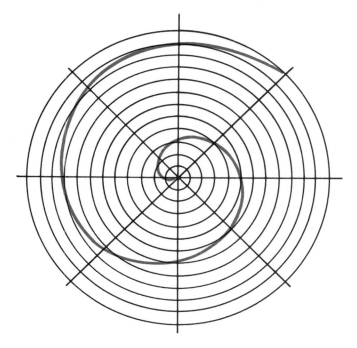

Fig. 7-15. SCROLLS may be developed using this technique.

Frequently, a scroll is required on both ends of the piece, Fig. 7-17. One curve should blend smoothly into the other curve.

Scroll ends are often flared or decorated, Fig. 7-18. This is done before the scroll is formed.

Fig. 7-18. Typical scroll ends.

The scroll is formed with the aid of a bending jig. A section is formed at a time, Fig. 7-16. Check the curve against the pattern during the forming operation to assure accuracy.

Curves of a given radius can be formed using a vise and a piece of pipe or rod with a diameter equal to the inside diameter of the required curve.

Clamp the metal in the vise as shown in Fig. 7-19. Pull the metal forward. As the

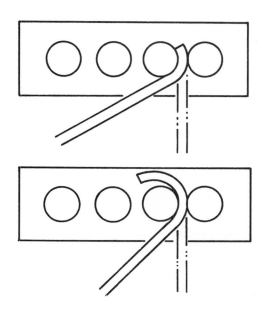

Fig. 7-16. Making a scroll on a bending jig.

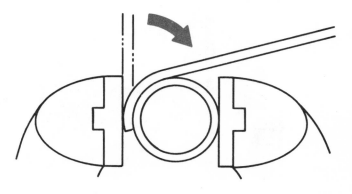

Fig. 7-19. Using a pipe held in a vise to form a scroll or curved section.

curve takes shape, move the work farther in and around the pipe.

Curves can also be formed using a hammer and a rod clamped in the vise, Fig. 7-20.

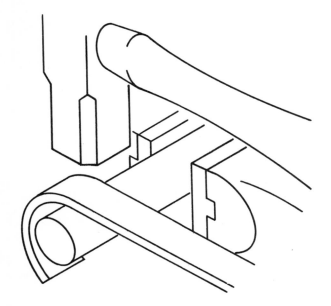

Fig. 7-20. *Making a curved section over a rod held in a vise.*

Bending with Special Tools

Bending can be done by using special machines, Figs. 7-21, 7-22, and 7-23. The machines provide additional leverage for bending heavier metal. In addition, special attachments permit intricate shapes to be formed easily.

Fig. 7-21. *The DI-ACRO BENDER can be used to form rod and bar stock mechanically.* (Di-Acro)

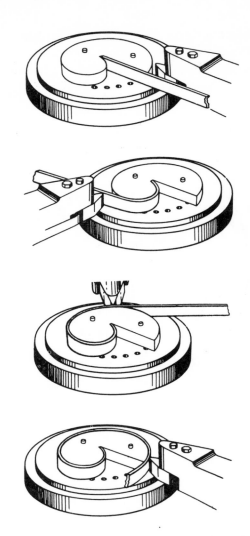

Fig. 7-22. *Scrolls and other shapes of irregular radii can be formed with bender, by using collar having same contour as the shape to be formed.*

It is essential that the bending sequence be planned BEFORE cutting the metal. Do not forget to make allowances for the bends.

Metal formed in a bending machine has some "springback" (the metal tries to return to its original shape). This can be eliminated by using a bending form with a radius slightly smaller than the required radius.

Springback varies with metal thickness. It may be necessary to make a sample bend using scrap metal of the required size to determine the correct form to use.

Be sure to study the instruction book supplied by the manufacturer of the machine being used.

Assembly

Wrought ironwork may be assembled by riveting or welding.

Fig. 7-23. The Metl-Former. (Swayne, Robinson and Co.)

Finishing Wrought Ironwork

Early wrought ironwork acquired a pleasing surface texture (finish) when the metal was forged to usable size. Today, with the

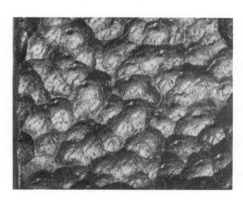

Fig. 7-24. Close-up of a peened surface.

availability of a large range of standard metal sizes, it is no longer necessary to forge the material to size. The resulting large smooth

surfaces brought about the development of PEENING (the work is struck repeatedly with the ball end of the hammer), Fig. 7-24. Today, peening is widely used. However the "real craftsman" still takes the time to forge the metal to size, Fig. 7-25.

Flat black lacquer or paint is applied for the final surface finish. It is easier to apply than the scorched linseed oil finish used by Colonial craftsmen.

Fig. 7-25. A very pleasing surface is produced when metal is forged to size. It is not an artificial surface finish like a peened surface.

Safety

1. Remove all burrs and sharp edges from the metal before attempting to shape it.
2. Wear your safety glasses when cutting, chiseling or grinding metal.
3. Have any cuts, bruises or burns treated promptly.
4. Handle long sections of metal with extreme care so that persons working nearby will not be injured.
5. Keep your fingers clear of the moving parts of the bending machine.
6. Do not use a bending machine unless you know how to operate it safely. When in doubt, consult your instructor.
7. Do not use finishing materials near an open flame or in an area that is not properly ventilated. Store oily and solvent soaked rags in an approved closed container.

What Do You Know About Wrought Metalwork? – Unit 7

1. The first wrought ironwork in America was made by the _____.

2. Today, wrought ironwork is also known as:
   a._____ b._____

3. Metal up to _____ in. thick can be bent _____. Heavier metal bends easier if it is _____.

4. There are many ways that metal can be bent. List four (4) of them.
   a._____
   b._____
   c._____
   d._____

5. Two things must be considered when making a bend in metal (check the answers that apply).
   a.____ Heavier metals must be used to allow extra metal for the bend.
   b.____ The length of the metal is reduced slightly by each bend and allowances must be made for this reduction.
   c.____ Bends should be made heated.
   d.____ Bends should be made with a hammer of the proper size.
   e.____ If several bends are to be made in the piece, the bending sequence must be planned very carefully.

6. Wrought metal may be sometimes twisted for additional _____ and _____.

7. Curves in wrought metal can be made by hand on the _____ or _____.

8. Scroll ends are often flared or decorated. Make a sketch showing four (4) such ends.

9. How can you determine how much material will be needed to make a scroll?

Special Activities

1. Make a collection of illustrations showing wrought ironwork.

2. Secure catalogs from historic developments (such as Williamsburg, Cooperstown, Greenfield Village, Old Sturbridge Village, Mystic Seaport, etc.) and develop wrought iron projects that can be made in the school shop.

3. Demonstrate the proper and safe way to make bends on the Di-Acro bender.

Dozens of different kinds and sizes of fasteners are used in the manufacture of this motorcycle. (Kawasaki)

Fig. 8-1. Fasteners typical of those found and used in the school shop.

Unit 8

FASTENERS

FASTENERS (nuts, bolts, rivets, screws, etc.) may be considered as small clamps that hold manufactured products together. They are available in a multitude of types and styles, Fig. 8-1.

Rivets

Many permanent assemblies (these cannot be taken apart without danger of damaging the project) are made with RIVETS. Rivets are made from soft iron, aluminum, copper and brass in many styles and sizes, Fig. 8-2.

Setting a Rivet

Select the style and length of rivet to be used---wrought iron projects should be joined with soft iron rivets.

Drill or punch a hole of the proper size for the rivet. Countersink both pieces if flat

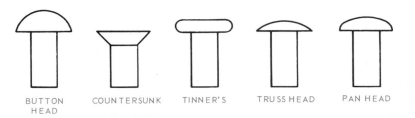

BUTTON HEAD   COUNTERSUNK   TINNER'S   TRUSS HEAD   PAN HEAD

Fig. 8-2. Rivet styles.

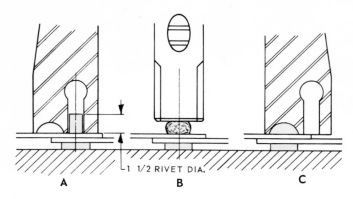

Fig. 8-3. Setting a rivet. A—Drawing the pieces to be riveted together. B—Flattening the rivet. C—Forming the rivet head.

head rivets are to be used. Remove all burrs and sharp edges.

1. Seat the rivet and draw the pieces together, A, Fig. 8-3.
2. Flatten the rivet, B, Fig. 8-3.
3. Form the rivet head, C, Fig. 8-3, with a RIVET SET, Fig. 8-4. Flatten flat head rivets to fill the countersunk holes. Complete the job with the flat face of the hammer. Support the work on a steel plate for the latter operations.

Fig. 8-4. Rivet set.

Threaded Fasteners

Threaded fasteners permit the work to be disassembled and reassembled without damage to the various parts.

Machine Screws

MACHINE SCREWS, Fig. 8-5, are widely used in the school shop. Many head styles with slotted or recessed heads are avail-

able. Machine screws clamp parts together by being screwed into tapped holes. However, square or hexagonal nuts may be used with the screws.

Fig. 8-5. Machine screws.

Machine Bolts

MACHINE BOLTS, Fig. 8-6, are used to assemble products that do not require close tolerance fasteners.

Fig. 8-6. Machine bolts.

Cap Screws

CAP SCREWS, Fig. 8-7, are similar to machine bolts. However, they are more accurately made and are used in assemblies that require a higher quality fastener. While nuts may be used with cap screws, their usual application involves passing them through a clearance hole (a hole slightly larger than the screw) in one of the pieces and screwing them into a threaded hole in the other piece, Fig. 8-8. Cap screws are available in a wide variety of head styles.

Fasteners

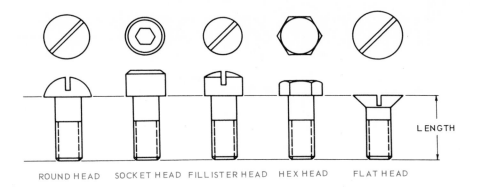

Fig. 8-7. Cap screws.

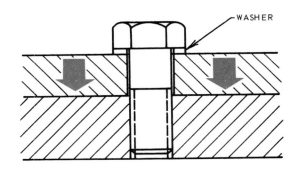

Fig. 8-8. How a cap screw clamps work together.

Stud Bolts

STUD BOLTS, Fig. 8-9, are threaded at both ends. One end is screwed into a tapped

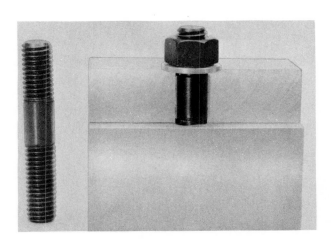

Fig. 8-9. Stud bolt.

hole, the piece to be clamped is fitted into place over the stud. A nut is screwed on to clamp the two pieces together.

Setscrews

Setscrews, Fig. 8-10, are used to prevent pulleys from slipping on a shaft, holding collars in place on a shaft, and to hold shafts in place on assemblies. Many types of setscrews are manufactured, Fig. 8-11.

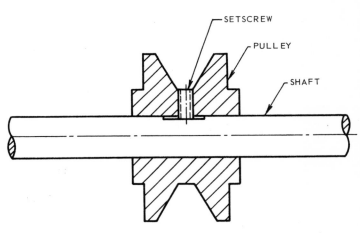

Fig. 8-10. Setscrew in use.

Fig. 8-11. Typical setscrews.

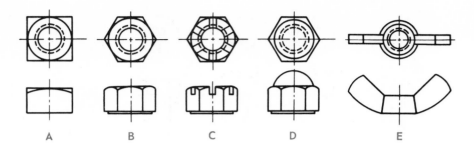

Fig. 8-12. Commonly used nuts. A—Square nut. B—Hex nut. C—Slotted nut. D—Acorn or cap nut. E—Wing nut.

Nuts

NUTS may be standard square or hexagonal in shape. They are used with bolts having the same shape heads. However, they are made in a number of styles for decorative and special applications, Fig. 8-12.

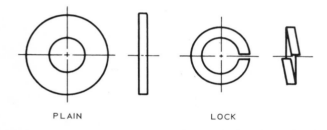

PLAIN   LOCK

Fig. 8-13. Washers.

Washers

WASHERS permit a bolt or nut to be tightened without damage to the work surface.

STANDARD and LOCK WASHERS, Fig. 8-13, are commonly found in the school shop.

Keys

Gears and pulleys are prevented from rotating on shafts by utilizing KEYS. Several key styles are shown in Fig. 8-14. One-half of the key fits into a KEYSEAT on the shaft. The remainder of the key fits into a KEYWAY in the hub of the gear or pulley. See Fig. 8-15.

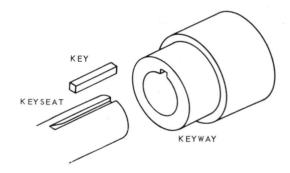

KEY

KEYSEAT

KEYWAY

Fig. 8-15. Key, keyway and keyseat.

Epoxy Adhesives

EPOXY ADHESIVES provide a practical way to join metal to metal, or metal to other

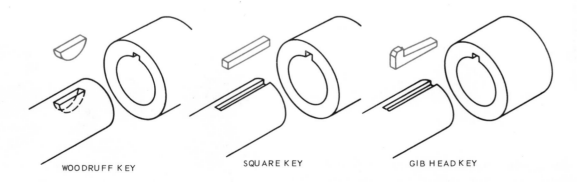

WOODRUFF KEY   SQUARE KEY   GIB HEAD KEY

Fig. 8-14. Types of keys.

materials. Many epoxy adhesives are available, Fig. 8-16.

In using epoxy adhesives, it is important that the surfaces to be joined are clean and that the adhesive is mixed and applied exactly as specified by the manufacturer.

CAUTION: EPOXY ADHESIVES MAY CAUSE SKIN IRRITATION. SHOULD YOU COME IN CONTACT WITH THE ADHESIVE, WASH THE AREA THOROUGHLY WITH SOAP AND WATER. KEEP THE ADHESIVE AWAY FROM YOUR EYES.

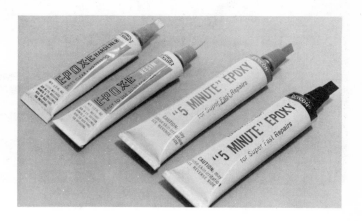

Fig. 8-16. Many types of epoxy adhesives are available. The surfaces to be joined must be clean and the adhesive mixed according to the manufacturer's instructions. *KEEP THE ADHESIVE AWAY FROM YOUR EYES AND WASH YOUR HANDS THOROUGHLY AFTER USING EPOXY ADHESIVES.*

What Do You Know About Threaded Fasteners? - Unit 8

1. Permanent assemblies are made with _____.
2. Why are threaded fasteners used?
3. _____ are similar to machine bolts but are more accurately made.
4. The _____ is threaded on both ends.
5. Setscrews are used to _____.
6. _____ permit a bolt or nut to be tightened without damaging the work surface.
7. Make a sketch showing how keys are used to prevent gears and pulleys from rotating on a shaft.
8. _____ is a practical method for bonding metal to metal, or metal to other materials.
9. Identify the fasteners shown in the illustration at the bottom of this page.

   A._____
   B._____
   C._____
   D._____
   E._____
   F._____
   G._____
   H._____

Special Activities

1. Prepare a collection of fasteners. Mount them on a display panel.
2. Research how threaded fasteners are manufactured.
3. Secure examples of fasteners in use.

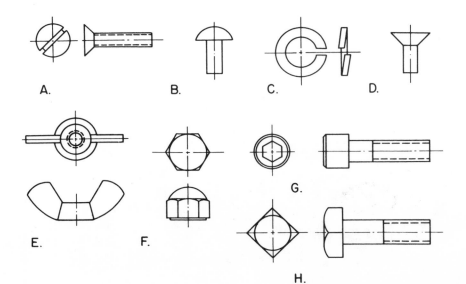

A.　　　B.　　　C.　　　D.

E.　　　F.

G.

H.

Fig. 9-1. Many thousands of square feet of metal is used in the manufacture of this Boeing 747. (Boeing Co.)

Unit 9
SHEET METAL

Great quantities of sheet metal are utilized in the manufacture of metal objects such as aircraft, Fig. 9-1, automobiles, furniture and household appliances. Sheet metal is also extensively used by the building trades (air conditioning, heating, roofing and prefabricated structures, Fig. 9-2).

The products made from sheet metal are given three-dimensional shape and rigidity by bending and forming the metal sheet into the required shape. In many manufacturing operations, the metal is cut to shape using a PATTERN as a guide. A PATTERN is a

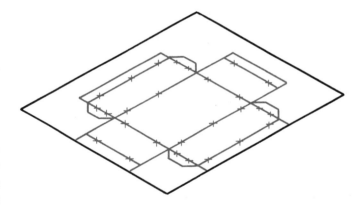

Fig. 9-3. A sheet metal layout or PATTERN. Folds are to be made as indicated by the letter X.

Fig. 9-2. A building made from sheet metal. (Stran-Steel)

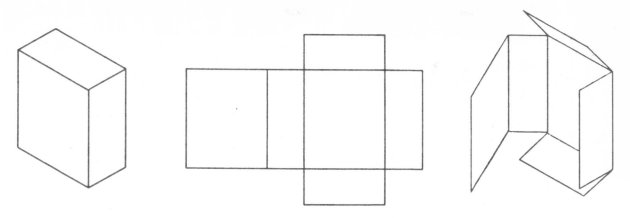

Fig. 9-4. A pattern made by parallel line development.

full-size drawing of the surfaces of the object stretched out as a single surface, Fig. 9-3. The pattern drawing is often called a STRETCHOUT. It is made employing a form of drafting called PATTERN DEVELOPMENT.

Developing Patterns

There are two basic types of pattern development:

PARALLEL LINE DEVELOPMENT. The technique used to make patterns of prisms and cylinders, Fig. 9-4.

RADIAL LINE DEVELOPMENT. Patterns for regular tapering forms (cones, pyramids, etc.) are developed utilizing this method, Fig. 9-5.

Patterns developed from more complex

geometric shapes are drawn by using variations and combinations of basic pattern development techniques.

The lines used in pattern development give additional meaning to the drawing. A heavy solid line (visible object line) indicates a sharp fold or bend, Fig. 9-6. Curved surfaces are shown on the pattern by construction or center lines, Fig. 9-7.

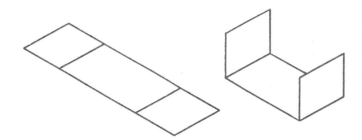

Fig. 9-6. A heavy solid line indicates a sharp fold.

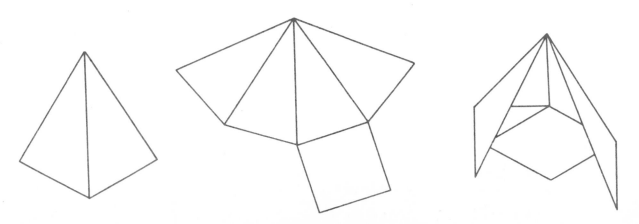

Fig. 9-5. A pattern made by radial line development.

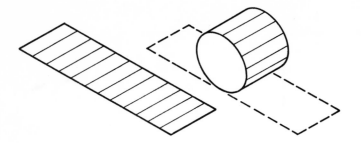

Fig. 9-7. Construction (light) or center lines indicate a curved or circular surface.

A word of caution. Be sure to allow for sufficient material to make the various JOINTS, HEMS and SEAMS needed to join the metal together and to give added rigidity to thin metal sheets, as explained later in this Unit.

The pattern may be developed on paper and transferred to the metal, or it can be drawn directly onto the metal. Plan the layout on the metal so there will be a minimum of waste, Fig. 9-8.

Pattern Development of a Rectangular Object

To develop rectangular or square objects, Fig. 9-9:

1. Draw front and top views.
2. The height of the pattern is the same as the height of the front view. Project light lines from the top and bottom of the front view. Number as shown.
3. Measure about 1 in. from the front view, and draw a vertical line between the extended lines to locate 1 - 5.

4. Set the compass or divider from 1 to 2 on the top view, and transfer this distance to the extended lines to locate line 2 - 6. Locate the other distances in the same manner.
5. Using 2 - 3 and 6 - 7 as one side draw the top and bottom.
6. Allow about 1/4 in. (more or less depending on the size of the object) for seams, and go over all outlines and folds with heavy lines (object lines).

Pattern Development of Cylindrical Objects

Cylindrical objects, Fig. 9-10, are developed by the following method:

1. Draw the front and top views. Divide the top view into twelve (12) equal parts and number as shown.
2. The height of the pattern is the same as the height of the front view. Project light lines from the top and bottom of the front view.
3. Measure about 1 in. from the front view, and draw a vertical line between the extended lines to locate line 1.
4. Set the compass or divider from 1 to 2 on the top view, and transfer this distance to the extended lines to locate points 1, 2, 3, etc. as shown. Draw light vertical lines at each point.
5. Draw the top and bottom tangent to the extended lines.
6. Allow material for the seams, and go over all outlines with heavy lines (object lines). The lines that represent curves or circular lines may be drawn in color, or left as light lines.

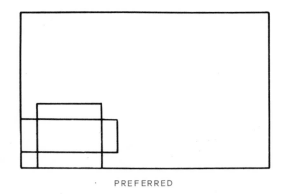

PREFERRED

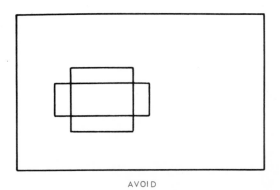

AVOID

Fig. 9-8. Locate the pattern on the metal so there will be a minimum of waste.

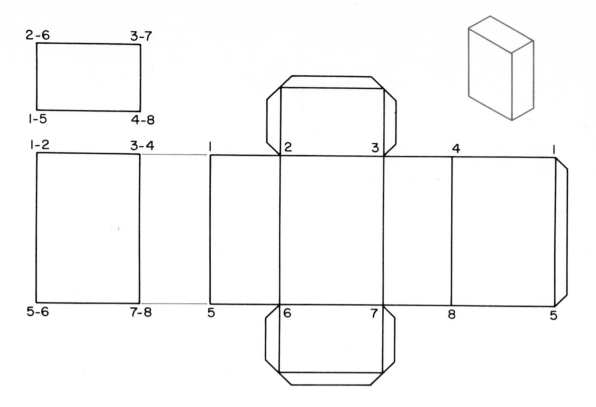

Fig. 9-9. Developing a pattern for a rectangular or square object.

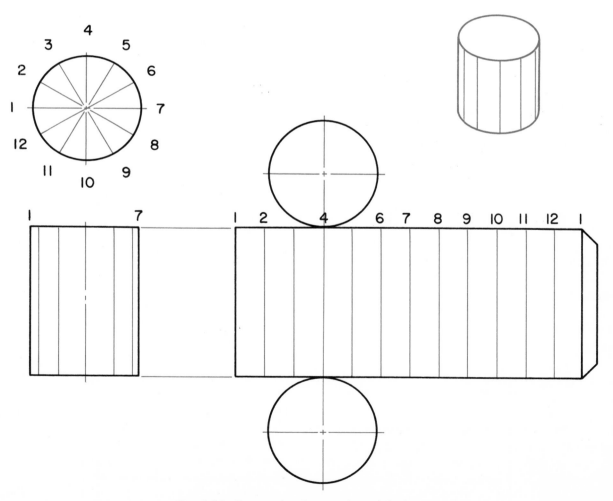

Fig. 9-10. Pattern development for a cylinder.

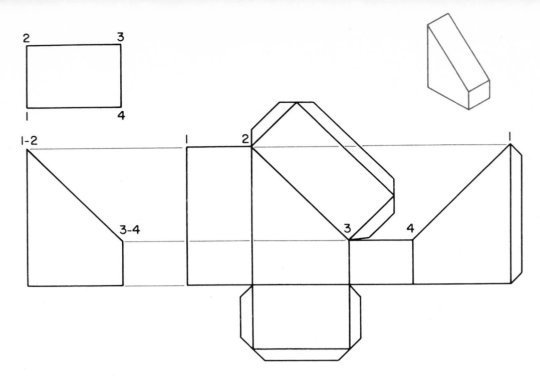

Fig. 9-11. Developing a pattern of a truncated prism.

Pattern Development of a Truncated Prism

A truncated (cut off at an angle to its base) prism development, Fig. 9-11, is made as follows:

1. Draw front and top views. Number views as shown.
2. Proceed as in the previous examples of parallel line developments.
3. Mark off and number the folding points. Project point 1 on the front view, to line 1 of the stretchout. Repeat with points 2, 3 and 4.
4. Connect the points 1 to 2, 2 to 3, 3 to 4, and 4 to 1.
5. Draw the top and bottom (if needed) in position.
6. Allow material for seams, and go over the outline and folds with visible object lines.

Pattern Development of a Pyramid

The pattern for a pyramid, Fig. 9-12, is developed as follows:

1. Draw front and top. Number as shown.
2. Locate center line X of the stretchout.
3. Set the compass to a radius equal to 0 - 1 on the front view and with X of the stretchout as the center, draw arc AB.
4. Draw a vertical line through center line X and arc AB.

5. Set the compass from 1 to 2 on the top view and using the place where the vertical line intersects the arc as the starting point, step off two (2) divisions on each side of the line (points 1-2-3-4-1 on the stretchout).
6. Connect the points, draw the bottom in place (if needed), and go over the outline and folds with object lines.

Pattern Development of a Cone

Develop the pattern for a cone, Fig. 9-13, as follows:

1. Draw front and top views. Divide the top view into twelve (12) equal parts and number as shown.
2. Locate center line X of the stretchout.
3. Set the compass from 0 to 1 on the front view and with X of the stretchout as the center line, draw arc AB.
4. Draw vertical construction line through center line X and the arc.
5. Set the compass from 1 to 2 on the top view, and using the place where the vertical line intersects the arc as the starting point, step off six (6) divisions on both sides of the line (points 1-2-3-4 etc. on the pattern).
6. Go over the outline with object lines. The lines that represent the curved portion are drawn in color, or are left as construction lines.

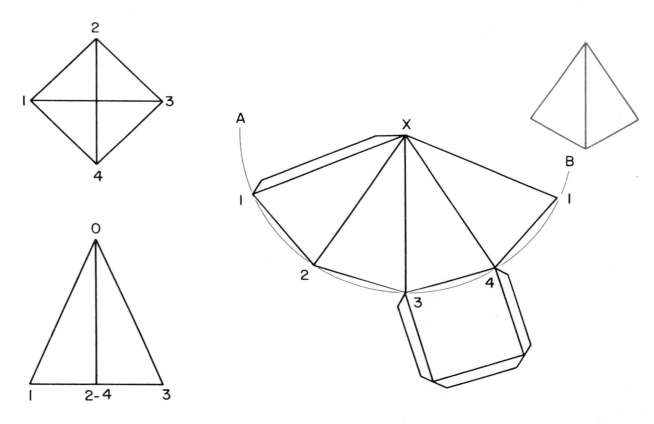

Fig. 9-12. Developing a pattern for a pyramid.

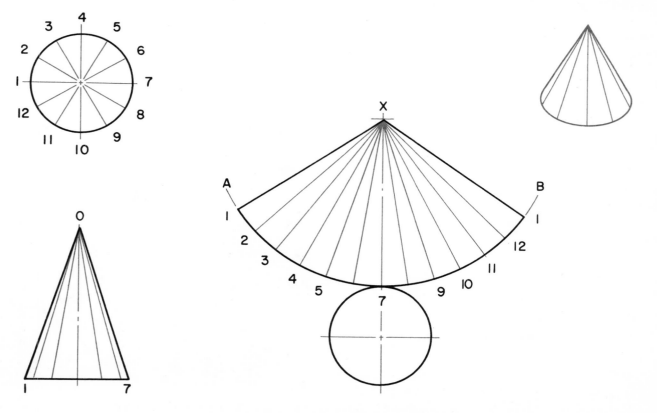

Fig. 9-13. Developing a pattern for a cone.

Metals Used in Sheet Metal

TIN PLATE, a mild steel with a tin coating; GALVANIZED STEEL, a mild steel with a zinc coating; and COLD FINISHED STEEL SHEET are the metals generally used in sheet metal work in the school shop.

These are available in standard thicknesses and sizes. The thickness can be measured with a micrometer or SHEET METAL GAUGE, Fig. 9-14.

Fig. 9-14. Measuring sheet metal thickness with a sheet metal gauge.

Fig. 9-15. Typical snips used to cut sheet metal. Above. Straight pattern snips. Center. Circular pattern snips. Below. Aviation snips, left cut. (Diamond Tool Co.)

Cutting Sheet Metal

SNIPS are employed extensively for cutting the metal sheets. They are manufactured in a number of sizes and styles, Fig. 9-15.

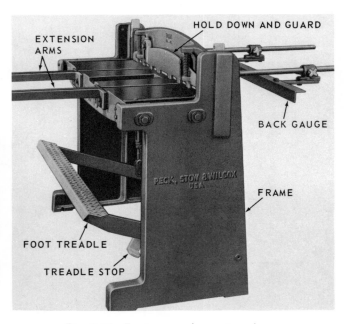

Fig. 9-16. Foot powered squaring shears.

Large sheet metal sections are cut on SQUARING SHEARS, Fig. 9-16. Smooth, clean cuts can be made with the electric powered tool, Fig. 9-17, when a quantity of sheet metal must be cut on the job.

Fig. 9-17. The NIBBLER cuts sheet metal cleanly and smooth with neither cut edge bending. (Skil Corp.)

Do not cut wire, band iron or steel rod with snips or squaring shears. This will damage the cutting edges.

KEEP YOUR HANDS CLEAR OF THE BLADE AND YOUR FOOT FROM BENEATH THE FOOT PETAL WHEN USING SQUARING SHEARS.

Making Small Diameter Holes in Sheet Metal

In addition to drilling, small diameter holes can be made in sheet metal with a HOLLOW PUNCH, Fig. 9-18, and a SOLID PUNCH, Fig. 9-19.

Fig. 9-19. Small diameter holes can be made in sheet metal with a solid punch. Use a bar of lead or end-grain wood block to support the work while making the hole.

by hand and square up the bend with a wooden mallet.

USE EXTREME CARE WHEN HANDLING SHEET METAL TO AVOID PAINFUL CUTS FROM THE SHARP EDGES OF THE MATERIAL.

Fig. 9-18. Using a hollow punch to cut holes in sheet metal.

Bending Sheet Metal

Sheet metal is very often bent into three-dimensional shapes. The bending gives the thin metal rigidity.

Some hand and machine bending techniques are described in the following paragraphs.

Bending Metal by Hand

Sheet metal may be bent by fitting it between two blocks of hardwood or pieces of angle iron, Fig. 9-20. Press the metal over

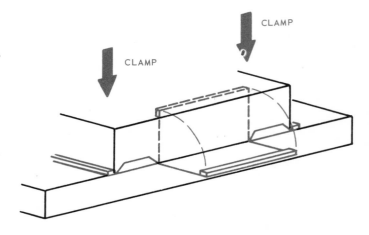

Fig. 9-20. Using blocks of wood to make a bend in sheet metal.

Bending can also be done using one of the many STAKES available, Fig. 9-21.

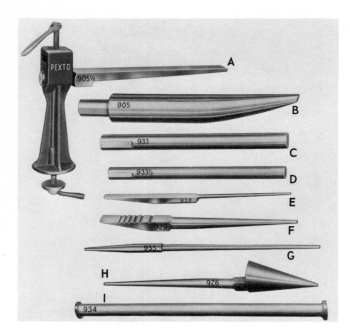

Fig. 9-21. A few of the many stakes available. A—Universal stake holder fitted with the rectangular end of a beakhorn stake. B—Beakhorn stake. C—Conductor stake, large end. D—Conductor stake, small end. E—Needle case stake. F—Creasing stake with horn. G—Candle mould stake. H—Blowhorn stake. I—Double seaming stake. (Pexto)

Bending Sheet Metal on Box and Pan Brake

The BOX AND PAN BRAKE, Fig. 9-22, makes accurate bends mechanically. Its upper jaw is made up of a number of blocks that are of different widths. These can be positioned

or removed to permit all four sides of a box to be formed.

Making Circular and Conical Shapes

Circular and conical shapes can be made by hand over a stake, Fig. 9-23. However it is difficult to make the curves smooth and accurate.

Fig. 9-23. Circular shapes can be formed by hand over a stake or metal rod.

Most cylindrical shapes can be formed rapidly and with accuracy on a SLIP ROLL FORMING MACHINE, Fig. 9-24. The rolls

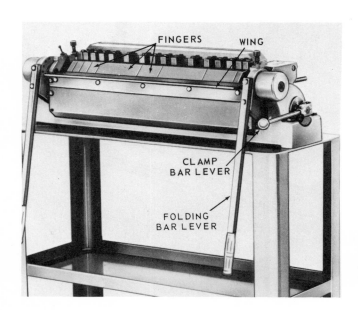

Fig. 9-22. Box and pan brake. (Di-Acro)

Fig. 9-24. Slip roll forming machine.

can be adjusted to accommodate different thicknesses of metal and to form the desired curvature, Fig. 9-25.

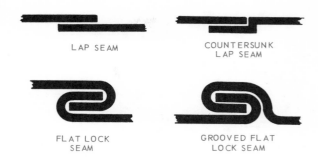

LAP SEAM   COUNTERSUNK LAP SEAM

FLAT LOCK SEAM   GROOVED FLAT LOCK SEAM

Fig. 9-26. Typical sheet metal seams.

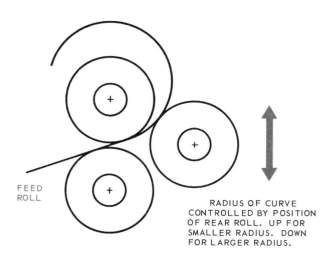

FEED ROLL

RADIUS OF CURVE CONTROLLED BY POSITION OF REAR ROLL. UP FOR SMALLER RADIUS. DOWN FOR LARGER RADIUS.

Fig. 9-25. The rolls can be adjusted to receive sheet metal of different thicknesses and to form the required curvature.

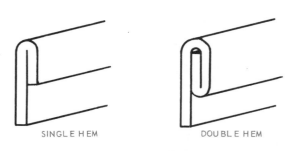

SINGLE HEM   DOUBLE HEM

Fig. 9-27. Hems are made on sheet metal to provide additional rigidity to the metal.

Common Sheet Metal Seams, Hems and Edges

Various SEAMS are used to join sheet metal sections, Fig. 9-26. Sheet metal seams are usually finished by soldering.

HEMS, Fig. 9-27, are used to strengthen lips of sheet metal objects. These are made in standard fractional sizes - 3/16, 1/4, etc.

The WIRE EDGE, Fig. 9-28, gives additional strength and rigidity to sheet metal edges.

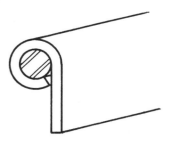

Fig. 9-28. Wire edge.

FOLDS that are basic to the making of seams, edges and hems are made on a BAR FOLDER, Fig. 9-29.

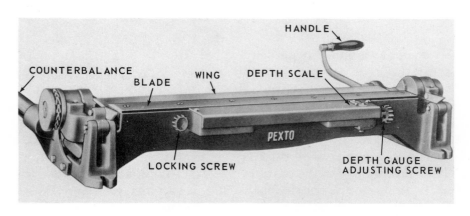

HANDLE

COUNTERBALANCE   BLADE   WING   DEPTH SCALE

PEXTO

LOCKING SCREW   DEPTH GAUGE ADJUSTING SCREW

Fig. 9-29. Bar folder. (Pexto)

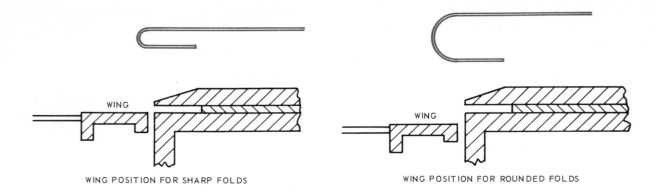

WING POSITION FOR SHARP FOLDS

WING POSITION FOR ROUNDED FOLDS

Fig. 9-30. Setting the wing of the bar folder to make different size folds.

The width of the folded edge is set on the DEPTH GAUGE of the machine. The sharpness of the folded edge, whether it is to be sharp for a hem or seam, or rounded to make a wire edge, is determined by the position of the WING, Fig. 9-30. The machine can also be adjusted to make 45 deg. and 90 deg. angle bends.

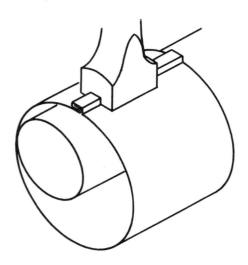

Fig. 9-31. Using a hand groover.

Folds necessary to make seams are made on a bar folder. After the sections are fitted together, the seams may be locked with a HAND GROOVER, Fig. 9-31.

A COMBINATION ROTARY MACHINE, Fig. 9-32, can be used to make a wire edge. See Fig. 9-33. The machine can be fitted with a variety of rolls to perform operations such as BEADING, Fig. 9-34, and CRIMPING, Fig. 9-35.

Sheet Metal Safety

1. Treat cuts and bruises immediately, no matter how minor.

2. Remove all burrs formed during the cutting operation before attempting further work on the metal.

3. Clean the work area with a brush. NEVER brush metal with your hands.

4. Use sharp tools.

5. Keep your hands clear of the blade on the squaring shears.

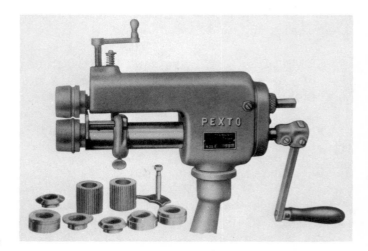

Fig. 9-32. Combination rotary machine with extra forming rolls.

6. Do not run your hand over metal that has just been cut or drilled. Painful cuts from the burrs may result.

7. Place scrap pieces of sheet metal in the scrap box.

8. Do not use tools that are not in first-class condition - - hammer heads that are

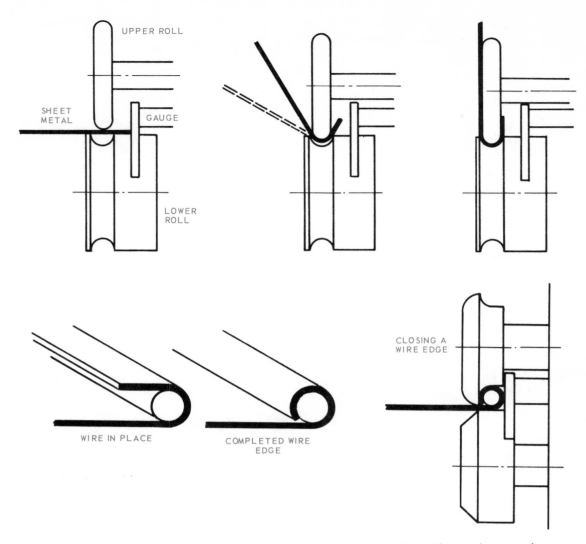

UPPER ROLL

SHEET
METAL

GAUGE

LOWER
ROLL

WIRE IN PLACE

COMPLETED WIRE
EDGE

CLOSING A
WIRE EDGE

Fig. 9-33. Above. Turning a wire edge with a rotary machine. Below. Closing the wire edge.

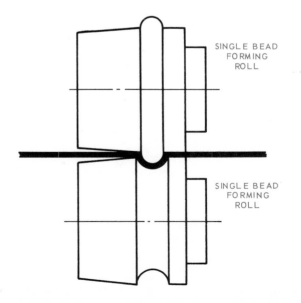

SINGLE BEAD
FORMING
ROLL

SINGLE BEAD
FORMING
ROLL

Fig. 9-34. Making a bead. The bead provides additional rigidity to the thin metal.

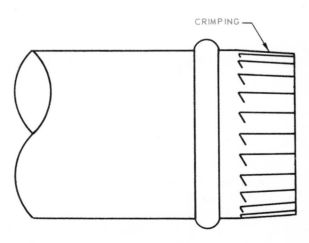

CRIMPING

Fig. 9-35. Crimping corrugates or makes one end of the metal
pipe smaller so it will fit easily into the end of another pipe
of the same diameter.

loose, files without handles, machines with guards removed, etc.

9. Always wear goggles when working in the shop.

Soldering

To SOLDER properly:

1. A 50-50 solder alloy (50 percent tin - 50 percent lead) is most commonly used.
2. The correct FLUX must be applied. A NONCORROSIVE flux such as RESIN works best on tin plate and brass.
3. The SOLDERING COPPER must furnish sufficient heat for the job.
4. The surfaces being soldered must be clean.

Fig. 9-36. Electric soldering copper.
(American Electrical Heater Co.)

Soldering Devices

Heat for soldering is usually applied with an ELECTRIC SOLDERING COPPER, Fig. 9-36, or a SOLID SOLDERING COPPER, Fig. 9-37, that is heated in a SOLDERING FURNACE.

Fig. 9-37. Solid soldering copper.

A soldering copper must be TINNED, Fig. 9-38, before it will solder properly. TINNING (coating the tip of the soldering copper with solder) is accomplished by first cleaning the copper tip with a file. Then heat it until it will melt solder freely and rub it on a sal ammoniac block on which a few drops of solder has been melted, Fig. 9-39. This will

Fig. 9-38. Properly tinned soldering copper.

clean the tip and cause the solder to adhere. Remove excess solder by rubbing the tip over a clean cloth.

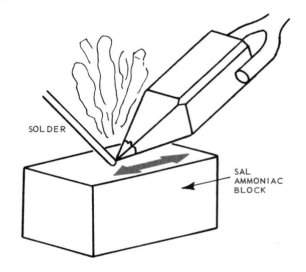

SOLDER

SAL AMMONIAC BLOCK

Fig. 9-39. Tinning soldering copper on a sal ammoniac block.

Soldering Sheet Metal

Clean the area to be soldered and apply flux. Place the pieces on a section of asbestos sheet.

Heat and tin the soldering copper. Hold the seam together with the tang of the file or stick of wood, Fig. 9-40, and tack it with small amounts of solder. Apply the solder directly in front of the soldering copper tip rather than on it.

Keep the seam pressed together with a file tang. With the soldering copper FLAT on the work, start moving the copper slowly toward the far end of the joint as the solder melts and begins to flow.

Clean the soldered seam with hot water to remove all traces of flux.

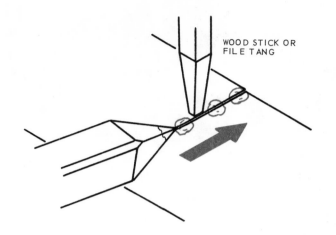

WOOD STICK OR FILE TANG

Fig. 9-40. Hold sheet metal pieces together with a wooden stick or file tang until the molten solder "freezes."

Soldering Safety

1. Wear safety glasses when soldering.
2. Wash your hands carefully after soldering to remove all traces of flux.
3. Have burns treated promptly.
4. Avoid touching joints that have just been soldered.
5. Use care when storing the soldering copper after use. Improper or careless storage can result in serious burns or a fire.

What Do You Know About Sheet Metal Work? - Unit 9

1. List several applications that use sheet metal.
2. A pattern is _____.
3. _____ are used to cut sheet metal. Large sections are usually cut on a _____.
4. _____ are often employed to join sheet metal sections.
5. _____ are used to strengthen the lips of some sheet metal objects.
6. _____ is a mild steel with a tin coating.
7. _____ is a mild steel with a zinc coating.
8. In addition to drilling, holes can be made in sheet metal with _____ and _____.
9. Folds that are basic to the making of seams, edges and hems are made on a _____.
10. Make a sketch of a wire edge, a bead and a crimped edge.
11. What does it mean when solder is referred to as 50-50 solder?
12. List the steps necessary to make a properly soldered joint.

Special Activities

1. Make a collection of illustrations that show examples of objects made from sheet metal. Prepare a bulletin board using the pictures.
2. Use an empty cereal box to demonstrate how a pattern is used.
3. Prepare posters on sheet metal safety.
4. Demonstrate the correct way to use tin snips.
5. Demonstrate the correct way to use the box and pan brake.
6. Prepare examples of hems, folds and the wire edge.
7. Demonstrate how to tin a soldering copper.
8. Prepare examples of properly soldered seams.

Fig. 10-1. Craftsmen in the James Geddy Silversmith Shop use 18th century methods to pound out handsome articles of colonial design from silver bars. (Colonial Williamsburg)

Unit 10
ART METAL

Hand Craftsmanship can easily be developed in ART METAL since most of the work is done by hand, Fig. 10-1. Machines are seldom used.

Fig. 10-2. This beautiful bowl is an example of hollow ware. (Shirley Pewter Shop, Williamsburg)

Fig. 10-3. This contemporary salad server set is typical of flatware work.

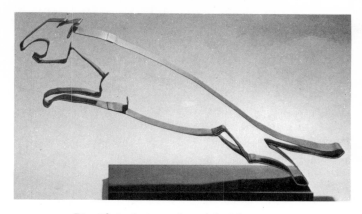

Fig. 10-4. Strip work model of leaping cat.

Four classifications of art metal are: hollow ware, Fig. 10-2; flatware, Fig. 10-3; strip work, Fig. 10-4 and jewelry making, Fig. 10-5.

Fig. 10-5. Jewelry making is one type of art metalwork.

Annealing and Pickling Metal

As metal is worked, it becomes hard and brittle. It must be ANNEALED (softened by heating) from time to time before further shaping and forming can be done. Otherwise, the metal may crack.

PICKLING is closely related to annealing. Annealing causes an oxide (a coating like rust) to form on the metal. The oxide must be removed or it will mar the surface of the metal when additional work is done on it.

Abrasives can be used to remove this oxide. However, it is a time consuming job. An easier method is to heat the piece and plunge it into a dilute solution of sulphuric acid. HAVE YOUR INSTRUCTOR DEMONSTRATE THIS OPERATION FOR YOU AND, WHEN YOU DO IT YOURSELF, WEAR A FACE SHIELD.

Anneal copper and sterling silver by heating to a dull red. Quench the hot metal in water or pickling solution.

Brass, bronze and German silver are heated to a dull red and allowed to cool slightly before plunging into water or pickling solution.

The metal may be heated with a torch or soldering furnace.

CAUTION: ASK YOUR INSTRUCTOR TO MIX THE PICKLING SOLUTION. THE ACID IT CONTAINS IS DANGEROUS AND CAN CAUSE SERIOUS BURNS IF NOT PROPERLY HANDLED.

Cutting and Piercing Metal

The metals used in art metal can be cut by conventional methods: hacksaw, snips, squaring shears, etc. However, these tools are not practical for cutting internal designs

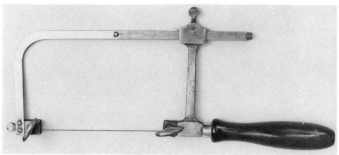

Fig. 10-6. Jeweler's saw.

often used in art metal for decorative purposes. This operation is known as PIERCING, and should be done with a JEWELER'S SAW, Fig. 10-6. Use a solid support when sawing, Fig. 10-7. The openings produced are cleaned up with JEWELER'S FILES, Fig. 10-8.

Hammers and Mallets

Many different HAMMERS, Fig. 10-9, are used to shape and form the metal. These are

Fig. 10-7. Support the work solidly when cutting with the jeweler's saw.

Fig. 10-8. Jeweler's files.

Fig. 10-9. Common types of art metal hammers.

made of steel. The hammer faces should be kept polished.

MALLETS, Fig. 10-10, are made of hardwood, plastic, rawhide and rubber. They are used to form the softer metals. After forming with the mallet, the piece is finished with a hammer.

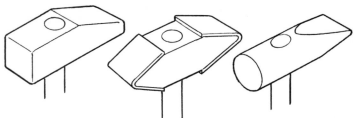

Fig. 10-10. Art metal mallets. Left. Hardwood forming mallet. Center. Leather faced forming mallet. Right. Round end forming mallet.

Forming by Beating Down

In this process, shallow trays and plates are formed by beating down portions of the metal over a hardwood stake or form.

Both methods require that a pattern be developed, Fig. 10-11. Guide lines indicate the portion to be beat down.

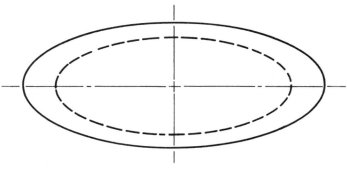

Fig. 10-11. Pattern with guide lines showing the portion to be formed.

Hold the metal over the stake with the guide lines about 1/8 in. from the edge of the stake, Fig. 10-12. Use a forming hammer to beat down the metal. Rotate the blank slightly after each blow until the correct

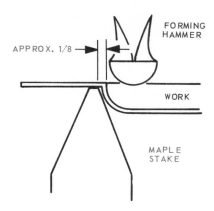

Fig. 10-12. Hold the metal on the stake.

depth is reached. A template may be used to check the progress of the forming operation.

A wooden form block, Fig. 10-13, may also be used to shape the piece.

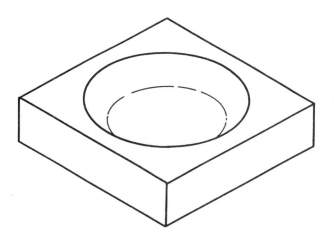

Fig. 10-13. Wooden form block for use when forming a piece by beating down.

Position the metal over the block and fasten it at the corners with small nails or screws. Use a mallet on soft metals (pewter and soft aluminum). For other metals, select a hammer having approximately the same contour (shape) as the form block sides.

Start working at the outer edges and slowly work toward the center.

The work will have a tendency to warp slightly and must be flattened. This is done on a flat, clean surface, using a wooden block

and a mallet to hammer the surface flat, Fig. 10-14.

Trim, planish (smooth by hammering lightly) and polish the piece.

Fig. 10-14. One method which may be used to flatten work that has been warped in the forming operation.

Planishing

PLANISHING is an operation used to make the surface of the metal smooth. See Fig. 10-15. It is done with a planishing hammer. Only a hammer with a mirror smooth face should be used.

Fig. 10-15. Note how the planish marks enhance the appearance of this brass mug. (Henry Kauffman)

Above. A pewter tea service of popular design. Below. Art metal requires a great deal of hand work. Here a craftsman finishes off a handle for a mug.

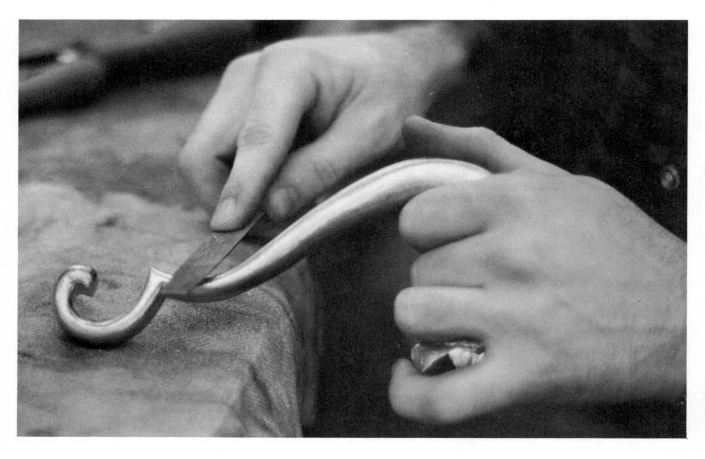

Lay the hammer blows on evenly. Rotate the piece so that no two blows fall in the same place, Fig. 10-15. Use a stake with a shape as near to the desired shape as possible.

Forming by Raising Metal

A bowl may be raised by one of several methods. The design of the project will determine the method to be used.

Shallow pieces can be raised using a block of hardwood having a shallow depression in one of the end grain sides, Fig. 10-16.

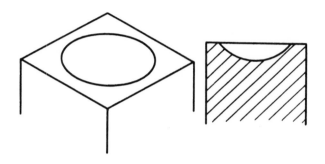

Fig. 10-16. A forming block.

Slowly form the metal into the depression. When the desired depth has been reached, clean the piece and planish it on a MUSHROOM STAKE, Fig. 10-17. Trim, Fig. 10-18, smooth the edges and polish.

Fig. 10-19 shows how to determine the diameter of the metal blank.

Bowls can be raised using a sandbag and mallet. Scribe concentric circles (several circles having the same center) on a disc of

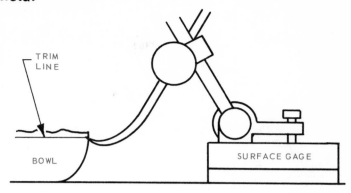

Fig. 10-18. Using a surface gauge to mark line for trimming.

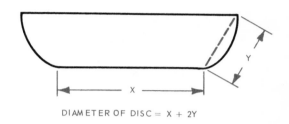

DIAMETER OF DISC = X + 2Y

Fig. 10-19. How to calculate the diameter of the metal disc.

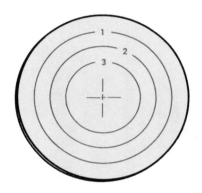

Fig. 10-20. Concentric circles on metal disc.

the proper size, Fig. 10-20. Place the disc on the sandbag and elevate the edge opposite the one to be struck with the mallet, Fig.

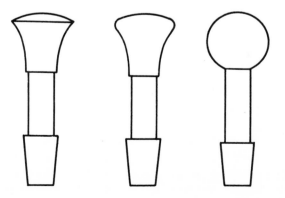

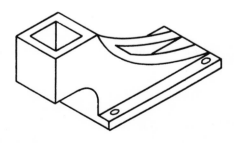

Fig. 10-17. Mushroom stakes with stake holder.

Fig. 10-21. *Starting to shape a bowl on a sandbag.*

10-21. Shape the bowl by striking the disc a series of blows around the outer circle. Continue working toward the center until the desired depth is obtained. Planish on a stake, trim to height and polish.

A form can also be raised over a stake. Forms of considerable height can be obtained using this method, Fig. 10-22.

Fig. 10-22. *Forms of considerable height can be raised.*

Cut the disc and scribe the concentric circles. Start the raising on the sandbag. Anneal the piece and place it on a RAISING STAKE, Fig. 10-23, and begin hammering by going round and round the scribed circles.

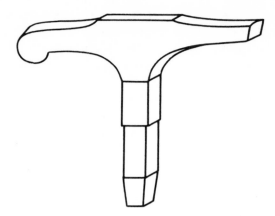

Fig. 10-23. *Stake used for raising work.*

To continue the raising operation, it is important that the work be held on the stake so the hammer blows land just ABOVE the point where the metal touches the stake, Fig. 10-24.

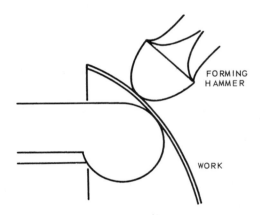

FORMING HAMMER

WORK

Fig. 10-24. *Hammer blows should be landed just above the point where the bowl rests on the stake.*

Continue the operation, annealing when necessary, until the desired height is reached.

Pickle, trim, planish and polish.

Hard Soldering

HARD SOLDERING or SILVER SOLDERING produces a joint much stronger than soft solder and is often used in art metal. A torch, Fig. 10-25, must be used because the temperatures needed range from 800 to 1400 deg. F. depending on the silver solder used. The solder is available in sheet and wire form.

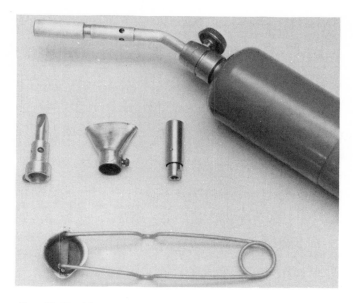

Fig. 10-25. The gas torch with a few of the tips available.

Most nonferrous metals (copper, brass and silver) can be joined by this method.

When silver soldering, the following steps should be followed:

1. CAREFULLY FIT THE PIECES TOGETHER, Fig. 10-26.

2. CLEAN THE METAL. This may be done with abrasive cloth or by pickling.

3. PROPER FLUXING. A suitable flux can be made by mixing borax and water to form a thick paste.

4. THE JOINT MUST BE SUPPORTED, Fig. 10-27, so the pieces cannot slip during the heating. Use clamps or binding wire.

5. HEATING AND FLOWING SOLDER. Cut the solder into pieces about 1/16 in. long.

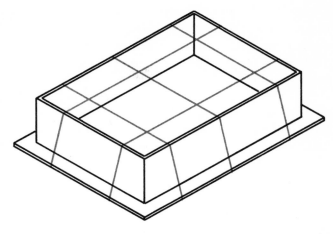

Fig. 10-27. Support the joints to be soldered. This can often be done by wiring them together with soft iron wire.

Dip them in flux and place them on the joint with a small brush or tweezers.

CAUTION: WHEN LIGHTING THE TORCH HOLD IT SO IT IS POINTING AWAY AND USE A SPARK LIGHTER, Fig. 10-28.

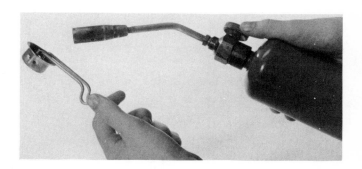

Fig. 10-28. The recommended way to light the torch. NEVER USE MATCHES.

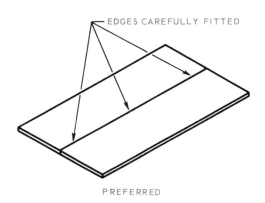

PREFERRED

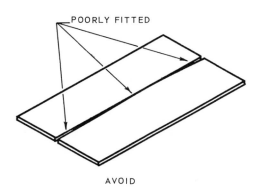

AVOID

Fig. 10-26. The pieces to be hard soldered (silver soldered) must be carefully fitted together.

Keep the torch in motion while heating the joint. This will assure a uniform heat. As the solder melts, it will be drawn into the joint.

If different size pieces are to be soldered, apply more heat to the larger section.

6. FINAL CLEANING. Remove all traces of flux and oxides from the joint. This can be done using abrasive cloth or pickling solution.

Safety

1. Remove all burrs and sharp edges from metal before attempting to work it.

2. Use caution when handling hot metal. Do not place it where it can start a fire.

3. HAVE YOUR INSTRUCTOR MIX THE PICKLING SOLUTION. It contains acid and may cause serious and painful burns.

4. Wear a face shield when using the pickling solution. Wear your regular goggles when working in the shop.

5. Use the pickling solution in a well ventilated area. DO NOT BREATHE THE FUMES.

6. Stand to one side when plunging hot metal into the pickling solution.

7. Clear the soldering area of solvents and other flammable material before soldering.

8. Place the heated soldering copper in its holder when you are finished with it.

9. Have cuts, bruises and burns treated promptly.

What Do You Know About Art Metal? – Unit 10

1. List some of the classifications of art metal.

a. _____
b. _____
c. _____

2. Why must metal be annealed?

3. Cleaning metal by heating it and plunging it into a dilute solution of acid is called _____.

4. Name the two methods used to form bowls and trays.

a. _____
b. _____

5. _____ is the name of the operation used to make the surface of art metal projects smooth.

6. How does soft soldering differ from hard soldering?

7. List a few of the safety rules that should be observed when working art metal.

a. _____
b. _____
c. _____

Special Activities

1. Make a collection of illustrations from old magazines, newspapers and catalogs that can be used for art metal project ideas.

2. Visit a museum and study examples of art metalwork made by well known craftsmen.

3. Demonstrate the technique of hard soldering.

4. Design and craft an outstanding craftsman award for the Industrial Arts department of your school.

5. Prepare posters on art metal safety.

6. Secure samples of the various classifications of art metalwork and describe them to your class. Emphasize what you consider their good points of design.

Fig. 11-1. This aircraft is painted to enhance its appearance and to make it easier to identify. (Gates-Learjet)

Unit 11
METAL FINISHES

Finishes are applied to metal to protect the surface from corrosion and to enhance its appearance, Fig. 11-1. Many types of finishes are available.

No matter what type of finish is applied, the surface of the metal must be clean.

Hand Polishing with Abrasives

Any hard, sharp material that can be used to wear away another material is considered to be an abrasive. For many purposes, man-made abrasives (aluminum oxide, silicon carbide, etc.) are superior to natural abrasives (emery and iron oxide).

Abrasive grains are bonded to a cloth or paper backing. The coarseness (grain size) of an abrasive is identified by number. The higher the number the smaller the grain and the finer the finish it will produce. Aluminum oxide and silicon carbide abrasive sheets used in the school shop usually range from 1 (one) extra coarse to 8/0 extra fine.

Properly filed work can be polished using only a fine-grain abrasive cloth. However, if there are deep scratches, it is best to start

with coarse-grain cloth. Change to medium-grain cloth, then finish with a fine-grain abrasive. A few drops of machine oil will speed the operation.

Support the abrasive cloth by wrapping it around a wood block or use a purchased sanding block, Fig. 11-2. Apply pressure and move

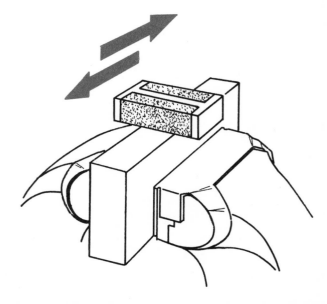

Fig. 11-2. When polishing, wrap the abrasive cloth around a block of metal or wood, or use a purchased sanding block.

the abrasive back and forth in a straight line. Rub it parallel to the long edge of the work if possible.

DO NOT POLISH MACHINED SURFACES.

Fig. 11-3. Buffing produces a highly polished surface on metal.

Buffing

BUFFING, Fig. 11-3, provides a bright mechanical finish. It is commonly applied to nonferrous metals like aluminum, copper, brass, pewter and silver. Copper base alloys must be covered by a clear plastic or lacquer coating to protect the polished surface. Buffing is done on a BUFFER-POLISHER, Fig. 11-4.

Fig. 11-4. A buffing machine typical of those found in the school metal shop. (Delta-Rockwell)

Remove all scratches with an abrasive before buffing.

To buff, use a fairly stiff wheel and charge it with tripoli or pumice. This will remove the small scratches formed by the abrasive cloth.

Final polishing is done with a loose flannel wheel and polishing compound.

Buffing should be done with the work held below the center line of the wheel, Fig. 11-5.

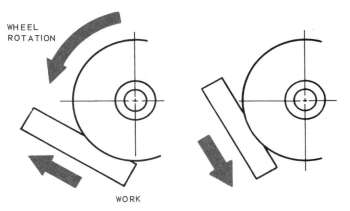

Fig. 11-5. Work below the center line of the buffing wheel. Pull the metal toward you when starting the operation as shown on the left. If the work is pulled from your grasp, your hands will not be pulled into the wheel and be injured. For the final high polish, pass the work lightly into the wheel as shown at the right.

Wire Brushing

WIRE BRUSHING produces a smooth satin sheen on the metal. Wire size will determine

Fig. 11-6. The painted finish on this factory built structure is not only attractive but also reduces maintenance and repair costs. (Stran-Steel)

Fig. 11-7. A wide selection of colors are available in pressurized spray cans. Project being finished is a barrel for a model cannon.

the smoothness of the finish - the finer the wire the smoother the finish.

Painting

PAINTING, Fig. 11-6, is another finishing technique. Many colors and finishes are available. They can be applied to the project by spraying, Figs. 11-7 and 11-8, brushing, rolling or dipping.

Fig. 11-8. An automatic rotary machine sprays porcelain enamel on metal parts for lighting fixtures. The machine boosted production 300 percent over hand spraying and had fewer rejects. (The DeVilbiss Co.)

MACHINED SURFACES SHOULD NOT BE PAINTED.

Coloring with Heat

This type of finish may be applied to steel. Clean the metal and slowly heat it. Watch the colors as they appear. Plunge the metal into cool water when the correct color is reached. Protect the resulting finish with clear lacquer.

Other Metal Finishes

There are several other finishes that can be applied to metal. However, some of them require special equipment to apply that is not readily available in a school shop.

HOT DIPPING, Fig. 11-9. This type of coating is applied to steel by dipping the metal into molten aluminum, zinc, tin or lead. GALVANIZED STEEL is an example of this finishing technique.

Fig. 11-9. Metal parts being hot dipped to produce a zinc (galvanized) coating on the parts.
(American Hot Dip Galvanized Assoc., Inc.)

ANODIZING is a process used to form a protective layer of aluminum oxide on aluminum parts. The anodized coating can be dyed a wide range of colors. The color becomes a part of the surface of the metal.

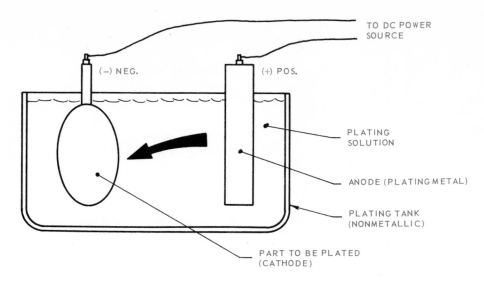

TO DC POWER
SOURCE

(−) NEG.

(+) POS.

PLATING
SOLUTION

ANODE (PLATING METAL)

PLATING TANK
(NONMETALLIC)

PART TO BE PLATED
(CATHODE)

*Fig. 11-10. Electroplating is the process by which one metal
is coated with another by electricity.*

ELECTROPLATING is a finishing technique whereby a metal coating is applied or deposited on a metal surface by the use of an electrical current, Fig. 11-10.

What Do You Know About
Metal Finishes? – Unit 11

1. Why are finishes applied to metal?
2. An abrasive is _____.
3. _____ and _____ are man-made abrasives and are superior to_____ and _____which are natural abrasives.
4. _____produces the brightest finish.
5. _____produces a smooth satin sheen.
6. Paints and lacquers may be applied by:
   a._____
   b._____
   c._____
   d._____

7. Galvanized steel is an example of a finish applied by_____.
8. _____is a finishing technique whereby the finish is deposited on a metal surface by the use of an electrical current.

Special Activities

1. Collect samples of metals with different types of finishes. Why was each finish used?
2. Look around your school shop and note the different types of finishes used on the tools and machinery. How many types can you identify?
3. Prepare samples of metal sheet with different kinds of painted finishes. Devise a method for testing the durability of each finish.
4. Demonstrate electroplating.

Fig. 12-1. The master blacksmith hand forges useful ironwork articles at the Deane Forge at Colonial Williamsburg, just as his 18th century predecessors did. (Colonial Williamsburg)

Unit 12

HAND FORGING

Metal is FORGED by heating it to less than the melting point and using pressure to shape the hot metal. Heating makes the metal PLASTIC (permits it to be more easily shaped). In HAND FORGING, pressure is applied by using a hammer, Fig. 12-1. FORGING improves the physical characteristics (strength, toughness) of the metal.

Equipment for Hand Forging

Forge

The metal is heated in a FORGE, Fig. 12-2. The forge may be gas or coal fired. Gas is preferred because it is cleaner to use.

Lighting a Gas Forge

1. Open the forge door. Check to be sure the gas valve is closed.

Fig. 12-2. A gas fired forge. (Johnson Gas Appliance Co.)

2. Start the air blower and open the air valve slightly.

3. Apply the lighter and slowly turn on the gas.

CAUTION: STAND TO ONE SIDE AND DO NOT LOOK INTO THE FORGE WHEN YOU LIGHT IT.

4. After the gas has ignited, adjust the gas and air valves for the best combination.

Anvil

Heated metal is shaped on an ANVIL, Fig. 12-3. The HORN which is conical in shape, is used to form circular sections.

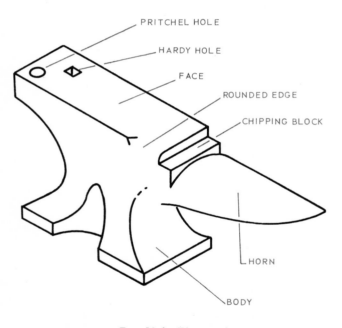

Fig. 12-3. The anvil.

PRITCHEL HOLE
HARDY HOLE
FACE
ROUNDED EDGE
CHIPPING BLOCK
HORN
BODY

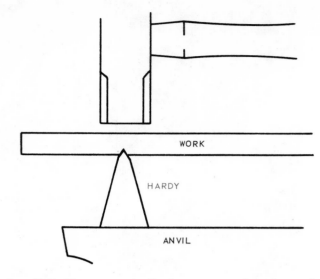

WORK
HARDY
ANVIL

Fig. 12-5. When using the Hardy to cut metal, nick it on both sides and bend it back and forth until it breaks. Metal thicker than 1/2 in. should be cut hot.

Various anvil tools can be mounted in the HARDY HOLE. The PRITCHEL HOLE is used to punch holes or to bend small diameter rods.

Anvil Tools

Many anvil tools are available. You will probably use the HARDY, Fig. 12-4, to cut metal. It is inserted in the HARDY HOLE. The metal to be cut is placed on the cutter and struck with a hammer, Fig. 12-5, until it is cut. If metal thicker than 1/2 in. is to be cut, it should be cut hot.

Hammers

Many different types of HAMMERS are available for hand forging. See Fig. 12-6. Use

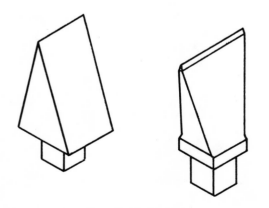

Fig. 12-4. Hardies.

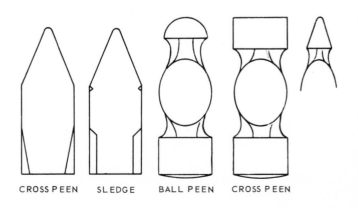

CROSS PEEN   SLEDGE   BALL PEEN   CROSS PEEN

Fig. 12-6. Forging hammers.

108

a 1 1/2 - 2 lb. hammer for light work. A 3 lb. hammer will be satisfactory for heavy work. Do not "choke-up" on the hammer handle - you may injure yourself.

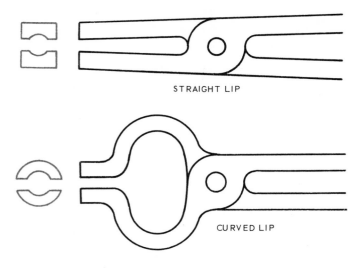

STRAIGHT LIP

CURVED LIP

Fig. 12-7. Typical forging tongs.

Tongs

TONGS are used to hold the hot metal while it is being forged, Fig. 12-7. Use tongs that are best suited for the work being done, Fig. 12-8.

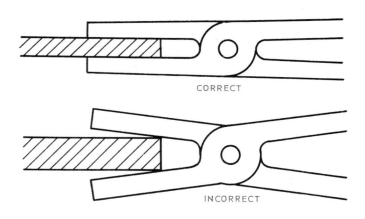

CORRECT

INCORRECT

Fig. 12-8. Use the correct tongs for the work to be forged.

Forging

It is necessary to heat the metal to the correct temperature before it can be forged. Mild steel should be heated to a BRIGHT RED. Carbon steel should not be heated beyond a DULL RED. A WHITE HEAT where sparks fly from the piece must be avoided.

CAUTION: WEAR A FACE SHIELD WHEN FORGING. THE SCALE THAT FLIES ABOUT IS HOT. GLOVES SHOULD BE WORN TOO.

Drawing Out Metal

The forging operation employed to stretch or lengthen the metal is called DRAWING OUT. Fig. 12-9 shows the sequence recommended for drawing out round stock. Square stock is drawn out in much the same way.

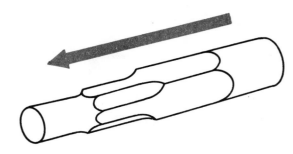

Fig. 12-9. Drawing out sequence.

Round stock can be pointed as shown in Fig. 12-10.

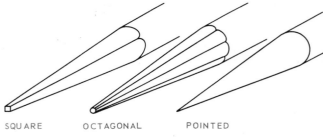

SQUARE   OCTAGONAL   POINTED

Fig. 12-10. Steps in drawing out a point.

Bending Metal

There are several ways to make a bend in stock. Unless a small size rod is to be bent, all require the metal to be heated to a red heat.

1. Bend the metal over the anvil face and edge, Fig. 12-11.
2. Place the stock in the hardy or pritchel

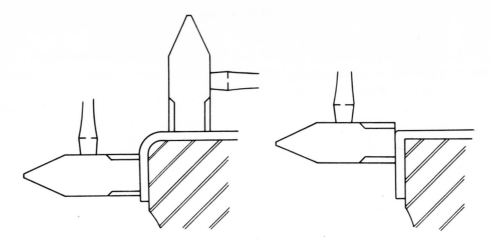

Fig. 12-11. Making a right angle bend over the edge of the anvil.

hole and bend it over, Fig. 12-12. Square the bend over the anvil edge.

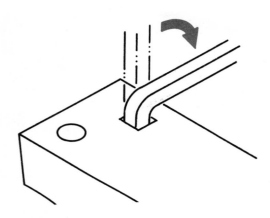

Fig. 12-12. Making a bend using the Hardy hole.

3. Curved sections are made on the anvil horn, Fig. 12-13.

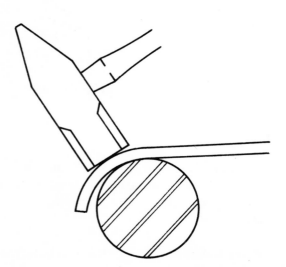

Fig. 12-13. Circular shapes can be made over the anvil horn.

Upsetting Metal

UPSETTING is a term given the operation used to increase the thickness of the metal at a given point, Fig. 12-14. The operation shortens the metal.

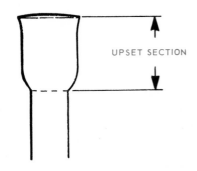

UPSET SECTION

Fig. 12-14. Upsetting decreases the length of the metal but increases the thickness.

1. Heat the metal to a red heat.
2. Short work is upset using the anvil face, Fig. 12-15.

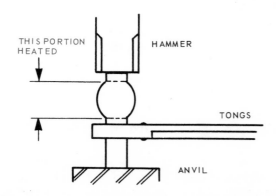

THIS PORTION HEATED   HAMMER

TONGS

ANVIL

Fig. 12-15. Short pieces can be upset on the face of the anvil.

3. Mount the work in a vise if it is short enough. The heated end extends above the vise jaws and is hammered to increase its size.

If the metal starts to work hard because of cooling, reheat it and continue the operation.

What Do You Know About Hand Forging? – Unit 12

1. How is metal forged?
2. Heating makes the metal _____ .
3. The metal is heated in a _____ . It is fired by_____or_____ .

4. Heated metal is held by_____while being shaped on an_____ .
5. _____ is the term given the forging operation that lengthens or stretches the metal.
6. What does the term "upsetting" mean?

Special Activities

1. Prepare posters on forging safety.
2. Demonstrate the proper way to light a gas forge.
3. Hand forge a cold chisel.
4. Secure examples of products that have been forged.

More than thirty different metals and alloys are needed to manufacture this radio controlled model car. (Jerobee)

Fig. 13-1. Familiar items made by the permanent mold process.

Unit 13
CASTING METALS

Fig. 13-2. Die casting machines are the most complex equipment used in any major casting method. Providing economical production of large quantities at very high output rates, die casting develops superior finish quality and surface detail. Shown: crane setting die in machine. (Aluminum Company of America)

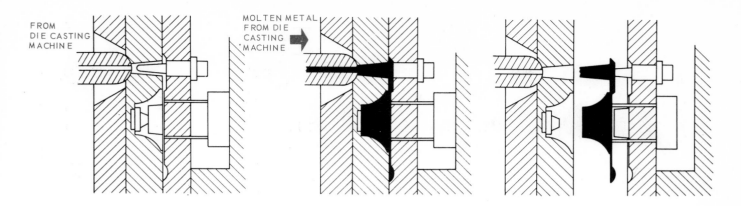

FROM DIE CASTING MACHINE

MOLTEN METAL FROM DIE CASTING MACHINE →

Fig. 13-3. Left. Here are the two sections of a die, closed and locked to receive the ''shot'' of metal to form a casting. Center. The cavity of the die is now completely filled. Note the metal in the overflow well at the bottom of the cavity which provides an outlet for the air entrapped in the die cavity. Right. The die is opened to permit ejection of the casting. Note the two pins which free the casting from the die.

Casting metals is one of the oldest metal-working processes used by man. It is a method of making objects by pouring molten metal into a mold. The mold forms a cavity the shape and size of the object to be cast, in a material suitable for holding the molten metal until it cools. The part made by this process is called a CASTING. In industry, castings are made in a FOUNDRY.

Permanent Mold Casting

PERMANENT MOLD CASTINGS are made in metal molds that are not destroyed when removing the casting. Many nonferrous metals (metals other than iron) can be cast this way.

The molds used to cast fishing sinkers and toy soldiers are examples of castings made in a permanent mold, Fig. 13-1. Many of the pistons used in the modern automobile are made by this technique.

Die Casting

DIE CASTING is a variation of the permanent mold process. The metal is forced into the mold or die under pressure, Figs. 13-2 and 13-3. Castings produced have smoother finishes, finer details and greater accuracy than regular sand castings, Fig. 13-4. Large quantities of die castings can be produced quickly on automatic casting machines.

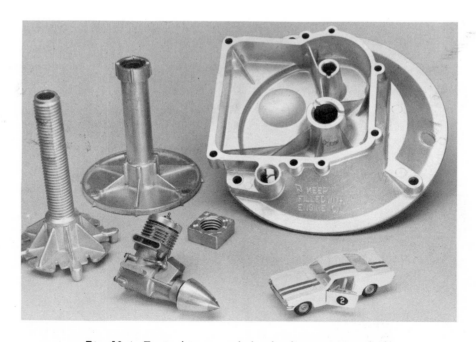

Fig. 13-4. Typical items made by the die casting method.

Fig. 13-5. *Jet engine turbine blade made by the investment or lost wax casting process.*

WAX PATTERNS

PATTERNS INVESTED IN REFRACTORY MOLD

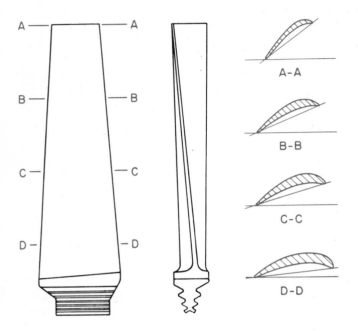

A-A

B-B

C-C

D-D

Fig. 13-6. *Note the complex shape of the turbine blade that made it expensive to manufacture by other methods.*

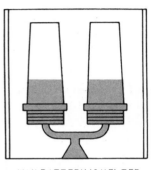

WAX PATTERN IS MELTED OR BURNED FROM MOLD

MOLD IS POURED

Fig. 13-7. *The investment casting process.*

Investment or Lost Wax Casting

INVESTMENT or LOST WAX CASTING is a foundry process used where a very accurate casting of a complex shape or intricate design must be produced, Figs. 13-5 and 13-6.

Fig. 13-8. **A shell mold.** *(Link-Belt)*

In the investment casting process, Fig. 13-7, patterns of wax or plastic are placed (invested) in a refractory mold (a mold that will withstand high heat). When the mold has hardened, it is placed in an oven and heated until the wax or plastic pattern is burned out (lost). This leaves a cavity in the mold the shape of the pattern. Molten metal is forced into the mold. It is allowed to cool and the mold is broken apart to remove the casting.

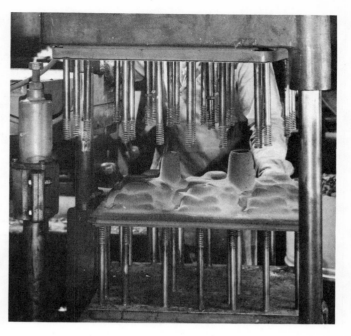

Fig. 13-9. The pattern halves ready to receive the specially prepared sand used in shell molding.

Fig. 13-10. Joining the two mold sections together.

Shell Molding

SHELL MOLDING is a fairly new foundry process that is a variation of sand casting. The molds are made in the form of thin sand shells, Fig. 13-8.

A metal pattern attached to a steel plate is fitted into the molding machine. After the

pattern has been heated to the required temperature, a measured amount of mix consisting of thermosetting resin (heat causes it to take a permanent shape) and sand is deposited on it, Fig. 13-9. The thin soft shells are then cured until the desired hardness is obtained. Upon cooling, the pattern is removed and the shell halves are bonded together using a special adhesive, Fig. 13-10. Like regular sand molds, shell molds must be destroyed to remove the casting.

Shell molding is well suited for mass-production. The casting produced, Fig. 13-11, has a superior finish with greater accuracy

Fig. 13-11. Shell molding is well suited to the quantity production of quality castings.

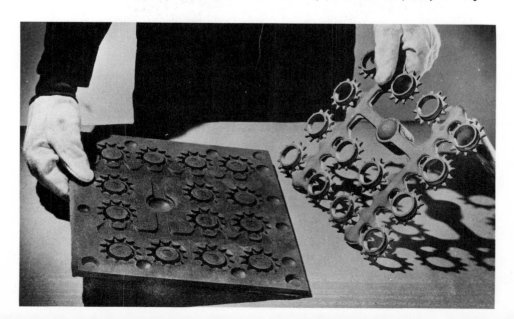

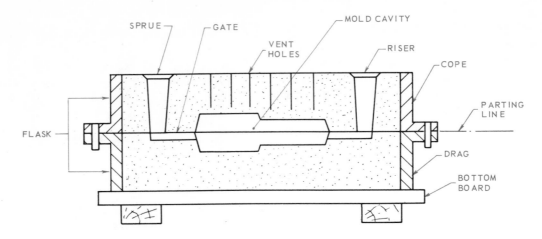

Fig. 13-12. Sand mold.

than castings made by the regular sand casting technique.

Metal Casting in the School Shop

While several of the above foundry processes can be used in the school shop, SAND CASTING is the method most commonly employed. It is also the most widely used of the industrial casting techniques.

Sand casting as practiced in the school shop is similar to that used by industry. The major differences being casting size and the quantity of castings produced.

Sand castings are cast in MOLDS made of a mixture of sand and clay, Fig. 13-12. The sand is used in the moist stage and is called a GREEN SAND MOLD. The mold is made by packing the sand in a box called a FLASK, around a PATTERN of the shape to be cast. Parts of the flask separate to allow easy removal of the pattern.

A GATING SYSTEM is used to get the molten metal to the mold cavity. This consists of vertical openings called SPRUES which

Fig. 13-13. The split pattern (above) is used to make castings of more complex shape than the simple pattern (below).

are connected to the mold cavity by grooves called GATES and RUNNERS.

Metals shrink as they cool and provisions must be made to supply additional metal to the parts of the casting that cool last. If this

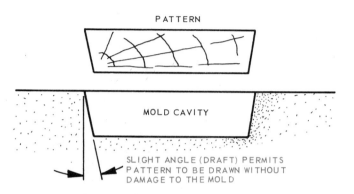

PATTERN

MOLD CAVITY

SLIGHT ANGLE (DRAFT) PERMITS PATTERN TO BE DRAWN WITHOUT DAMAGE TO THE MOLD

Fig. 13-14. A slight angle (draft) on the pattern permits it to be easily drawn from the mold.

is not done, hollow parts may occur in the finished casting. These reservoirs of extra metal are called RISERS or FEEDERS.

Sand molds can be used only once as they are destroyed in removing the finished casting.

How to Make a Sand Mold

In order to produce a sound casting in the school shop, a certain sequence of operations should be followed:

Patternmaking

The cavity in the sand mold is made with a PATTERN, Fig. 13-13. A SIMPLE PATTERN is made in one piece. SPLIT PATTERNS (patterns with two or more parts) are used to make castings of more complex shape.

A pattern must have DRAFT, Fig. 13-14. Draft is a slight taper that permits the pattern to be lifted from the sand without damaging the mold.

The pattern must be made slightly larger than the casting because metal shrinks as it cools from the molten state. The amount of shrinkage will depend on the metal being cast.

Openings or hollow spaces are made in a casting with a sand CORE, Fig. 13-15. Cores are made from a special sand mix. When baked, this is hard enough to withstand casting pressures.

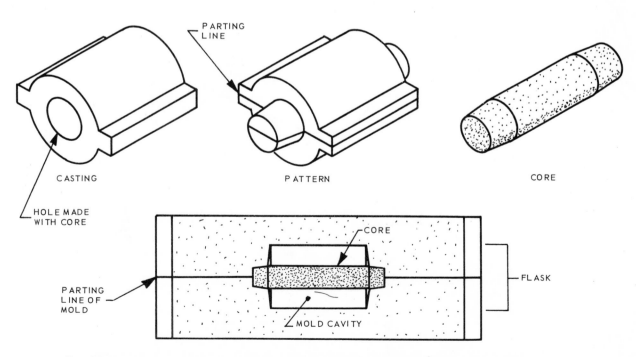

PARTING LINE

CASTING

HOLE MADE WITH CORE

PATTERN

CORE

CORE

PARTING LINE OF MOLD

MOLD CAVITY

FLASK

Fig. 13-15. Cores are made of a special sand and are used to produce openings in castings.

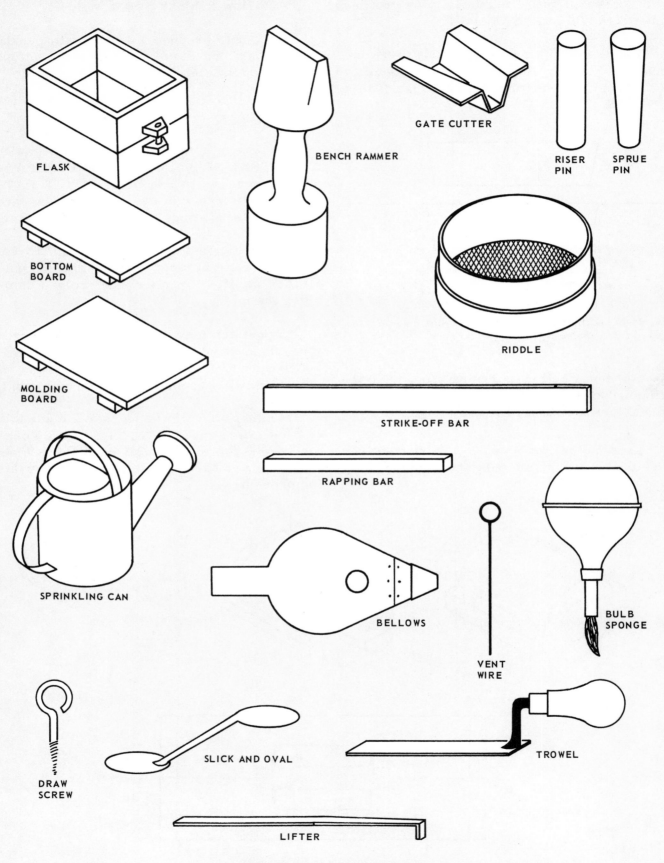

Fig. 13-16. Tools used in the foundry.

Tools and Equipment

Typical foundry tools and equipment are shown in Fig. 13-16. Their use will be described in MAKING A SIMPLE MOLD.

Molding Sands

Good molding sand is essential if good castings are to be made. Two types of sand are commonly used in the school foundry. NATURAL SAND which is used as it is dug from the ground and SYNTHETIC SAND. Synthetic sands have an oil binder and no water is needed.

If a synthetic sand is not used, the sand must be TEMPERED or dampened enough to be workable. Water which is added serves as a binder. After mixing the sand until it is uniformly moist, test by squeezing a handful of sand and breaking it in half. Properly tempered sand will break cleanly and retain the imprint of your fingers, Fig. 13-17. The sand will cling to your hand if it is too moist, and will crumble if too dry.

Fig. 13-17. Notice how cleanly properly tempered sand breaks.

Parting Compound

A light dusting of PARTING COMPOUND (a waterproofing material) will prevent the moist sand from adhering to the pattern or to the mold faces.

Making and Casting a Simple Mold

1. Temper the molding sand.
2. Clean and wax the pattern.
3. Position the DRAG (aligning pins down) on the MOLDING BOARD and place the PATTERN in position, Fig. 13-18. The flat back of the pattern is placed on the board.

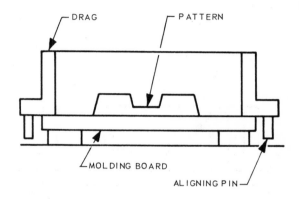

Fig. 13-18. Position the drag on the molding board and position the pattern near its center.

4. Dust the pattern with PARTING COMPOUND.
5. Fill the RIDDLE with sand and sift a 1 in. layer of sand over the pattern, Fig. 13-19.

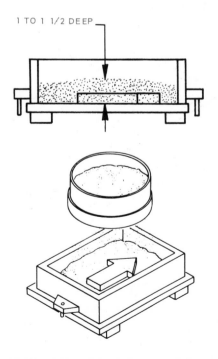

Fig. 13-19. Riddle (sift) about 1 to 1 1/2 in. deep layer of sand over the pattern.

6. Using your fingers, pack the riddled sand around the pattern. Roughen the surface of the packed sand and fill the drag with unriddled sand.

7. Pack loose sand around the pattern and inside edges of the drag with the PEEN edge of the BENCH RAMMER, Fig. 13-20. Be careful not to hit the pattern. Ram the sand firmly enough around the pattern to give a good, sharp impression.

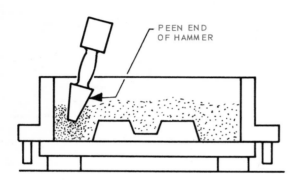

Fig. 13-20. Ram the mold using the peen end of the rammer. Be careful not to hit the pattern.

8. Add extra sand if necessary to fully pack the drag. Use the BUTT end of the rammer for the final packing.

9. Use a STRIKE-OFF BAR to remove the excess sand, Fig. 13-21.

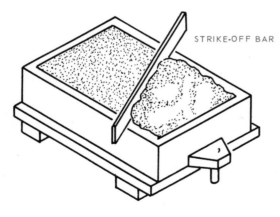

Fig. 13-21. Remove excess sand with the strike-off bar.

10. Place the BOTTOM BOARD on top of the drag and roll (turn) it over.

11. Remove the molding board to expose the pattern. Examine the surface of the sand and, if necessary, smooth and level it with a TROWEL or SLICK.

12. Place the COPE on the drag. Locate the SPRUE and RISER PINS in the drag about 1 in. away from each end of the pattern, Fig. 13-22. Place the riser pin near the heaviest section of the pattern.

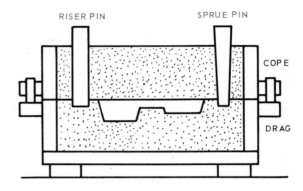

Fig. 13-22. Locate the riser and sprue holes approximately 1 in. from the pattern. Place the riser hole near the heaviest section of the pattern.

13. Dust parting compound over the face of the mold to prevent the surfaces from sticking together when the cope is separated from the drag.

14. Riddle, ram and strike off the sand in the cope as was done before.

15. Gases are generated when the molten metal is poured into a mold. To permit these gases to escape, vent the mold with a VENT WIRE, Fig. 13-23. The vent holes should almost, but not quite, touch the pattern.

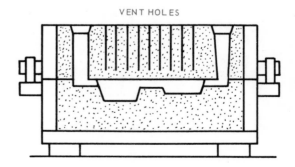

Fig. 13-23. Vent holes permit the gases generated when the molten metal contacts the moist sand to escape without damaging the mold.

16. Remove the sprue and riser pins from the mold. Smooth the edges of the holes with your fingers.

17. Carefully lift the cope from the drag and place it on edge away from the immediate work area.

18. Use a BULB SPONGE to moisten the sand around the pattern. This will lessen the chance that the sand will break up when the pattern is DRAWN (removed from the sand).

19. Withdraw the pattern from the mold. Insert a DRAW SCREW into the back of the pattern. Tap the screw lightly with a RAPPING BAR to loosen the pattern. DO NOT HIT THE BACK OF THE PATTERN.

20. Draw the pattern from the mold. Repair defects with a SLICK and/or SPOON, Fig. 13-24.

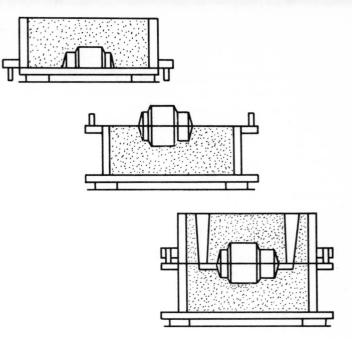

Fig. 13-26. Ramming up a split pattern. Above. Pattern half with aligning holes is rammed up first. Center. After drag is rolled over, the pattern half with the aligning pins is put in place. Below. Mold is rammed up in conventional manner.

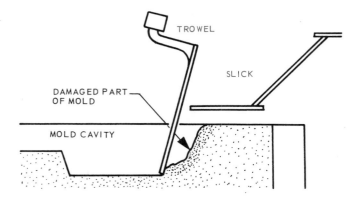

Fig. 13-24. Defects in the mold can often be repaired using the trowel and slick.

21. Cut a GATE from the mold cavity to the sprue hole and riser hole with a GATE CUTTER, Fig. 13-25. The gate is about 1/2 in. wide and 1/2 in. deep. Smooth the gate surfaces with your finger or a slick.

22. Use a BELLOWS to remove any loose sand that has fallen into the mold cavity.

23. Replace the cope on the drag.

24. Move flask to the pouring area. Allow to dry for a short time before pouring.

25. Pour metal into sprue hole carefully and rapidly. Hold the LADLE or CRUCIBLE close to the mold. Large molds are weighted or clamped to prevent the molten metal from lifting the cope and allowing molten metal to flow out of the mold at the parting line.

26. Allow the casting to cool, then break the sand from around it.

The mold is made in much the same manner when a SPLIT PATTERN, Fig. 13-26, is

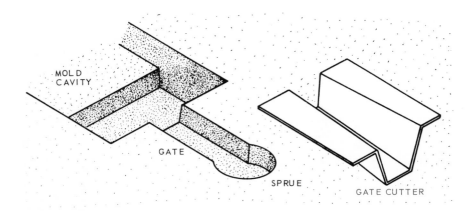

Fig. 13-25. The gate cutter is used to make the trough that connects the riser and sprue holes to the mold cavity.

used. As the pattern is made in two parts, one fitted with aligning pins, the other has holes to receive the pins. The pattern half with the holes is rammed in the drag, Fig. 13-26. The other half is placed in position after the drag has been rolled.

Foundry Safety

1. Wear protective clothing and goggles when pouring and handling molten metal.

2. CAUTION: UNDER NO CONDITION SHOULD MOIST OR WET METAL BE ADDED TO MOLTEN METAL. A violent explosion might result.

3. Place hot castings in an area where they will not cause accidental burns.

4. Stand to one side of the mold as you pour, never directly over it. Steam is generated when molten metal meets the moist sand and may burn you. Also, molten metal may spurt from the mold if the sand is too moist.

5. Keep the foundry area clean.

6. Do not wear oily or greasy shop clothing when working with hot metals.

7. Follow instructions carefully. DO NOT TAKE CHANCES. WHEN YOU ARE NOT SURE WHAT MUST BE DONE, ASK YOUR INSTRUCTOR.

8. Never look into the furnace when it is lighted. Stand to one side. DO NOT ATTEMPT TO LIGHT THE FURNACE UNTIL YOU HAVE BEEN INSTRUCTED IN THE PROPER WAY TO DO IT.

Melting Metals

A CRUCIBLE FURNACE, Fig. 13-27, is used to melt aluminum and brass. A SOLDERING FURNACE, Fig. 13-28, can be used to melt metals with lower melting temperatures like lead, pewter and zinc alloys (garalloy).

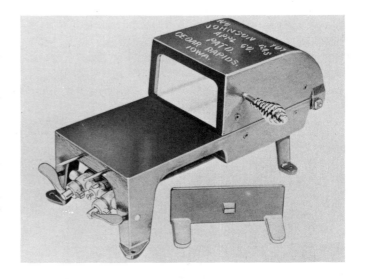

Fig. 13-28. Gas fired soldering furnace.
(Johnson Gas Appliance Co.)

A CRUCIBLE, Fig. 13-29, is used to hold aluminum and brass being melted. It is removed from the furnace with CRUCIBLE TONGS, Fig. 13-30, and placed in a CRUCIBLE SHANK for pouring.

Fig. 13-27. Melting furnace (gas fired) with safety features.
(Johnson Gas Appliance Co.)

Fig. 13-29. The crucible.

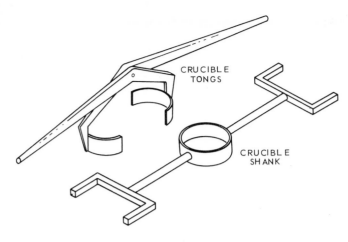

Fig. 13-30. Tongs are used to lift the crucible from the furnace. The crucible of molten metal is placed in the shank for pouring into the mold.

TURN OFF THE GAS BEFORE REMOVING THE CRUCIBLE FROM THE FURNACE.

Pouring Metal

Get enough metal together before lighting the furnace. Be careful not to mix different metals. Use a crucible large enough to hold sufficient metal for the casting. Place the crucible in the furnace.

Light the furnace and allow the metal to come to pouring temperature, Fig. 13-31. Use a PYROMETER, Fig. 13-32, to check the temperature of the metal. If additional metal must be added to the crucible, take every precaution to prevent metal with moisture from being added to the molten metal. WATER AND MOLTEN METAL REACT VIOLENTLY WHEN THEY COME IN CONTACT. BE SURE TO KEEP THEM APART.

When the metal has been heated to the correct temperature (be careful not to overheat or a poor casting will result), turn off the furnace. Remove the crucible from the furnace with tongs. Place it in a crucible shank for pouring. Add FLUX and skim the SLAG or DROSS (impurities in the metal) from the surface of the molten metal.

Fig. 13-32. The probe of the pyrometer is placed in the molten metal and the temperature is read on the direct reading gauge.

Pour the molten metal rapidly. STAND TO ONE SIDE OF THE MOLD AS YOU POUR, NEVER DIRECTLY OVER IT. Stop when the riser and sprue holes become full.

Allow the casting to cool, then SHAKE OUT (break up) the mold.

After cutting off the sprue and riser, the casting is ready for machining and finishing.

MELTING POINTS OF METAL

Tin	449°	Gar-alloy	830°
Lead	621°	Aluminum	1217°
Zamak	736°	Brass	1751°
Zinc	787°	Copper	1981°

Fig. 13-31. Chart of melting temperatures. Temperature is in degrees Fahrenheit.

Exploring Metalworking

What Do You Know About Casting Metals? – Unit 13

MATCHING QUESTIONS. Match the words in the column below with the sentences below. Place the letter of the word in the appropriate blank.

a. flask
b. cope
c. drag
d. green sand mold
e. mold
f. gating system
g. parting line
h. core
i. split pattern
j. simple pattern
k. draft
l. riddle
m. bench rammer
n. crucible

1. ____The container in which metal is melted.
2. ____The box into which the sand is packed to make the mold.
3. ____The sieve that breaks the sand into fine loose particles.
4. ____Mold made with moist sand.
5. ____The opening or cavity in the sand into which the molten metal is poured to produce a casting.
6. ____The bottom half of the mold.
7. ____The tool used to pack sand into the flask.
8. ____How the molten metal reaches the mold.
9. ____The top half of the flask.
10. ____A single piece pattern.
11. ____Necessary if the pattern is to be removed from the sand without damaging the mold.
12. ____A pattern made in two or more parts.
13. ____Point at which the flask comes apart.
14. ____Inserts to make holes and other openings in castings.
15. Identify the parts of a simple mold shown in the drawing below.

A._____   G._____
B._____   H._____
C._____   I._____
D._____   J._____
E._____   K._____
F._____

Special Activities

1. Secure samples of various types of castings.
2. Prepare a series of posters on safe foundry operations.
3. Demonstrate to the class the proper way to make a sand mold.
4. Certain products require molds made of plaster. Research and prepare a paper on the plaster casting process.

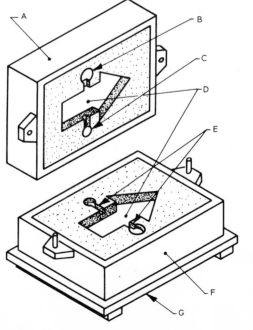
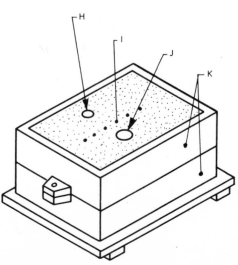

Unit 14
WELDING
AND BRAZING

Fig. 14-1. Workman puts finishing touches on a crosshead for a large press fabricated in the weldment shop of Bethlehem Steel Corporation.

WELDING is a technique used to fabricate metal parts, Fig. 14-1. It is a process in which two or more pieces of metal are joined into a single unit by heating them to a temperature high enough to cause them to melt and combine. A permanent joint is produced.

Pressure may be applied to force the pieces together, or filler metal may be added to fill the joint.

Many welding methods are available, including ARC, OXYACETYLENE, and SPOT WELDING. Welding makes it possible for most metals and their alloys to be welded to themselves, and often to each other.

With careful design, parts fabricated by welding standard stock metal shapes are often simpler, lighter and, in many applications, stronger and less expensive than their cast counterparts, Fig. 14-2. Frequently, welding

Fig. 14-2. A comparison can readily be made between the two surface grinder models illustrated. The grinder to the left was fabricated from castings. The grinder to the right has been redesigned to make use of welded and cast components.

is used to fabricate combinations of castings, forgings and stock steel shapes.

Arc Welding

ARC WELDING uses an electric current to generate the heat necessary to make the weld. The tip of the electrode (welding rod) and a small portion of the work becomes molten in the intense heat, Fig. 14-3.

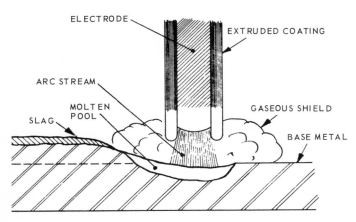

Fig. 14-3. Close-up showing electric welding procedure.

Typical arc welding equipment is illustrated in Fig. 14-4.

Fig. 14-4. AC welding machine.

Welding

When welding, be sure you are shielded from the direct rays of the arc. Protect your eyes, face, and neck with an arc welding helmet. NEVER USE GAS WELDING GOGGLES FOR THIS PURPOSE.

Keep your sleeves down and wear gauntlet type leather gloves to protect your arms and hands from "arc burn" and molten weld metal.

Turn your trouser cuffs down to prevent catching hot particles. WEAR LEATHER (NOT CANVAS) SHOES WHEN WELDING.

Wearing a leather apron or jacket which will protect your clothing from weld "splatter" is desirable.

Preparing Work for Welding

Metal to be welded should be clean. It may also be necessary to shape the joint to a V so electrode metal will fuse with the parent metal better, Fig. 14-5. Special welding symbols are used on drawings to show the type and size of the weld that is to be made. Fig. 14-6 shows the meaning of some of these symbols.

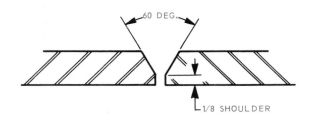

Fig. 14-5. A joint prepared for welding.

Striking the Arc

Adjust the machine to the correct power setting. Your instructor will help you do this. He will also help you select the correct type and size of welding rod.

Clamp the electrode into the holder, Fig. 14-7. It should be at an angle of 90 deg. to the jaws.

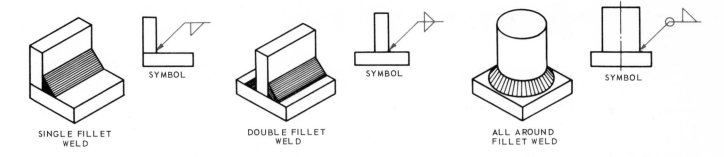

SINGLE FILLET
WELD

SYMBOL

DOUBLE FILLET
WELD

SYMBOL

ALL AROUND
FILLET WELD

SYMBOL

Fig. 14-6. Typical symbols used in welding.

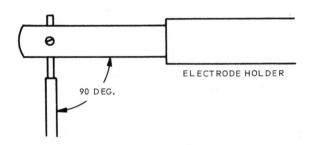

ELECTRODE HOLDER

90 DEG.

Fig. 14-7. The electrode is clamped into the holder as shown.

Two methods of striking an arc are the SCRATCHING METHOD, Fig. 14-8, and the TAPPING method, Fig. 14-9.

Once the arc is established, a short arc (1/16 to 1/8 in.) should be held.

Depositing Weld Metal

The electrode should be held at a right

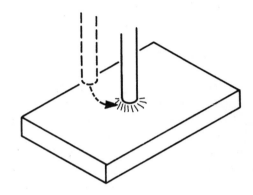

Fig. 14-9. In the TAPPING METHOD, the electrode is brought straight down on the work. It is immediately raised on contact to provide the proper arc length.

angle to the bead, and slightly tilted in the direction of travel, Fig. 14-10.

Do not watch the arc. Watch the puddle of molten metal directly behind the arc and the

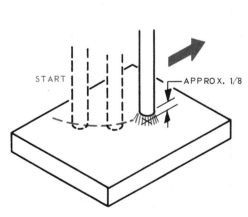

START

APPROX. 1/8

Fig. 14-8. In the SCRATCHING METHOD of striking the arc, the striking end of the electrode is dragged across the work. It might be compared to striking a match. To prevent the electrode from "freezing" to the work, withdraw the rod from the work immediately after contact has been made.

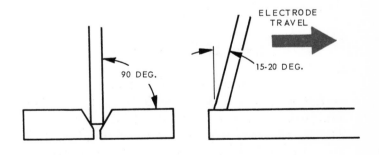

ELECTRODE
TRAVEL

90 DEG.

15-20 DEG.

Fig. 14-10. The electrode is held at a slight angle in the direction of travel.

ridge that forms as the molten metal solidifies. Move the electrode at a uniform speed. The correct speed is indicated when the ridge formed is about 3/8 in. behind the arc. Fig. 14-11 shows weld characteristics.

AMPERAGE   AMPERAGE   CORRECT
TOO LOW   TOO HIGH   PENETRATION

Fig. 14-11. Arc weld characteristics.

Arc Welding Safety

1. NEVER arc weld or watch arc welding being done without using a protective shield. Gas welding goggles or sun glasses are not satisfactory.
2. Wear goggles when chipping slag (the coating formed on the weld).
3. Wear suitable clothing for welding.
4. Do not weld where solvent or paint fumes may collect. Remove all flammable materials from the welding area.
5. Weld only in a well ventilated area.
6. Treat any cut or burn promptly.
7. Safety goggles should be worn under your welding shield for additional safety.
8. Do not attempt to weld a container until you have determined whether flammable liquids were stored in it. Get them steam cleaned or fill them with water before welding.
9. Use care when handling metal that has just been welded. A serious burn could result.

Oxyacetylene Welding

GAS WELDING EQUIPMENT, Fig. 14-12, includes two heavy CYLINDERS; one for acetylene gas, one for oxygen. PRESSURE REGULATORS are used to reduce the high pressure in the cylinders to useable pressures, and to maintain constant pressure at the torch. One gauge of the regulator shows the cylinder pressure, the other shows the pressure being delivered to the torch.

HOSES are used to transfer the acetylene and oxygen from the cylinders to the torch.

For easy identification, the oxygen hose is green and the acetylene hose is red.

The TORCH mixes the gases in proper proportion for welding.

You also need a WRENCH to fit the various connections, a SPARK LIGHTER to light the torch (NEVER USE MATCHES), and a pair of suitable GOGGLES and ASBESTOS GLOVES for hand protection.

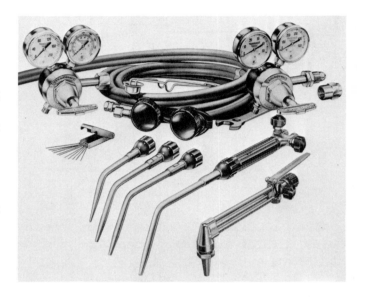

Fig. 14-12. Typical oxyacetylene welding equipment. (Marquette Mfg. Co.)

Fluxes

FLUXES are needed when gas heating certain metals to be joined with solder, or by welding or brazing. The flux helps to promote better fusion of the metals and to prevent harmful oxides (which cause poor weld joints) from forming.

How to Weld

Attach the torch tip best suited for the job (check with your instructor). Be sure it is clean, and that both valves on the torch are closed.

Open the oxygen tank valve SLOWLY until the Oxygen High Pressure Gauge shows tank pressure, then open valve as far as it will go.

Turn the handscrew until the Oxygen Low Pressure Gauge shows the pressure needed for the torch tip being used. Your instructor will provide this information.

Do the same with the acetylene cylinder except the cylinder valve should be opened only 1 to 1 1/2 turns - do not open it any more.

It is good practice to stand to one side of the regulator valves when the cylinder valves are opened.

Have your instructor show you how to light and adjust the welding flame. He should also check you out on preparing the equipment for welding.

To close down the welding unit:

1. Shut off the acetylene valve ON THE TORCH, then the oxygen valve.
2. Turn off each tank valve.
3. Open both valves on the torch to drain the gases from the hoses.
4. When both gauges read "zero," turn the adjusting screws on both regulators all the way out.
5. Close the torch valves and store the torch and hoses.

Making a Weld

Welds can be made with or without the use of welding rod. Either type of weld is made holding the torch at a 45 deg. angle to the work, Fig. 14-13. Position the torch until the cone of the flame is about 1/8 in. from the metal. When the metal begins to

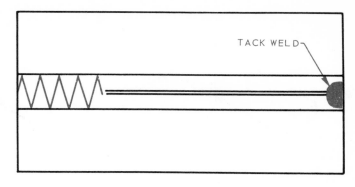

Fig. 14-14. When the metal begins to melt into a "puddle," move the torch along in a zigzag motion. The tack weld at the end is made to prevent the pieces from spreading apart when they expand from being heated.

melt into a "puddle," move the torch along in a zigzag motion, Fig. 14-14, as fast as the metal will melt and form a smooth, uniform weld, Fig. 14-15.

Fig. 14-15. Producing a smooth, strong, uniform weld using the BACKHAND GAS WELDING TECHNIQUE. With this technique the weld progresses from left to right and the welding rod is between the completed weld and the torch flame. For a FOREHAND WELD, the weld progresses from right to left. The flame is then between the completed weld and the welding rod.

If welding rod is used, preheat it by bringing it to within 3/8 in. of the flame. Preheating causes the rod to melt faster when it is dipped into the molten puddle as more metal is needed.

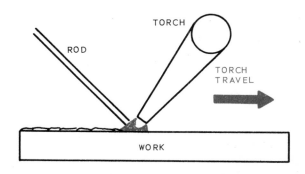

Fig. 14-13. Torch position for gas welding.

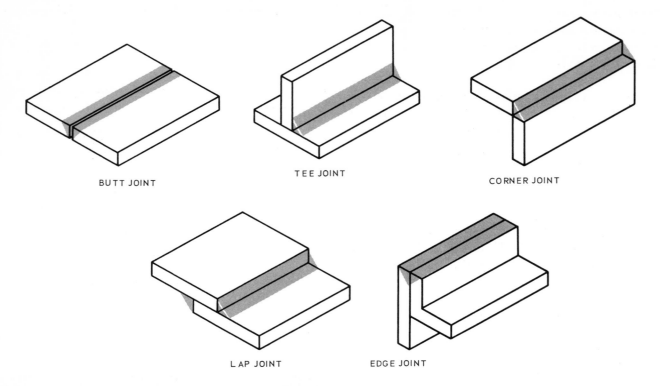

Fig. 14-16. *Typical weld joints.*

Enough rod should be added to raise the metal in the joint into a slight crown.

A number of typical weld joints are illustrated in Fig. 14-16.

Brazing

The difference between welding and brazing is that the base metal is not melted in brazing and a nonferrous rod is used as filler metal. Gas welding equipment is used.

The joint must be clean. Heat the pieces until they are red hot, then heat the end of

the brazing rod and dip it in flux. Hold the rod just ahead of the flame and allow it to melt and flow into the joint. An example of a properly deposited brazed joint is shown in Fig. 14-17.

Fig. 14-18. *Hold the torch away from the cylinders and pointed away from the body when lighting it. Note the gloves worn by the welder.* (Linde Co.)

Gas Welding Safety

1. Do not attempt to gas weld until you have received instructions on how to use the equipment.
2. Wear appropriate welding goggles.
3. Remove all flammable material from

Fig. 14-17. *An example of a properly deposited brazed joint.*

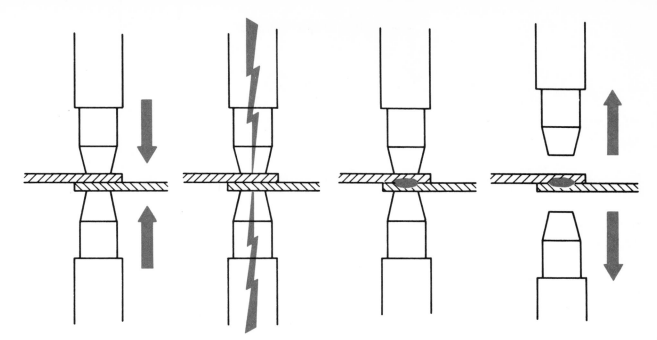

Fig. 14-19. How a spot weld is made.

the welding area.

4. Never light the torch with matches. Use a spark lighter, Fig. 14-18.

5. Never attempt to blow dirt from your clothing with gas pressure. Your clothing may become saturated with oxygen and/or acetylene and may literally explode if a spark comes in contact with it.

6. For added protection, dress properly for the job. Wear welder's gloves.

7. Use care when handling work that has just been welded to avoid serious burns.

8. It is only necessary to turn off the torch if your work needs to be repositioned. However, the entire unit should be turned off when the job is completed. Carefully hang up the torch.

Spot Welding

A SPOT WELD is a resistance type weld in which the metals to be welded are clamped between two electrodes. An electric current is passed between the two electrodes and resistance to the current of the metal between the electrodes heats the metal at the point of contact and fuses the pieces together, Fig. 14-19. The addition of filler metal is not required. Spot welding can be done with a portable unit or a larger stationary unit, Fig. 14-20.

Fig. 14-20. Portable spot welding equipment. (Ace-Sycamore, Inc.)

131

Exploring Metalworking

What Do You Know About Welding and Brazing - Unit 14

1. List the three welding techniques most frequently used.
   a. _____.
   b. _____.
   c. _____.
2. What precautions should you take to protect yourself when arc welding?
3. The two methods recommended for striking the arc are:
   a. _____.
   b. _____.
4. Gases used in oxyacetylene welding are stored in _____.
5. _____ cleans the metal and prevents oxidation from forming during the welding operation.
6. How does brazing differ from welding?
7. What precautions should be observed when gas welding?
8. How does spot welding differ from other forms of welding?

Special Activities

1. Prepare a series of posters on arc welding safety.
2. Prepare a series of posters on gas welding safety.
3. Secure samples of work that have been:
   a. Arc welded.
   b. Gas welded.
   c. Brazed.
   d. Spot welded.
4. Acquire drawings that show parts that must be fabricated by welding.
5. Make a chart showing the various symbols used on drawings to denote different kinds of welds.

Fig. 15-1. Many parts on this tractor and scraper must be heat-treated to prevent them from wearing out rapidly. (Caterpillar Tractor Co.)

Unit 15
HEAT-TREATING METALS

Metals must be soft enough to machine, and hard and tough enough so that they will perform the job they were designed to do, without quickly dulling or wearing down, Fig. 15-1. It would be difficult to meet these conditions in the manufacture of many metal products if it were not for the science of HEAT-TREATING METALS. Most metals and alloys can be heat-treated.

The heat treatment of metal includes a number of processes. All of them involve the CONTROLLED HEATING and COOLING of a metal to obtain certain desirable changes in properties such as toughness and hardness. One heat-treating process, ANNEALING, can be used to soften some metals for easier machining. Another, CASE HARDENING, can be used to produce a very hard surface on steel to make the metal more resistant to wear.

Fig. 15-3. The thermocouple is set to the desired attention (1500 deg. F). The furnace has attained a temperature of 800 deg. F.

Heat-treating is done by heating the metal to a predetermined temperature, Figs. 15-2, 15-3, and 15-4, then cooling rapidly (QUENCHING) in water, oil or brine. Another

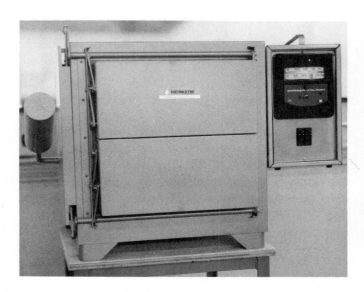

Fig. 15-2. Electric heat-treating furnace.

Fig. 15-4. The parts have reached the required temperature and are ready for quenching. Note how the parts are placed in the furnace so they will be uniformly heated.

133

heating (but at a lower temperature) and cooling cycle may be needed to give the metal the desired degree of hardness and toughness.

Heat-Treating in the School Shop

Of the many heat-treating processes used by industry, the following techniques can be used in the school shop. However, before attempting any of them, the following safety precautions are recommended.

Wear a face shield and asbestos gloves because heat-treating requires the handling of very hot metals. Get any burns, no matter how small, treated promptly.

Annealing

Some metals become hardened as they are worked. They will fracture or be very difficult to work if something is not done to soften them. ANNEALING is the heat-treating process used to reduce the hardness of these metals to make them easier to machine and shape.

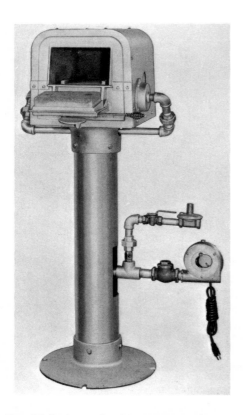

Fig. 15-5. A gas fired heat-treating furnace.
(Johnson Gas Appliance Co.)

Annealing is accomplished by heating the metal in a HEAT-TREATING FURNACE, Fig. 15-5, and letting it cool slowly in an insulating material such as ashes or vermiculite. The temperature and the time the metal is to be heated depends on the kind of metal being annealed and its size. Your instructor can help you find this information in a machinist's handbook.

Metals like copper, silver and nickel silver require an annealing operation different from those of steel. These metals are heated and cooled very rapidly by quenching in water.

Some aluminum alloys are annealed by letting the heated metal cool in still air.

Case Hardening

CASE HARDENING is a process that adds carbon to low carbon steel so that a hard shell or case is produced, Fig. 15-6. The in-

Fig. 15-6. Only a thin outer case is hardened when steel is CASE HARDENED. The center portion of the metal remains soft.

terior of the metal remains soft. The process is employed on steel parts that need a tough, hard wearing surface such as gears and roller bearings.

Case hardening is accomplished by heating the steel to a bright red (1650-1700 deg. F.). Use a PYROMETER, Fig. 15-7, to measure the temperature. Dip, roll or sprinkle on one of the commercial nonpoisonous carburizers similar to Kasenit, Fig. 15-8. These powders add carbon rapidly to the surface of the steel.

Reheat according to the instructions furnished with the carburizing compound used and quench in clean, cold water.

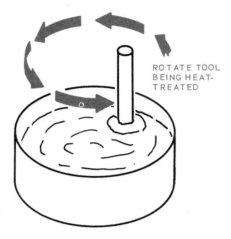

Be careful when quenching the heated metal. Dip it into the liquid, Fig. 15-9. NEVER drop it in. This may cause sections of the metal to cool faster than other sections causing it to warp or crack.

ROTATE TOOL BEING HEAT-TREATED

Fig. 15-9. General work can be quenched using a rotary motion. However, long, slender work should be plunged into the quenching fluid in an up-and-down motion to prevent the piece from warping.

Fig. 15-7. A PYROMETER is used to measure the high temperatures needed in the heat treatment of metals. (Johnson Gas Appliance Co.)

Properly hardened steel will be "glass hard" and too brittle for most uses. Hardness can be tested by trying to file the metal with an OLD file. The file will not cut if the steel has been properly hardened.

Hardened steel is "glass hard" and very brittle. Another heat-treating process must be performed to make it usable. This process is called TEMPERING.

Fig. 15-8. Roll, dip or sprinkle the case hardening compound on the heated piece until a coating of uniform thickness forms. Then reheat and plunge in the quenching fluid according to the manufacturer's instructions.

Tempering

TEMPERING should follow immediately after hardening. The brittle steel may crack if exposed to sudden changes in temperature.

The process removes some of the hardness and reduces brittleness.

To do tempering:

1. Polish the piece to be tempered with abrasive cloth.

2. Reheat to the correct tempering tem-

Hardening

HARDENING is accomplished by heating carbon or alloy steel to a certain temperature (CRITICAL TEMPERATURE) and cooling it rapidly by quenching in water, oil or brine (salt water). The exact temperature is determined by the type of steel being hardened. This information can be found in a machinist's handbook.

perature. Use a COLOR SCALE, Fig. 15-10, as a guide. Quench the steel when the proper color has been reached.

Degrees Fahrenheit	Temper Colors	Tools
380	Very Light Yellow	Tools that require maximum hardness — lathe centers, lathe tools
420	Light Straw	Drills, taps, milling cutters
460	Dark Straw	Tools that need both hardness and toughness — punches
500	Bronze	Cold chisels, hammer faces
540	Purple	Screwdrivers, scribers
580	Dark Blue	Wrenches, chisels
620	Pale Blue	Springs, wood saws

Fig. 15-10. Tempering colors and temperatures for 0.95 percent carbon steel.

3. Temper small tools by placing them on a steel plate that has been heated red hot. Have the point of the tool extending beyond the edge of the plate, Fig. 15-11. Quench the piece when the correct color has reached the tool point.

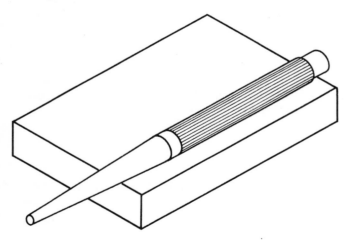

Fig. 15-11. Temper small tools on a steel plate that has been heated red hot. It is very important that the tool be in continuous motion during the tempering process or portions of the tool will be overheated.

Safety

1. Wear goggles and the proper protective clothing - - asbestos gloves, apron (never one that is greasy or oil soaked).

2. Heat-treating involves metal heated to very high temperatures. Handle it with the appropriate tools.

3. Never look at the flames of the furnace unless you are wearing tinted goggles.

4. Do not light the furnace until you have been instructed in its operation. If you are not sure how it should be done ask for further instructions.

5. Be sure the area is properly ventilated and all solvents and flammable materials have been removed.

6. Do not stand over the quenching bath when immersing heated metal.

What Do You Know About Heat-Treating? - Unit 15

1. What is meant by the term heat-treating?
2. How is metal heat-treated?
3. Annealing is done by _____.
4. Case hardening means that the low carbon steel has _____.
5. Furnace temperature may be checked by a _____.
6. Why is hardened steel frequently tempered?
7. List the safety precautions that should be followed when heat-treating.

Special Activities

1. Secure examples of products that have been heat-treated.
2. Demonstrate how to anneal a piece of metal.
3. Demonstrate how to case harden a piece of low carbon steel.
4. Demonstrate how to harden and temper a center punch made from carbon steel.
5. Prepare a poster on one of the safety precautions that should be observed when heat-treating.

Fig. 16-1. Many machined parts are used in this British-French CONCORDE SST.

Unit 16
MACHINE SHOP

Many different kinds of MACHINE TOOLS are found in the MACHINE SHOP. Machine tools are power driven tools. They may be used to "mass produce" accurate and uniform parts that are assembled into such things as automobiles, washers, airplanes, Fig. 16-1, and thousands of other every day items.

The Lathe

The LATHE is a very versatile machine tool. Rotating work is shaped by a cutting tool that is fed against the work, Fig. 16-2.

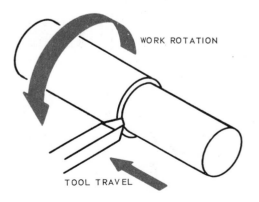

WORK ROTATION

TOOL TRAVEL

Fig. 16-2. The lathe operates as the rotating work is shaped by a cutting tool that is fed against the material.

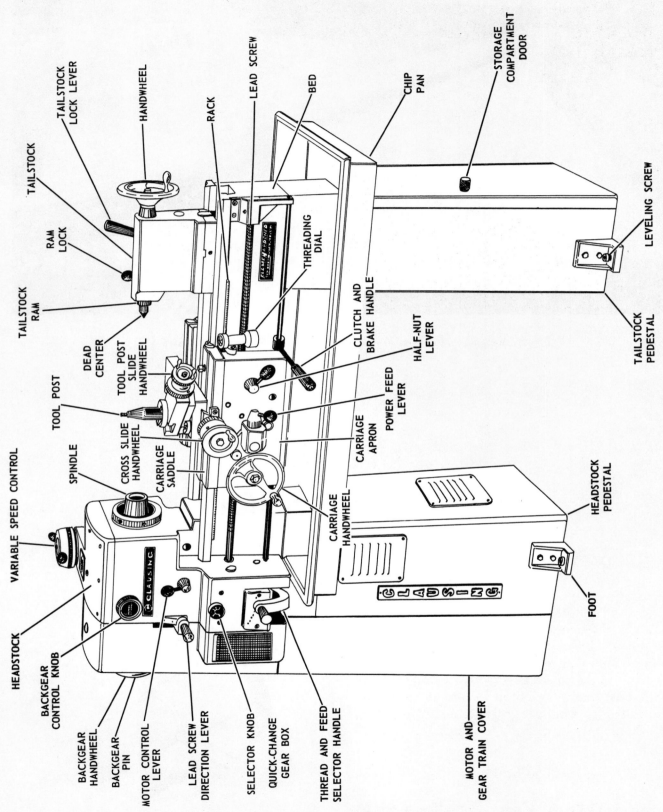

TAILSTOCK LOCK LEVER

TAILSTOCK

HANDWHEEL

RACK

LEAD SCREW

BED

CHIP PAN

STORAGE COMPARTMENT DOOR

RAM LOCK

THREADING DIAL

LEVELING SCREW

TAILSTOCK RAM

DEAD CENTER

TOOL POST SLIDE HANDWHEEL

CLUTCH AND BRAKE HANDLE

TAILSTOCK PEDESTAL

TOOL POST

HALF-NUT LEVER

POWER FEED LEVER

SPINDLE

CROSS SLIDE HANDWHEEL

CARRIAGE APRON

CARRIAGE SADDLE

VARIABLE SPEED CONTROL

CARRIAGE HANDWHEEL

HEADSTOCK PEDESTAL

HEADSTOCK

FOOT

BACKGEAR CONTROL KNOB

BACKGEAR HANDWHEEL

BACKGEAR PIN

MOTOR CONTROL LEVER

LEAD SCREW DIRECTION LEVER

SELECTOR KNOB

QUICK-CHANGE GEAR BOX

THREAD AND FEED SELECTOR HANDLE

MOTOR AND GEAR TRAIN COVER

Fig. 16-3. The metal cutting lathe. (Clausing)

The major parts of the lathe are shown in Fig. 16-3.

Preparing to Operate the Lathe

First become familiar with the names and location of the lathe parts. Learn what each does. Get permission to operate the various handwheels and levers of the lathe WITH THE POWER OFF. The parts should move freely. There should be no binding.

The lathe should be lubricated before it is used. Use the lubricants specified by the manufacturer.

Clean the lathe after each working period. Use a paint brush to remove the chips - - - NEVER USE YOUR HANDS. Wipe all surfaces with a soft cloth.

Lathe Cutting Tools and Tool Holders

On the lathe, the cutting of the metal is done by a small piece of metal called a CUTTER BIT, Fig. 16-4. The cutter bit used in the school is usually made from a special alloy steel called HIGH SPEED STEEL (HSS).

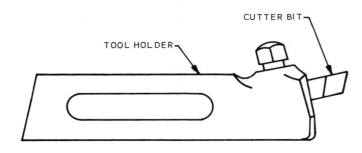

Fig. 16-4. Lathe tool holder and cutter bit.

On most lathes, the cutter bit must be supported in a TOOL HOLDER. Tool holders are made in STRAIGHT, RIGHT-HAND and LEFT-HAND shapes, Fig. 16-5. This permits many different machining operations to be done.

Cutting Tool Shapes

Some cutting tools for general turning are shown in Fig. 16-6. The cutter bit should have a keen, properly shaped cutting edge.

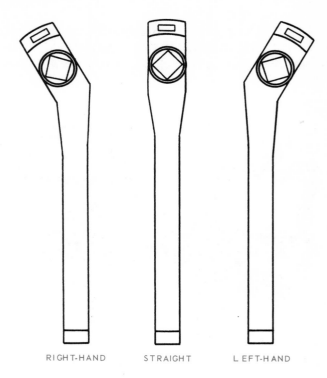

RIGHT-HAND   STRAIGHT   LEFT-HAND

Fig. 16-5. Shapes of tool holders available.

The class of work (ROUGHING or FINISHING) and the kind of metal being cut will determine the shape to grind the cutter bit.

ROUGHING CUTS are used to reduce the work diameter quickly to approximate size (about 1/32 in. oversize).

The FINISH CUT brings the work to EXACT size. The work surface is also made smooth.

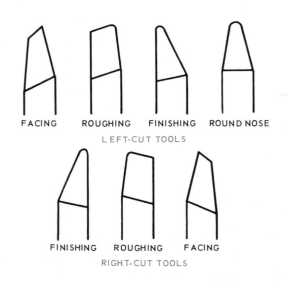

Fig. 16-6. Common cutting tools used on the lathe.

The cutter bit is sharpened on a BENCH or PEDESTAL GRINDER, Fig. 16-7. The bench grinder is a grinder fitted to a bench

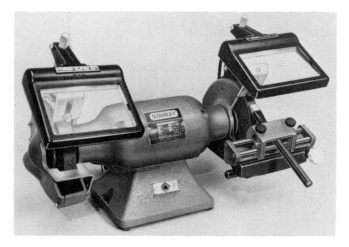

Fig. 16-7. Typical bench grinder. (Stanley Tools)

or table. The grinding wheel mounts directly to the motor shaft. The pedestal grinder is usually larger than the bench grinder, and is equipped with a base (pedestal) that is fastened to the floor.

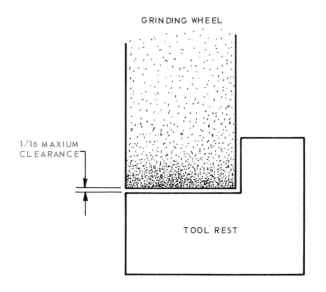

GRINDING WHEEL

1/16 MAXIUM CLEARANCE

TOOL REST

Fig. 16-8. How the tool rest should be adjusted for grinding.

Before attempting to grind a cutter bit, be sure the tool rest is positioned so that there is a space of about 1/16 in. between the tool rest and the grinding wheel, Fig. 16-8.

Holding Work on the Lathe

As you work on the lathe, you will find that different kinds of work will require different methods for holding the work.

CHUCKS, Fig. 16-9, are the easiest and fastest method for mounting work for turning. They fit on the headstock spindle.

Fig. 16-9. Above. The 3-jaw universal chuck. Below. 4-jaw independent chuck. (L. W. Chuck Co.)

The jaws on a 3-JAW UNIVERSAL CHUCK all operate at one time and automatically center round or hexagon shaped stock.

Each jaw on a 4-JAW INDEPENDENT CHUCK operates individually. This permits irregular shaped work (square, rectangular, octagonal, etc.) to be centered.

The jaws can be reversed on the 4-jaw independent chuck to hold large diameter work, Fig. 16-10. Another set of jaws must be used with the 3-jaw universal chuck.

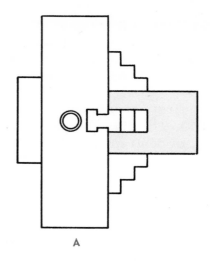

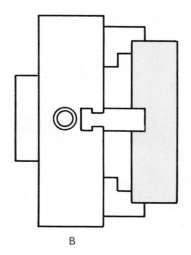

Fig. 16-10. A—Chuck jaw position when holding small diameter work. B—Chuck jaw position when holding large diameter work.

At first, it may appear difficult to center work on a 4-jaw chuck. Practice is all that is required. Center the work approximately by using the concentric rings on the chuck face as a guide, Fig. 16-11. Final centering

work is centered. The cutter bit may be used instead of chalk if the work is large enough.

REMOVE THE CHUCK KEY FROM THE CHUCK BEFORE TURNING ON THE LATHE.

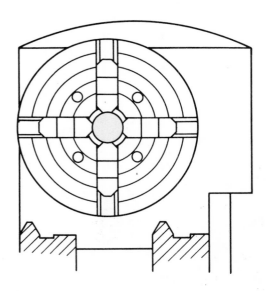

Fig. 16-11. The concentric rings on the face of the 4-jaw independent chuck can be used for approximate centering of work.

Fig. 16-12. Using chalk to center work in a 4-jaw chuck. The chalk mark indicates the "high point." Loosen jaw opposite chalk mark then tighten jaw on chalked side. Use gradual adjustments rather than large movements.

can be done using a piece of chalk, Fig. 16-12. Rotate the chuck slowly and bring the chalk into contact with the work. Loosen the jaw(s) opposite the chalk mark slightly. Then tighten the jaw(s) on the side where the chalk mark is located. Continue the operation until the

Facing Stock Held in a Chuck

FACING is the term used when the end or face of the stock is machined square. The tool is positioned on center and mounted as shown in Fig. 16-13.

The cut can be made in either direction.

141

Fig. 16-13. The FACING operation. Note that a right-hand tool holder is used.

Plain Turning

PLAIN TURNING, Fig. 16-14, is done when the work must be reduced in diameter. One precaution must be noted. If the work projects from the chuck more than a few inches, it should be center drilled (see Fig. 16-27) and supported with the tailstock center, Fig. 16-15. This will prevent the work from springing away from the cutting tool while it is being machined. DO NOT FORGET TO LUBRICATE THE TAILSTOCK (DEAD)

CENTER; OTHERWISE, IT WILL HEAT UP AND "BURN" OFF. This can be done with a dab of white lead mixed with machine oil or a commercially prepared center lubricant.

The first operation is called ROUGH TURNING. The diameter is reduced to within 1/32 in. of desired size. Use a LEFT-HAND

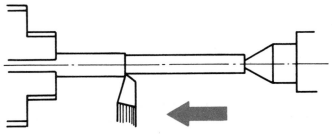

Fig. 16-15. Support long or slender work with the tailstock center. Otherwise, the resulting "chatter" will cause a very poor surface finish or the work will be cut on a slight taper.

TOOL HOLDER to hold the cutter bit. Position the tool holder as shown in Fig. 16-16.

CAUTION: Before starting the lathe, check to be sure that the cut can be made without danger of the rotating chuck striking the tool holder or compound, Fig. 16-17.

Fig. 16-14. PLAIN turning. In this situation, a left-hand tool holder is used for most operations of this type. It will permit maximum clearance between the rotating chuck and the lathe carriage.

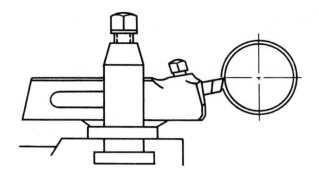

Fig. 16-16. Tool set up for general turning.

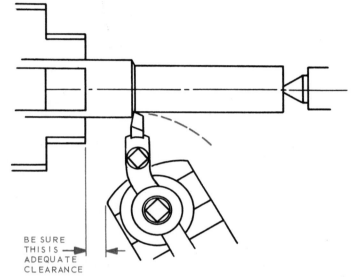

BE SURE
THIS IS
ADEQUATE
CLEARANCE

Fig. 16-17. Check to be sure that the cut can be made without danger of the rotating chuck striking the tool holder or compound. Also, position the tool holder so it will swing clear of the work if the tool holder slips in the tool post.

The tool cutting edge should be on center or slightly above center without too much overhang, Fig. 16-18.

Adjust the lathe to the proper CUTTING SPEED (Revolutions Per Minute) and FEED (the distance the cutter travels each revolution of the work). This will vary for different metals, Fig. 16-19.

STOCK DIA. IN IN.	MACHINE STEEL	BRASS	ALUMINUM
3/8	960	1700	2100
1/2	720	1200	1600
5/8	576	960	1280
3/4	500	800	1066
1	360	600	800
1 1/4	288	480	640
1 1/2	240	400	540
2	180	300	400

Fig. 16-19. SPEEDS for the various metals are given in revolutions per minute (rpm) and are only approximate. Increase or decrease as necessary for the job being machined. FEEDS will vary from 0.010–0.020 in. for ROUGHING CUTS to 0.002–0.010 in. for FINISHING CUTS.

Make the cut from the tailstock to the headstock. Feed the cutter into the stock. Engage the power feed and make a trial cut about 1/4 in. wide. Check with a micrometer or caliper. You may have to make several roughing cuts to get the work to the desired size plus 1/32 in.

Insert a finishing tool,—INCREASE the speed but DECREASE the feed. Again, make a trial cut 1/4 in. wide. DO NOT CHANGE THE CROSS FEED SETTING. Measure the diameter with a micrometer. If, for example, the work is 0.006 in. oversize, the cross feed micrometer dial is fed in 0.003 in. and another cut is taken. Check your lathe. Some

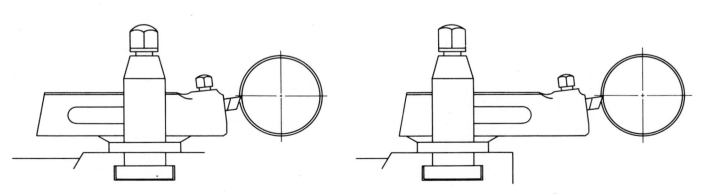

Fig. 16-18. Left. Recommended tool set up for general turning. Right. Avoid excessive overhang of the tool holder.

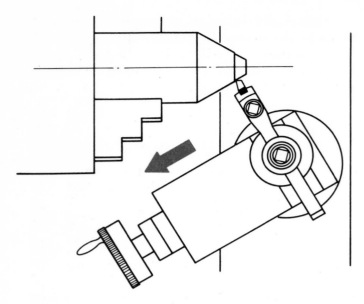

Fig. 16-20. *Turning a taper using the compound rest method.*

of them are set differently. The cross micrometer dial must be fed in 0.006 in. if 0.006 in. of metal is to be removed.

When the correct diameter is attained, finish the cut.

Cutting Tapers

The lathe center is cut on a TAPER. There are several ways to cut tapers on the lathe. The COMPOUND REST method of turning tapers, Fig. 16-20, is perhaps the easiest. However, the taper length is limited to the compound rest travel. The base of the compound is graduated in degrees.

When cutting tapers, the compound rest is ALWAYS set parallel to the desired taper.

Long tapers can be cut using the TAILSTOCK SET-OVER METHOD, Fig. 16-21. To calculate the amount of set-over use the following formulas (it is suggested that all fractions be converted to decimal fractions):

When taper per inch is known - -

$$\text{SET-OVER} = \frac{\text{Total length of piece} \times \text{Taper per inch}}{2}$$

When taper per foot is known - -

$$\text{SET-OVER} = \frac{\text{Total length of piece} \times \text{Taper per foot}}{24}$$

When the dimensions of the tapered section are known - -

$$\text{SET-OVER} = \frac{\text{Total length of piece} \times (\text{Major Dia.} - \text{Minor Dia.})}{2 \times \text{Length of Taper}}$$

The set-over can be measured by using center points to determine amount of tailstock set-over, Fig. 16-22, or by measuring the distance between the witness marks on base of the tailstock, Fig. 16-23.

When using the tailstock set-over method of turning tapers the work must be mounted between centers. See Fig. 16-24.

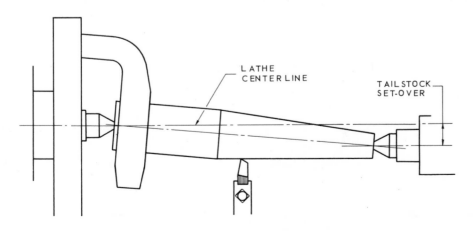

Fig. 16-21. *Tailstock set-over method of turning tapers. The work must be mounted between centers.*

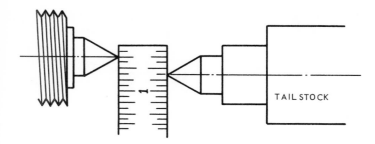

Fig. 16-22. The set-over can be measured using the center points.

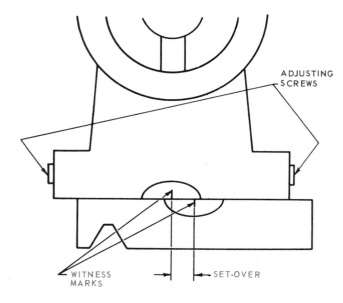

Fig. 16-23. The distance between the witness marks on the base of the tailstock can be used to measure the amount of set-over.

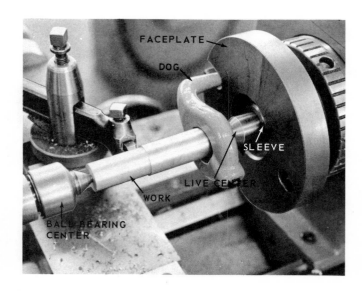

Fig. 16-24. Working between centers.

You can also cut tapers by using a taper attachment that is built on many lathes. See Fig. 16-25.

Fig. 16-25. Lathe fitted with taper attachment. When using this method to cut tapers the work can be mounted in a chuck or between centers. (Clausing)

Turning Between Centers

Much lathe work is done with the stock mounted between centers, Fig. 16-24. The chuck is replaced with a FACEPLATE. A LIVE CENTER and a SLEEVE is inserted in the headstock spindle. A DEAD CENTER is placed in the tailstock. The work is connected to the faceplate with a DOG.

Before stock can be turned between centers, it is necessary to drill a CENTER HOLE in each end. Center holes are drilled with a COMBINATION DRILL AND COUNTERSINK, Fig. 16-26.

Fig. 16-26. Combination drill and countersink (center drill). (Greenfield Tap and Die)

There are several ways to locate the center of the stock. An easy way is to mount the work in a 3-jaw chuck. Face the stock to length and drill the center holes. Fig. 16-27 shows a properly drilled center hole.

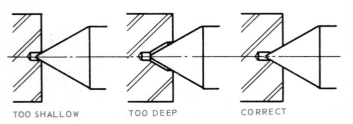

Fig. 16-27. Drilling center holes.

Center holes can also be located using the CENTER HEAD of the combination set, Fig. 16-28. The holes are drilled on a drill press.

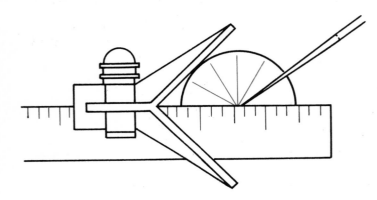

Fig. 16-28. Using the center head to locate the center of round stock.

The centers must run true if accurate work is desired. Check center alignment by bringing them together, Fig. 16-29. A tapered piece will result if they are not aligned. Adjust the tailstock to bring them into alignment.

Clamp a dog on one end of the stock. Place a dab of lubricant (white lead and oil) in the center hole at the tailstock end. Insert the centers in the holes. Adjust the tailstock center until it is snug enough to prevent the lathe dog from "clattering." Check the adjustment from time to time. The heat generated during the machining operation causes the work to expand. The tailstock center may burn off if too much heat is generated.

Fig. 16-29. Center alignment can be checked by bringing them together.

The cutting operation is identical to machining work mounted in a chuck.

If the work must be reversed to machine its entire length, protect the section under the dog setscrew by inserting a piece of soft copper or aluminum sheet, Fig. 16-30.

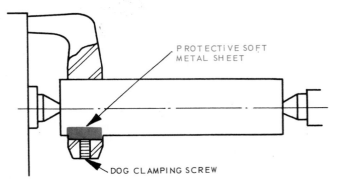

Fig. 16-30. Protect the work by placing a piece of soft aluminum or copper under the clamping screw.

Fig. 16-31. Drilling with a straight shank drill held in a Jacobs chuck.

Fig. 16-32. Drilling on the lathe.

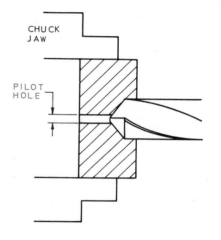

Fig. 16-33. A pilot hole permits the larger drill to cut easier and faster.

Drilling

DRILLING can be done on the lathe. Hold the work in a chuck and mount a Jacobs chuck in the tailstock to grip the drill, Fig. 16-31.

Start the hole by first "spotting" the work with a center drill.

Drills up to 1/2 in. diameter are held in a Jacobs chuck. Larger drills are mounted in the tailstock spindle. See Fig. 16-32.

A PILOT HOLE (small hole) should be drilled first if a drill larger than 1/2 in. diameter is used, Fig. 16-33.

Boring

BORING, Fig. 16-34, is done when a hole is not a standard drill size. It is also done when a very accurate hole diameter is needed.

A BORING TOOL HOLDER supports the BORING BAR. A cutter bit is inserted in the boring bar. The hole is first drilled slightly smaller than the desired diameter. The cutting tool is set on center with the boring bar parallel to the center line of the hole. The cutting is done in much the same manner as is external turning.

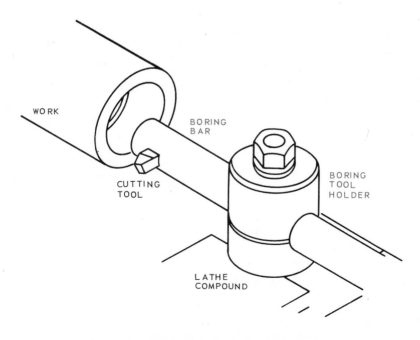

Fig. 16-34. Boring on the lathe.

Knurling

KNURLING, Fig. 16-35, is the operation that presses horizontal or diamond shaped serrations on the circumference of the stock. This provides a gripping surface.

To knurl:

1. Mark off the section to be knurled.
2. Put the lathe into back gear (slow speed) with a fairly rapid feed.
3. Position the knurling tool so that both knurl wheels bear uniformly and squarely on the work.
4. Start the lathe and feed the knurl slowly into the work until a pattern develops. Engage the automatic feed. USE A LUBRICANT ON THE KNURL WHEELS. After the knurl has traveled the desired distance, reverse the spindle rotation and apply additional pressure. Repeat until a satisfactory knurl has been formed.

Fig. 16-35. Knurling.

Filing and Polishing on the Lathe

If the cutter bit is properly sharpened, there should be NO NEED to file or polish work machined on the lathe. However, because of a lack of experience, it may be desirable to smooth and polish a machined surface.

A fine mill file or long angle lathe file should be used, Fig. 16-36. Take long even

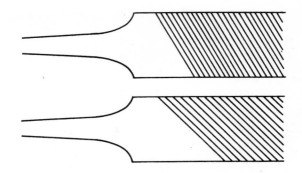

Fig. 16-36. Long angle lathe file, above, compared with regular file, below.

strokes across the rotating work. Hold the file as shown in Fig. 16-37. Keep the file clean and free from chips.

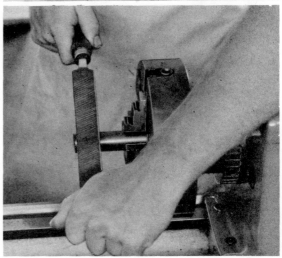

Fig. 16-37. Above. Left-hand method of filing. The hands are clear of the rotating chuck. Below. Right-hand method of filing. Note how the left hand and arm must be over the revolving chuck.

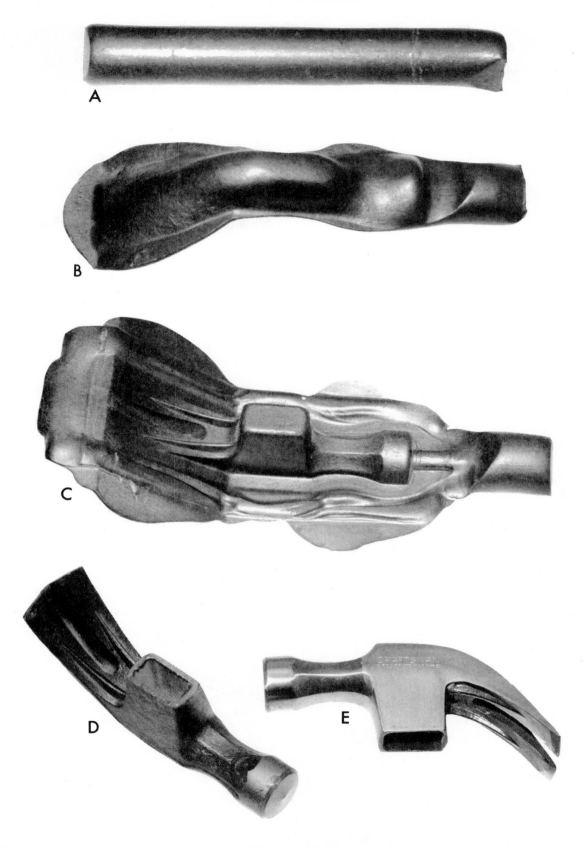

Sequence followed in forging a hammer head. A—Piece of high carbon steel sheared to length. B—After heating, it is forged to this rough shape. C—Further heating and forging brings it to this shape. Note the flashing. The opening for the handle is partially made on the underside. D—The handle opening is completed and the flashing removed. E—The completed hammer head. It has been heat treated and polished.

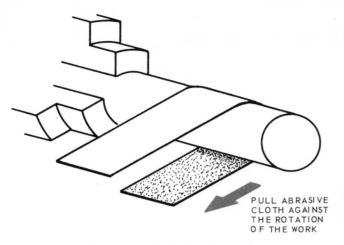

PULL ABRASIVE
CLOTH AGAINST
THE ROTATION
OF THE WORK

Fig. 16-38. Polishing on the lathe. Do not forget to protect
the lathe ways from the abrasive particles.

Fig. 16-39. Cutting threads.

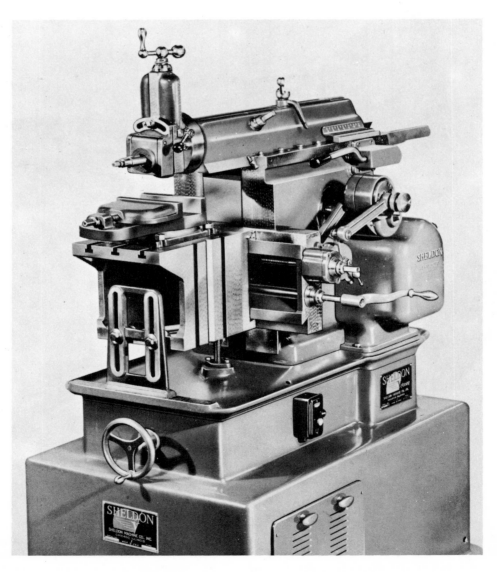

Fig. 16-40. The shaper.   (Sheldon Machine Co., Inc.)

A filed surface can be made very smooth by using fine grades of abrasive cloth, Fig. 16-38. Apply oil to the abrasive cloth and keep it moving across the rotating work. It is recommended that you protect the lathe ways from the abrasive particles.

Cutting Threads on the Lathe

Threads can be cut on many lathes, Fig. 16-39. The cutter bit is sharpened to the shape of the desired threads and the feed and speed selector controls are adjusted to move the carriage and cutter bit across the work at a rate that will cut the desired number of threads per inch. Because cutting threads is a complex operation, the correct way to set up the lathe and how threads are cut is best demonstrated by your instructor. Ask him to show you how threads are cut on the lathe.

The Shaper

The SHAPER, Fig. 16-40, is another machine tool frequently found in the school shop. It is used primarily to machine flat surfaces, Fig. 16-41. However, a skilled machinist can manipulate it to cut curved and irregular shapes, grooves and keyways. The cutting tool is mounted to a ram which moves back and forth across the work, Fig. 16-41.

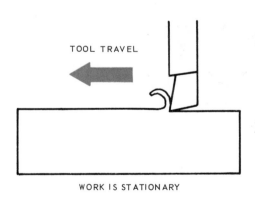

TOOL TRAVEL

WORK IS STATIONARY

Fig. 16-41. How a shaper works.

Mount the work in the vise or clamp it directly to the worktable. The table can be moved horizontally or vertically. The head, to which the tool holder is mounted, can be pivoted for angular cutting, Fig. 16-42.

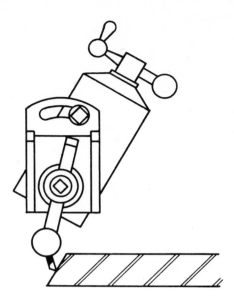

Fig. 16-42. The head of the shaper can be pivoted to make angular cuts.

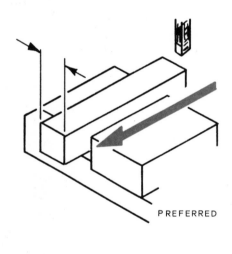

PREFERRED

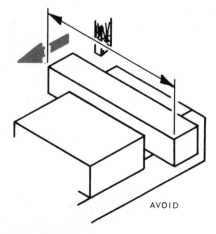

AVOID

Fig. 16-43. Mount the work in the shaper so that the work will be done in the least amount of time.

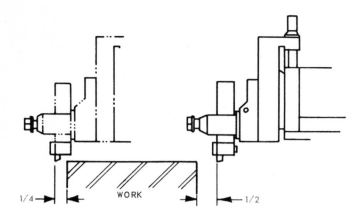

Position the work so that the cut can be made in the shortest possible time, Fig. 16-43. The STROKE (length of cut) is adjustable and should be positioned as shown in Fig. 16-44.

Fig. 16-44. The correct way to position the shaper stroke for cutting.

Shaper Safety

KEEP YOUR FINGERS CLEAR OF THE CUTTING TOOL WHILE ADJUSTING THE STROKE.

DO NOT RUB YOUR FINGERS ACROSS THE WORK WHILE THE TOOL IS CUTTING.

Fig. 16-45. The vertical milling machine. (Clausing)

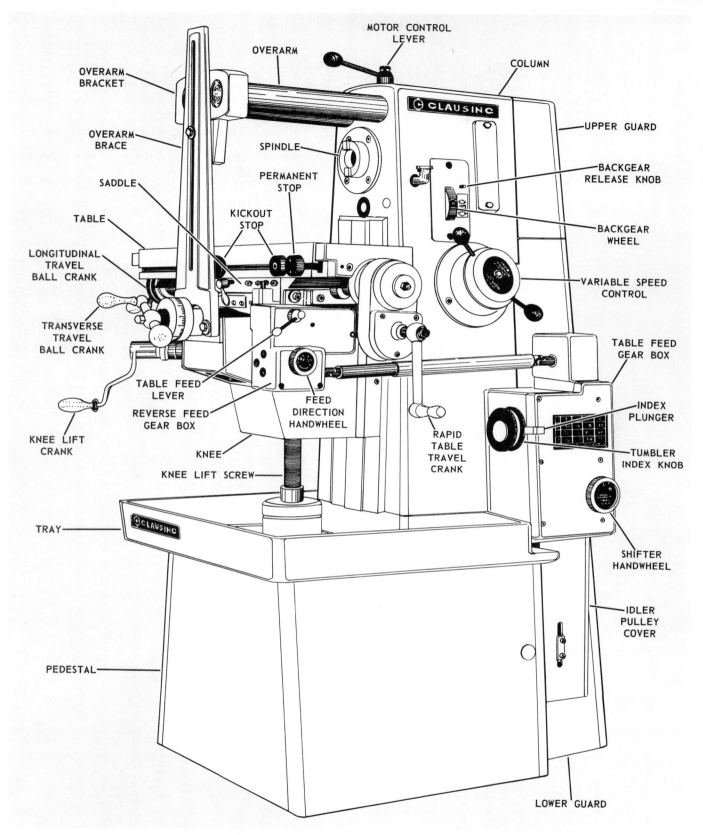

OVERARM BRACKET

OVERARM

MOTOR CONTROL LEVER

COLUMN

OVERARM BRACE

SPINDLE

PERMANENT STOP

SADDLE

TABLE

KICKOUT STOP

LONGITUDINAL TRAVEL BALL CRANK

TRANSVERSE TRAVEL BALL CRANK

TABLE FEED LEVER

REVERSE FEED GEAR BOX

KNEE LIFT CRANK

FEED DIRECTION HANDWHEEL

KNEE

KNEE LIFT SCREW

RAPID TABLE TRAVEL CRANK

TRAY

PEDESTAL

CLAUSING

CLAUSING

UPPER GUARD

BACKGEAR RELEASE KNOB

BACKGEAR WHEEL

VARIABLE SPEED CONTROL

TABLE FEED GEAR BOX

INDEX PLUNGER

TUMBLER INDEX KNOB

SHIFTER HANDWHEEL

IDLER PULLEY COVER

LOWER GUARD

Fig. 16-46. The horizontal milling machine with parts identified.

The Milling Machine

While industry utilizes many types of MILLING MACHINES, the VERTICAL MILL-

ING MACHINE, Fig. 16-45, and the HORI-ZONTAL MILLING MACHINE, Fig. 16-46, are most commonly found in the school shop. Milling machines operate on the principle of

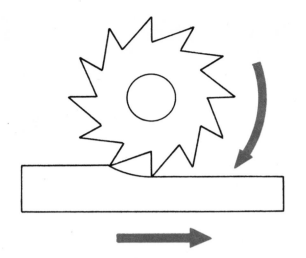

Fig. 16-47. How the milling machine works.

a rotating multitoothed cutter being fed into a moving piece of work, Fig. 16-47. The horizontal milling machine uses a cutter mounted on an arbor to smooth and shape metal, Fig. 16-48. The cutter used on a vertical milling machine is called an END MILL and it clamps in the machine spindle, Fig. 16-49.

Special attachments permit gears to be cut on the horizontal milling machine, Fig. 16-50.

Fig. 16-50. Cutting gears. A dividing head is used to space the gear teeth.

Fig. 16-48. The cutter on the horizontal milling machine is mounted on an arbor.

Fig. 16-51. The lathe/miller is a combination lathe and milling machine. (Hamilton Associates)

Fig. 16-49. An end mill is used to do the cutting in a vertical milling machine.

Fig. 16-52. *The milling machine portion of the lathe/miller.*

A unique machine tool that is a combination LATHE/MILLING MACHINE, Figs. 16-51 and 16-52, is finding considerable acceptance for school use. The machine tool is capable of performing basic milling and lathe operations.

Milling machines range in size from the small vertical milling machine similar to those in the school shop, to the 50 hp horizontal milling machine shown in Fig. 16-53.

Other Machine Tools

Many other types of machine tools are used by industry. Several of the more widely used machines are listed.

Fig. 16-53. *This 50 hp horizontal milling machine can make a cut 1/8 in. deep by 12 in. wide.*
(National Machine Tool Builders Assoc.)

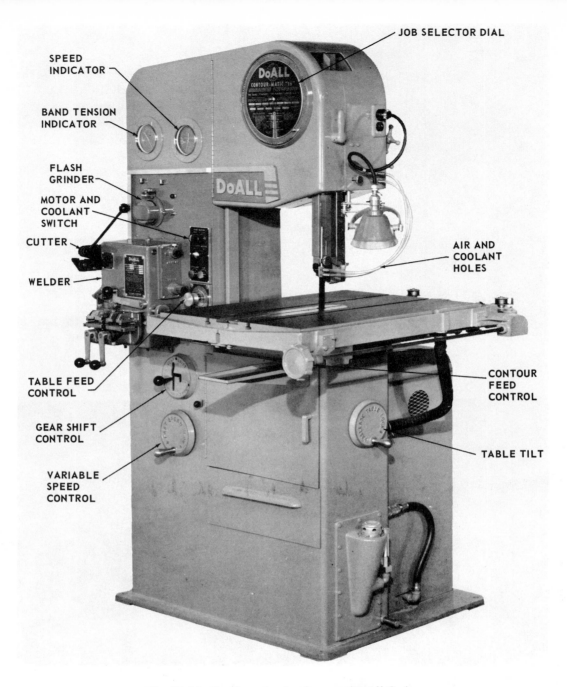

JOB SELECTOR DIAL

SPEED
INDICATOR

BAND TENSION
INDICATOR

FLASH
GRINDER

MOTOR AND
COOLANT
SWITCH

CUTTER

WELDER

TABLE FEED
CONTROL

GEAR SHIFT
CONTROL

VARIABLE
SPEED
CONTROL

AIR AND
COOLANT
HOLES

CONTOUR
FEED
CONTROL

TABLE TILT

Fig. 16-54. Metal cutting band saw. (DoAll Co.)

Band Saw

The cutting operation done on the METAL CUTTING BAND SAW, Fig. 16-54, is called BAND MACHINING. The machine tool employs a continuous saw blade to do the cutting which can be done at any angle or in any direction, Fig. 16-55.

UNRESTRICTED
MACHINING
GEOMETRY

Fig. 16-55. Band machining permits machining at any angle or direction. The length of the cut is unlimited.

Precision Grinding Machines

There are many types of precision grinding machines. The SURFACE GRINDER, Fig. 16-56, is the type frequently found in the school shop. The machine uses a grinding wheel to produce a smooth, accurate surface on material regardless of its hardness. The work moves back and forth under the grinding wheel, Fig. 16-57.

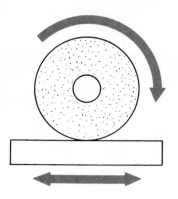

Fig. 16-57. How the surface grinder works.

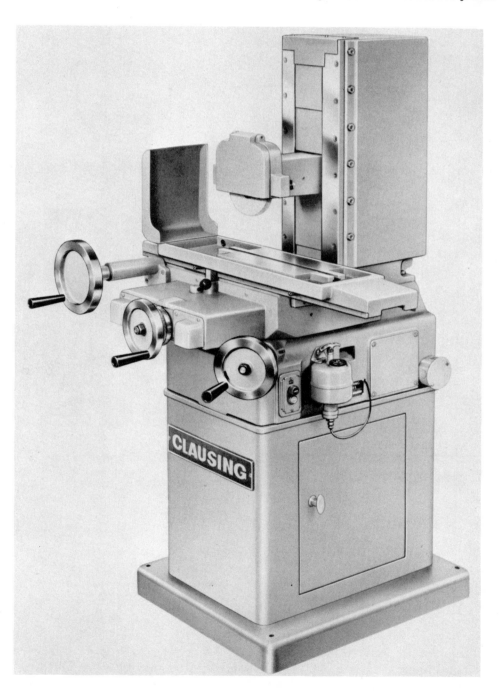

Fig. 16-56. Surface grinder.

Fig. 16-58. Large planer. Note the size of the work being machined. (G. A. Gray Co.)

Planing Machines

PLANING MACHINES produce horizontal, vertical and angular surfaces on metal in much the same way the shaper does.

On the PLANER, Fig. 16-58, the material is mounted on the worktable which moves back and forth under the cutting tool, Fig. 16-59. The planer is used to machine large, flat surfaces.

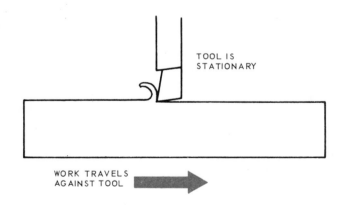

TOOL IS STATIONARY

WORK TRAVELS AGAINST TOOL

Fig. 16-59. How the planer works.

The BROACH employs a long tool with many cutting surfaces. Each tooth is slightly higher than the one before and increases in size to the exact size required, Fig. 16-60.

The tool is pushed or pulled across the surface to be machined, Fig. 16-61. Many flat surfaces on automobile engines are broached.

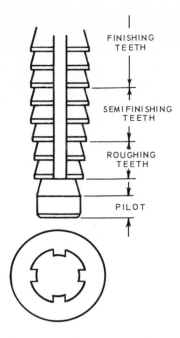

FINISHING TEETH

SEMIFINISHING TEETH

ROUGHING TEETH

PILOT

Fig. 16-60. Typical broaching tool.

BROACH

Fig. 16-61. Vertical broach machining the flat surface of compressor cylinder heads. (National Machine Tool Builders Assoc.)

Numerical Control

The machine tools in your shop are operated by conventional controls. That is, you must turn a handwheel or pull a lever to move the cutting tool against the work.

Industry makes extensive use of machine tools that perform machining operations by utilizing electrical impulses to tell the machine where to cut, Figs. 16-62 and 16-63.

158

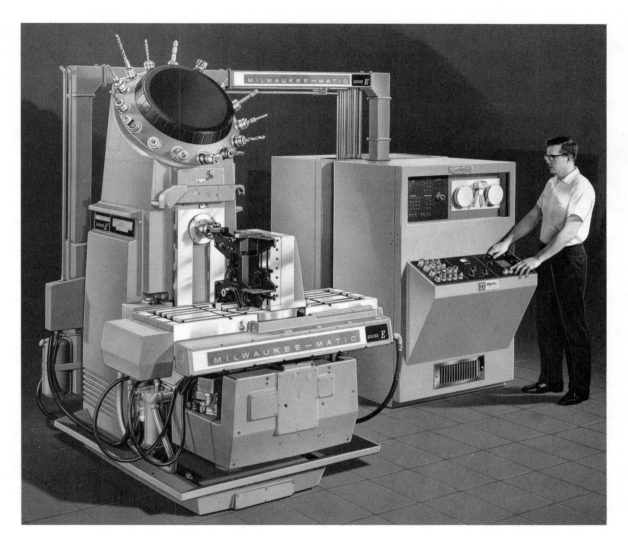

Fig. 16-62. Industrial type N/C machine. Note the location of the various cutting tools. They are automatically fitted into the spindle when instructed to by the tape.

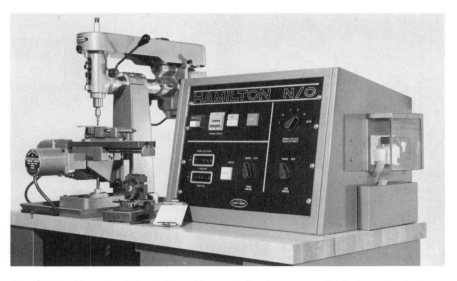

Fig. 16-63. Numerical Control machine tool that is now available for school shops.
(Hamilton Associates)

This technique is called NUMERICAL CONTROL (N/C) and means that the machine is directed by coded numerical instructions on a punched paper or plastic tape such as that shown in Fig. 16-64.

Fig. 16-64. Section of tape similar to that used on N/C machines.

Instructions for the machine are punched into the tape. A full set of instructions is called a PROGRAM.

The punched tape is fed into a TAPE READER which senses the presence or absence of the holes. The number and the location of the holes in each row has a specific

meaning, Fig. 16-65. The reader interprets this code and stores each BIT of information until a complete BLOCK of information (instructions to complete an operation) is stored. When the END OF BLOCK (EOB) signal is received the control unit directs the motors that operate the table movements to move the work to the desired position.

Work positioning is accomplished using the CARTESIAN COORDINATE SYSTEM, Fig. 16-66, which is the basis of all N/C programming. The X and Y axes are horizontal table motions and the Z axis is vertical tool or table movement.

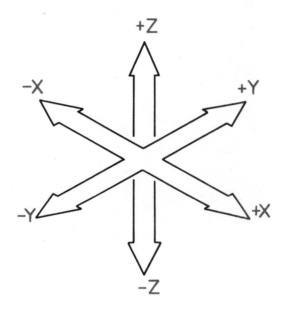

Fig. 16-66. The coordinate system that is the basis of all N/C programming.

A sample program and the drawing of the part to be manufactured are shown in Figs. 16-67 and 16-68. Program notes are given in Fig. 16-69.

Safety in the Machine Shop

1. Have ALL guards in place before operating any machine.
2. When using the drill press, clamp the work to the table or mount it solidly in a vise. Otherwise, a "merry-go-round" (the work spins very rapidly) might occur.
3. Never reverse a machine before it comes

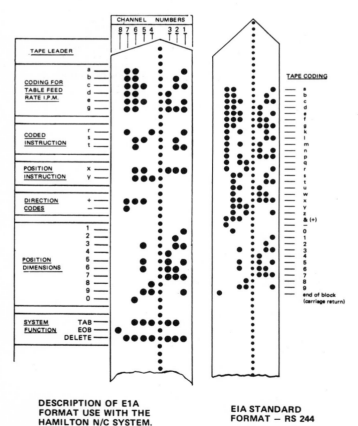

DESCRIPTION OF E1A FORMAT USE WITH THE HAMILTON N/C SYSTEM.

EIA STANDARD FORMAT – RS 244

Fig. 16-65. Tape code.

HAMILTON N/C

NUMERICAL TAPE CONTROL PROGRAM

PART NO. **1375**		PART NAME	**HINGE SPACER DRILLING SAMPLE No. 1**			TAPE NO. **21**		FILE NO.

PREPARED BY **R.F.S.**	DATE **6/2/70**	CK'D. BY **S.F.R**	DATE **6/3/70**	DEPT. **ENG.**	SHEET **1** OF **1**

REMARKS
DRILL 3 HOLES — ¼" DIA.
FEED RATE OF TABLE 12 I.P.M.
TOOLS — ¼" DIA. H. S. S. JOBBERS LENGTH DRILL.

SEQ. NO.	TAB or EOB	CODED INST.	TAB or EOB	TABLE SPEED	TAB or EOB	X	+ or −	X INCREMENT				TAB or EOB	Y	+ or −	Y INCREMENT				EOB	INSTRUCTIONS
0	TAB	s	EOB																	START TAPE
1	TAB	t	TAB	e	TAB	X	+	2	0	0	0	TAB							EOB	TOOL DOWN — DRILL HOLE — TOOL UP
2	TAB	t	TAB		TAB	X	+	1	0	0	0	TAB							EOB	TOOL DOWN — DRILL HOLE — TOOL UP
3	TAB	t	TAB		TAB	X	+	1	0	0	0	TAB							EOB	TOOL DOWN — DRILL HOLE — TOOL UP
4	TAB		TAB		TAB	X	−	4	0	0	0	TAB							EOB	
5	TAB	r	EOB																	REWIND TAPE

Fig. 16-67. Sample program.

to a full stop. This could cause the chuck on some lathes to spin off.

4. Get into the habit of ALWAYS removing the chuck key from the lathe or drill press chuck.

5. Stop machines before making measurements and adjustments.

6. Do not operate portable electric power tools in areas where thinners and solvents are used and stored. A serious fire or explosion might result.

7. Roll up your sleeves, remove jewelry and necktie before starting to work.

8. ALWAYS WEAR GOGGLES.

9. Get cuts, burns and bruises, no matter how small, properly treated.

10. Do not wear loose clothing when operating machines.

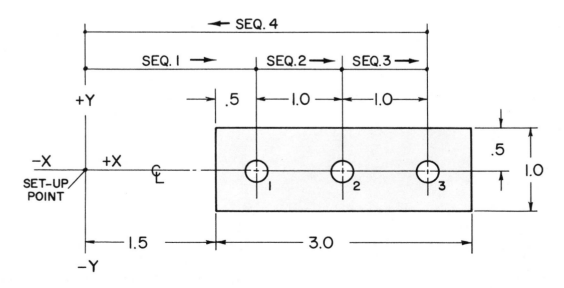

Fig. 16-68. Part made from program.

PROGRAMMING SAMPLE DRILLING

ARRANGEMENT NO. 1

PROGRAM NOTES:

1. Select the set-up point and establish sequence of operations.

2. Program begins with Sequence No. 0 containing the coded instruction "s" for Rewind Stop. Rewind Stop instructs the tape reader to stop at this point in the tape after rewinding. At this point, "Tool Change" light comes on. Press the "Start" button to continue the program.

3. Sequence No. 1 — The tool moves on the X axis at table speed "e" (12 I.P.M.) to location of hole (1). At this location, the unit stops, "Tool Change" light comes on, signalling the operator to manually drill the hole. After the hole has been drilled and the quill retracted, press "Start" button to continue the program.

4. Sequence No. 2 — Tool moves on the X axis from hole (1) to hole (2). Repeat operations described in Sequence No. 1.

5. Sequence No. 3 — Tool moves on the X axis from hole (2) to hole (3). Again, operations described in Sequence No. 1 must be repeated in this sequence.

6. Sequence No. 4 — Tool moves from hole (3) back to the set-up point along the X axis.

7. Sequence No. 5 — At this point in the program the tape reader is instructed to use the coded instruction "r" for rewinding the tape to Sequence No. 0.

Fig. 16-69. Program notes for preparing the program to drill the part shown in Fig. 16-68.

What Do You Know About The Machine Shop – Unit 16

1. Name the parts of the lathe indicated in the drawing on the top of page 163.
2. Make a sketch showing how the lathe works.
3. List the safety precautions that should be observed when operating the lathe and other machine tools.
4. Chips should be removed from the lathe using a _____ _____ .
5. The cutter bit is held in a _____.
6. A _____ cut is used to reduce the work diameter rapidly. This machined surface may not be very smooth. The _____ cut machines the work to exact size and this machined surface is smooth.
7. Round work is easily centered in the ___ _____ chuck.
8. _____ is the term used to describe the operation that machines the end or face of the stock.
9. List two methods used to hold work in the lathe for machining.
   a. _____.
   b. _____.
10. What is knurling?
11. How does the machining done on the lathe differ from the machining done on the shaper?
12. Name the parts indicated in the drawing on the bottom of page 163.
   A. _____.
   B. _____.
   C. _____.
   D. _____.
   E. _____.
   F. _____.
13. Make a sketch of a COMBINATION DRILL and COUNTERSINK.

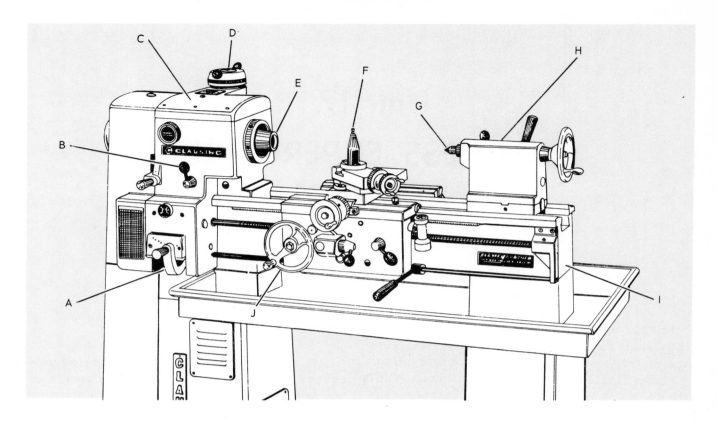

14. A lubricant must be placed in the center hole of the "dead center"; otherwise, _____.

15. The shaper is primarily used to machine _____ surfaces.

16. Prepare sketches showing the difference between the vertical milling machine and the horizontal milling machine.

17. End mills are used in the _____.

18. The symbol N/C means _____.

19. How are N/C machines controlled?

20. Describe how N/C machines operate.

Special Activities

1. Carefully clean and lubricate a lathe in your school shop. Use the lubrication chart furnished with the lathe to be certain that you do not overlook critical points.

2. After securing permission from your instructor, AND WITH THE POWER OFF, operate the various handwheels and levers on the lathe. Learn what each does. Do not force any movement.

3. Sharpen a cutter bit.

4. Prepare a check list and keep a record of the various operations you perform on the lathe. Prepare a similar chart for other machines that you operate.

5. Prepare a series of safety posters on the operation of machine tools.

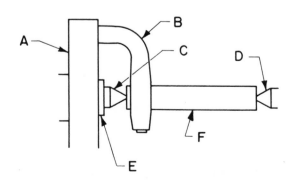

Unit 17
BUSINESS EXPERIENCE ACTIVITY

In this activity you will obtain first-hand experience in the business world... experience in Organizing, Financing and Operating your own Small Manufacturing Business. You will do many of the things a large business does, on a miniature scale. You will obtain experience that will make you a better employee when you are ready for your first full-time job.

Typical Activity

The business activity discussed in this Unit may be changed to meet local conditions and restrictions.

The procedure to follow in a typical setup includes:

1. Deciding on a product.
2. Selecting a name for your new company.
3. Electing company officials.
4. Determining approximate amount of operating capital needed to finance the business.
5. Selling shares of stock to raise operating capital.
6. Determining the manufacturing steps required, and sequence of operations.
7. Providing jigs and fixtures needed for mass production.
8. Developing sales plan; promoting product sales.
9. Dissolving the business and reimbursing stockholders.

Decide on Product

At your first meeting (with your instructor serving as advisor) you should decide on the product to be manufactured. Selecting one of the tested products covered later in this Unit is suggested.

Select Company Name

The name selected should be appropriate, businesslike, and not too long.

Since this is a class activity in which all students are expected to participate, each member of the class should make an effort to come up with a good name for the new company which is being organized.

It is suggested that each class member write one or more names on a slip of paper. The slips should be collected, proposed names discussed, and a vote taken to determine which company name is to be used.

Caution: Do not include Incorporated, or Corporation after the company name. Each of these is a legal term which can be used only in cases where a state charter has been obtained.

Company Officials

If your company is to be successful, it must be operated in an efficient, business-

A-1 PRODUCTS, 123 W. Taft, South Holland, Ill. 60473

R E C E I P T S

Date	Item	Quantity	Sold To	Sold By	Amount

Fig. 17-1. Business activity records - - cash receipts.

like manner. This means you will need capable company officials, also capable workers. It is suggested that you elect:

1. General Manager.
2. Office Manager.
3. Purchasing Agent.
4. Sales Manager.
5. Safety Director.

Duties of the company officials as described in the following paragraphs, should be discussed before holding an election.

Duties of General Manager

Your General Manager will be expected to:

1. Exercise general supervision over entire activity.
2. Train workers, assign workers to jobs.
3. Check on, and be responsible for product quality and manufacturing efficiency.
4. OK bills to be paid by Office Manager; OK purchase orders before making purchases.
5. Prepare and submit reports as required by your Advisor (Instructor).
6. Cooperate with your Advisor, and other Company officials.

Duties of Office Manager

He should:

1. Maintain attendance records. Check absentees for valid excuses.
2. Keep Company's financial records (8 1/2 x 11 loose leaf notebook suggested).

3. Keep a record of all money received on RECEIPTS page of record book, Fig. 17-1.
4. All cash receipts should be deposited in a local bank and a checking account established.
5. Pay all bills, invoices previously OK'd by your General Manager, by writing checks. Make a complete record in your check book, which shows date and amount of money deposited in checking account and checks written. Show balance - - amount in bank, after each check is written. See Fig. 17-2. Be sure your figures are accu-

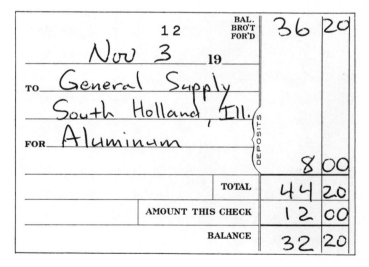

Fig. 17-2. Business activity records - - checkbook record of bills paid.

rate because this is the only record your Company has of the cash on hand.
6. Keep stock sales and ownership records.
7. Cooperate with your Advisor and other Company officials.

Duties of Purchasing Agent

He should:

1. Check with Advisor relative to materials and supplies needed to manufacture product selected.
2. Arrange to have printed, or run off on school duplicator, stock certificates, purchase orders, and other forms needed.
3. Have purchase orders OK'd by General Manager before issuing order.
4. Obtain materials required from school stock or purchase from outside source.
5. Cooperate with Advisor and other Company officials.

Duties of Sales Manager

He should:

1. After product sample is available, he should help decide on how product is to be packaged, and provide instructions on product use, to include in the package.
2. Plan sales program; help decide on price to charge for product, where and how product is to be sold. Note: All students participating in this activity will be expected to sell your Company's products (also stock).
3. Cooperate with Advisor and other Company officials.

Duties of Safety Director

He should:

1. Enforce safety rules.
2. Stop all horseplay and call attention to undesirable conduct.

3. Be alert to hazards.
4. Take steps to eliminate possible accident causes.
5. See to it that equipment and tools are in good operating condition.
6. Check to make sure machine guards are in place and students are using eye protection and protective clothing as specified by Advisor.
7. If someone is injured, even slightly, contact Advisor immediately.
8. Cooperate with Advisor and other Company officials.

All Company officials should be provided with identification badges, Fig. 17-3.

Fig. 17-3. Identification badge for company official - - typical.

Raising Capital

In operating your new business, you will need money (capital) to pay bills until you start taking in cash from the sale of your product. Most corporations raise money by selling stock to the public. It is suggested you do the same.

Getting stock certificates printed, stock sold, and keeping the necessary records, is the responsibility of your Office Manager. See Fig. 17-4.

A-1 PRODUCTS, 123 W. Taft, South Holland, Ill. 60473

STOCK RECORD

Date	Certif. No.	Sold To	Sold By	Amount

Fig. 17-4. Business activity - - stock ownership record.

STOCK CERTIFICATE

A-1 PRODUCTS
South Holland, Ill.

One Share

Par Value 50¢

Certificate Number

_____

Redeemable Within
One Year After Issue

Date Issued

_____

This Certifies That (please print)

_____

First Name   Initial   Last Name

_____

Street Address   City   State   Zip

Is the Owner of One Share, Par Value 50¢, of the stock of A-1 Products.

_____   _____

Stockholder's Signature   for A-1 Products

Stockholder by signature, okays operation of Company by Student Officials elected
by Student Stockholders.

Fig. 17-5. Stock certificate, form suggestions.

Let's assume that you need $40.00. This may be raised by selling 80 shares of stock at $.50 each. See Fig. 17-5 for a suggested Stock Certificate form.

This should be run off on a duplicating machine on two different colors of stock... 100 copies of each, yellow and white suggested. Number the certificates 1 to 100.

Each student will be expected to purchase a share of stock at $.50. When starting to sell stock (on your own time) it is a good idea to make your first sale to yourself. Using a ball point pen and carbon paper, fill out the stock certificate form in duplicate, with the white copy on top. On the share you sell to yourself sign in two places, where the stockholder's signature is required, and as a representative of your company. Keep the white copy. Turn in the yellow copy (carbon) and the $.50 to your Office Manager. It is his job to keep an accurate record of stock sales, and to see to it that the cash turned in is deposited in the bank. See Fig. 17-6.

It is suggested you limit stock sales to one share per customer. The stock should

Fig. 17-6. All cash received from product sales is deposited in the bank and bills are paid by check.

DEPOSITED WITH

South Holland Trust & Savings Bank
SOUTH HOLLAND, ILLINOIS

NAME A-1 PRODUCTS

ADDRESS SOUTH HOLLAND, ILL.

DATE 11-1 19____

ACCOUNT NUMBER
_487_

	DOLLARS	CENTS
CURRENCY	7	00
COIN	3	40
CHECKS		
TOTAL	10	40
LESS CASH DEDUCTION		
TOTAL DEPOSIT	10	40

LIST ADDITIONAL CHECKS ON REVERSE SIDE

CHECKS DEPOSITED CANNOT BE DRAWN AGAINST
UNTIL THEY HAVE BEEN COLLECTED BY THE BANK.

be divided so each student has approximately the same number of shares to sell. In contacting prospective purchasers ... local business men, parents, neighbors, friends, be businesslike. Describe your Company and its operations briefly. Be enthusiastic. Try to give your prospect the impression he is buying a share in a GOING BUSINESS, and is NOT "donating to charity." Tell him you cannot guarantee results in advance, but that your Company expects to operate profitably and when the business is closed out to redeem the stock at full par value ($.50 per share) and pay a small dividend.

After a share of stock has been sold, fill out the stock certificate as previously described. Be sure to print. Ask your purchaser to read the certificate to make sure everything is understood and is agreeable, then ask him to sign. Hand the top (white) copy to your purchaser. As you leave don't forget to say "thank you" (like you really meant it).

Establishing Price, Selling Product

In establishing a selling price for your product, it is suggested you determine the total cost per item, then add to this about 25%. The extra 25% is to cover the cost of material wasted, and to pay a dividend to stockholders when the business is closed out.

Each student participating in the project (he is also a stockholder) is expected to help sell his company's product.

If the product selected is small such as the two items described in this Unit, you will probably find it advisable to make up the products in advance so you can provide "on the spot" delivery.

Keep an accurate record of all sales -- quantity sold, name of customer, and amount collected. Turn these records and the cash collected over to your Office Manager for handling.

At the completion of the mass production project, the Company you formed should be liquidated and the money in the bank (after all bills are paid) divided equally among your stockholders.

Including with each of the checks a "thank you" note (mimeographed) worded something like this is suggested:

Date _____

MEMO TO STOCKHOLDER:

A-1 Products, the business experience activity you helped finance by purchasing a share of stock, is being liquidated.

The check, in amount of _____ which is enclosed, is intended to redeem the stock you purchased. The stock certificate you have, need not be returned to us.

Thank you very much for supporting our project.

(signature)
General Manager

Fig. 17-7. Project suggestion — Tie Rack.

Mass Production in the School Shop

Two projects for mass production with proven student interest are the Tie Rack, Fig. 17-7, and the Contemporary Lamp, Fig. 17-26.

Mass-Producing Tie Rack

The TIE RACK, Fig. 17-8, provides interesting production problems but is simple enough to be produced in a relatively short time.

Using Flow Chart

The PRODUCTION FLOW CHART, Fig. 17-9, shows a suggested sequence of manu-

Fig. 17-8. Tie rack suitable for mass production.

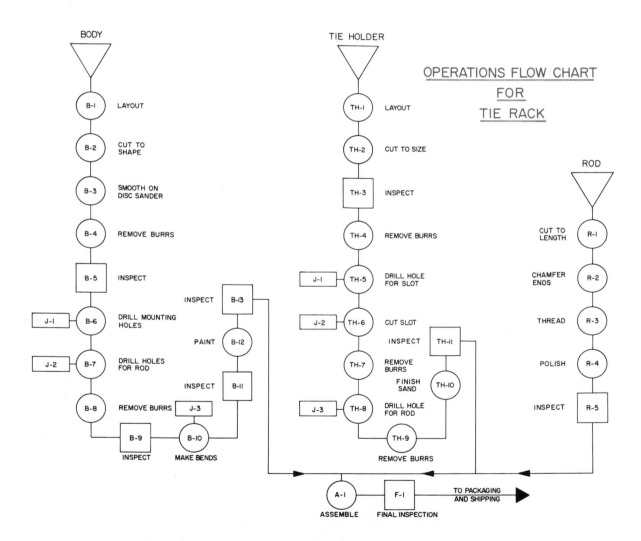

Fig. 17-9. A PRODUCTION FLOW CHART for the tie rack. Only one method is shown for the manufacture of the tie holder.

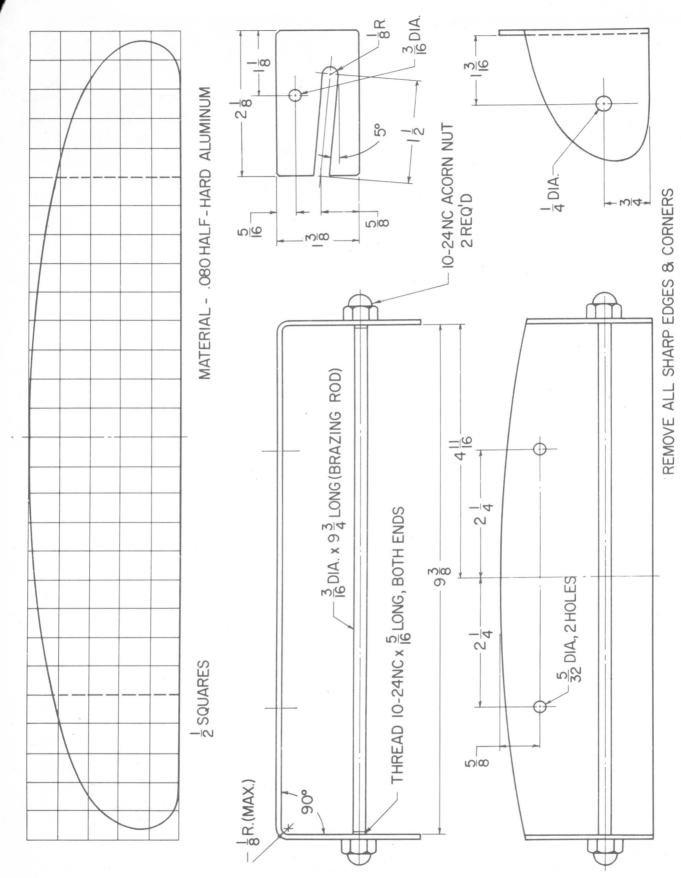

MATERIAL — .080 HALF-HARD ALUMINUM

$\frac{1}{2}$ SQUARES

REMOVE ALL SHARP EDGES & CORNERS

Fig. 17-10. Plans for the tie rack.

facturing, inspecting, assembling and finishing operations. The facilities and equipment available in your shop may require making some changes.

Tie rack plans are shown in Fig. 17-10. A tie rack of the size indicated will hold about 20 ties. A smaller rack may be made up by using shorter body pieces.

Body

The body (main part) is made from .080 in. half-hard aluminum sheet. After making a pattern on .030 aluminum, trace the body outline on the metal, Fig. 17-11. A soft lead

Fig. 17-13. *Using disc sander to smooth edges.*

pencil or fine point magic marker may be used. The metal may be cut to shape on a jig saw, Fig. 17-12, utilizing a fine toothed (24T-32T) blade, or a band saw if available.

Rough edges of the metal are smoothed on a disc sander, Fig. 17-13, using a fine (3/0 - 4/0) abrasive disc, or by hand. Be sure all burrs are removed.

The 1/4 in. holes for the 3/16 in. rod are drilled using a simple jig to hold the part in position, as in Fig. 17-14. The same jig can

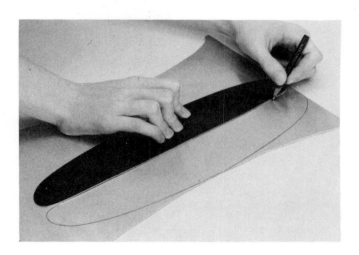

Fig. 17-11. *Use a metal template to transfer the outline to .080 in. thick aluminum sheet.*

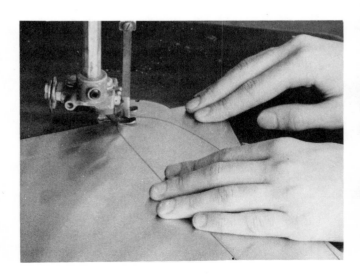

Fig. 17-12. *Cutting to outline shape on a jig saw.*

Fig. 17-14. *Jig used to position metal for drilling holes to hold rod.*

Fig. 17-15. Jig shown in Fig. 17-14 may also be used to position the work for drilling the mounting holes.

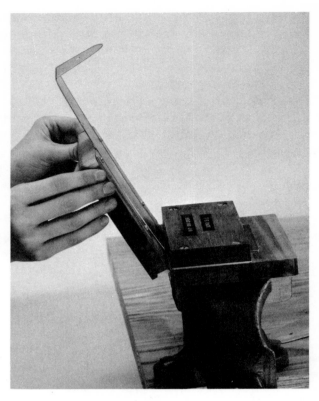

Fig. 17-16. Making bends with a shop made bending jig.

be used to position the work for drilling the mounting holes, Fig. 17-15. Remove all burrs.

The 90 deg. bends are formed using a shop made bending jig, Figs. 17-16 and 17-17.

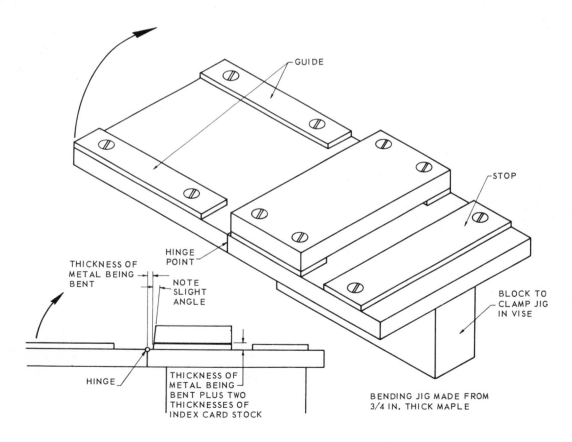

GUIDE

STOP

HINGE POINT

THICKNESS OF METAL BEING BENT

NOTE SLIGHT ANGLE

BLOCK TO CLAMP JIG IN VISE

HINGE

THICKNESS OF METAL BEING BENT PLUS TWO THICKNESSES OF INDEX CARD STOCK

BENDING JIG MADE FROM 3/4 IN. THICK MAPLE

Fig. 17-17. Drawing of jig shown in Fig. 17-16.

There are two guides on the device so it may be used to make both of the required bends.

After a careful inspection the tie rack body is ready to be cleaned and painted, Fig. 17-18. Using paint in aerosol type spray cans will eliminate a lot of clean-up mess. After inspection, store the completed bodies until needed for final assembly.

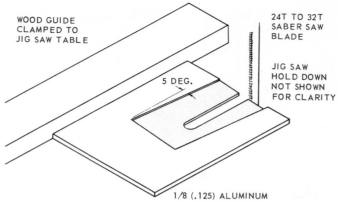

Fig. 17-20. Fixture and setup for cutting slot in individual tie holders.

Fig. 17-18. Painting tie rack body with aerosol type spray paint.

Tie Holders

There are several ways the holders (for individual ties), Fig. 17-19, can be made. These may be cut to individual size on squaring shears or on a jig or band saw, Fig. 17-20. Or, the slots may be cut quickly by using a small milling machine, Fig. 17-21. After removing burrs, round corners to remove the sharp edges. Smooth by sanding.

Inspect to be sure that each part has been properly cleaned and smoothed.

Fig. 17-21. Cutting slot on small vertical milling machine.

When the slot in the holder is to be cut on a jig saw or band saw, a hole should be drilled at the end of the slot. A drill jig can be used to position the part to drill the hole. It will not be necessary to lay out each holder separately if the fixture shown in Fig. 17-20 is utilized.

Fig. 17-19. Sequence to be followed in making individual tie holders.

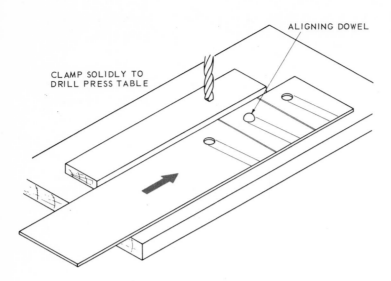

Fig. 17-22. Drill jig utilized to drill hole at bottom of slot when tie holders are made in strip form.

It is also possible to manufacture the holders in strip form. Using squaring shears, cut a strip of aluminum sheet as wide as the tie holder is long. The length of the strip will be determined by the capacity of the squaring

shears. The strip can also be cut on a jig saw or band saw.

Lay out tie holders on the strip. Do not forget to allow material for the cut if a saw is to be used to cut the strip into individual tie holders.

The holes at the base of the slots are drilled first. The procedure is to drill a hole in the first tie holder on the strip. Then place the hole over the aligning dowel on the drill jig, Fig. 17-22. After CAREFULLY aligning the jig, drill a hole in the second holder (do not forget to clamp the jig solidly to the drill press) and drill the second hole. Succeeding holes are positioned for drilling by moving the strip over so the last drilled hole is fitted over the aligning pin. Drill holes required and remove the burrs. This may be done by using a countersink mounted in the drill press.

The slots in the tie holder are cut using the fixture shown in Fig. 17-23. A guide must

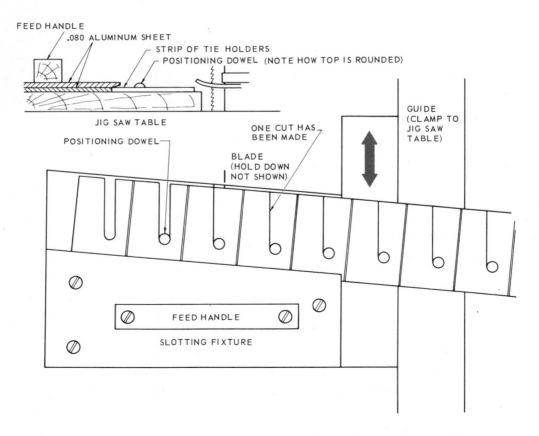

Fig. 17-23. Fixture used to position strip of tie holders so slots can be cut.

be clamped to the jig saw table. Make first cut in all holders, then adjust position of guide for second cut. The fixture can be mounted on the miter gauge if the slots are to be cut on a band saw.

The same fixture can be utilized if a jig saw or band saw is to be used to cut the individual holders from the strip.

Fig. 17-24. Jig that positions holder for drilling mounting hole. It is important that the part be fitted in the jig as shown.

Remove all burrs and rough edges with a file.

The hole to mount the tie holder on the rod can now be drilled using the jig shown in Fig. 17-24 to position the piece. In drilling it is important that the parts be fitted into the jig as illustrated.

After burrs are removed, the holder is sanded clean and inspected. Store until needed for final assembly.

Rod

The rod is made from 3/16 in. dia. brazing rod. However, 3/16 in. dia. cold finished steel rod may be substituted.

Cut the material to length. Using a grinder, round each end slightly to make threading easier.

Thread both ends. Remove any burrs, polish and inspect.

Final Assembly

Parts ready for assembly are shown in Fig. 17-25. The assembly line can be set up as follows:

1. Attach one acorn nut to rod.
2. Slide rod through one end of body.
3. Fit holders to rod.
4. Attach second acorn nut to rod.
5. Final inspection.

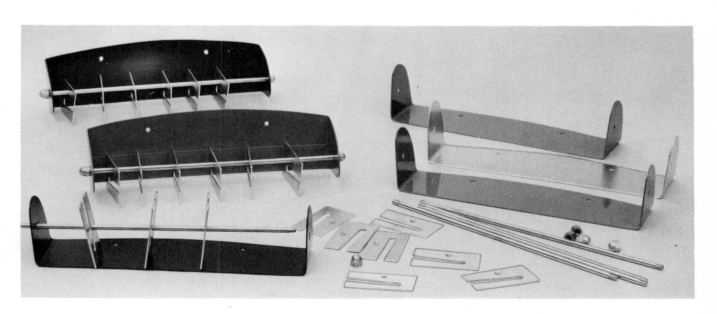

Fig. 17-25. Final assembly — shown are all parts ready for assembly.

Exploring Metalworking

Mass-Producing Contemporary Lamp

Mass-producing the lamp, Fig. 17-26, involves a number of interesting metalworking procedures. For constructional details on the lamp, see Fig. 17-27 on pages 177 and 178.

An OPERATIONS FLOW CHART is given in Fig. 17-28. At each step, the student group assigned to the task of preparing production equipment should ask the question, "Is there a way to make it better, or a better way of making it?" Any approved suggestions should be incorporated in the plan.

Fig. 17-26. Table lamp that was mass-produced.

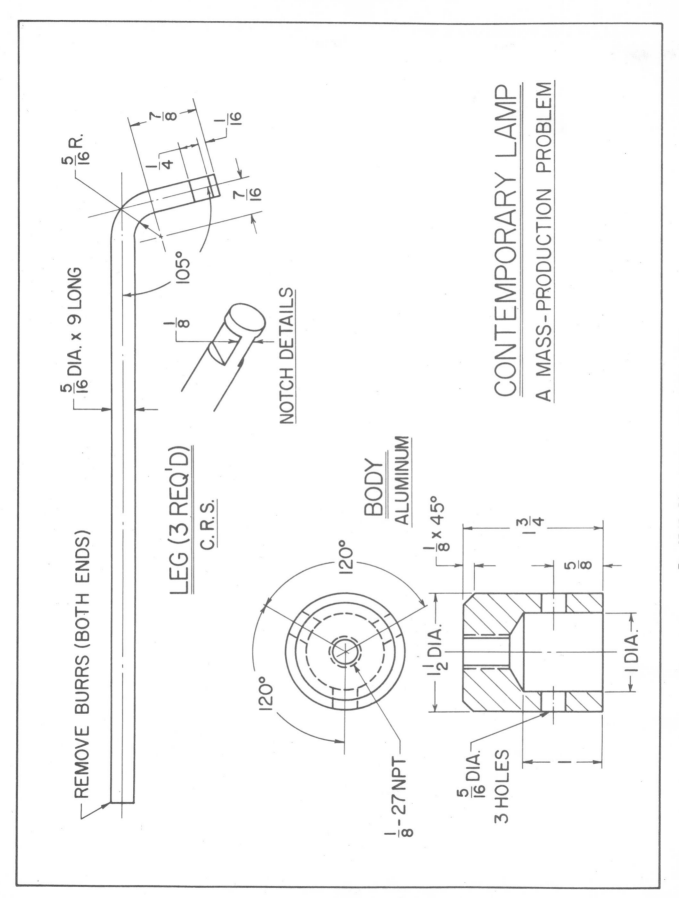

REMOVE BURRS (BOTH ENDS)

$\frac{5}{16}$ DIA. x 9 LONG

$\frac{5}{16}$ R.

$\frac{7}{8}$

$\frac{1}{16}$

$\frac{1}{4}$

$\frac{7}{16}$

105°

NOTCH DETAILS

$\frac{1}{8}$

LEG (3 REQ'D)
C.R.S.

BODY
ALUMINUM

120°

120°

$\frac{1}{8}$ x 45°

$1\frac{3}{4}$

$\frac{5}{8}$

$1\frac{1}{2}$ DIA.

1 DIA.

$\frac{5}{16}$ DIA.
3 HOLES

$\frac{1}{8}$ - 27 NPT

CONTEMPORARY LAMP
A MASS-PRODUCTION PROBLEM

Fig. 17-27. Plans for lamp shown in Fig. 17-26.

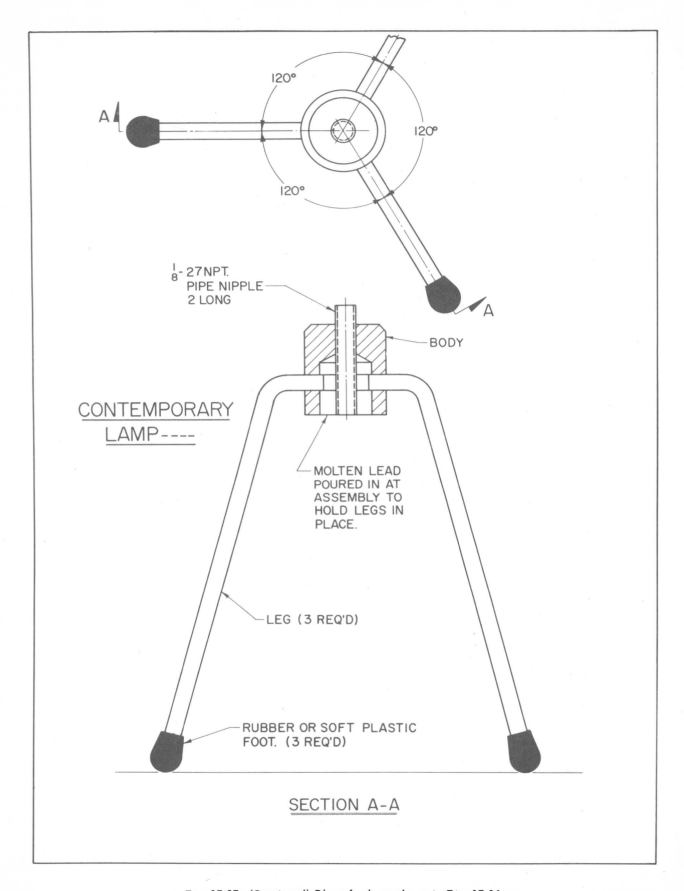

120°

120°

120°

A

A

$\frac{1}{8}$- 27NPT.
PIPE NIPPLE
2 LONG

BODY

CONTEMPORARY
LAMP----

MOLTEN LEAD
POURED IN AT
ASSEMBLY TO
HOLD LEGS IN
PLACE.

LEG (3 REQ'D)

RUBBER OR SOFT PLASTIC
FOOT. (3 REQ'D)

SECTION A-A

Fig. 17-27. (Continued) Plans for lamp shown in Fig. 17-26.

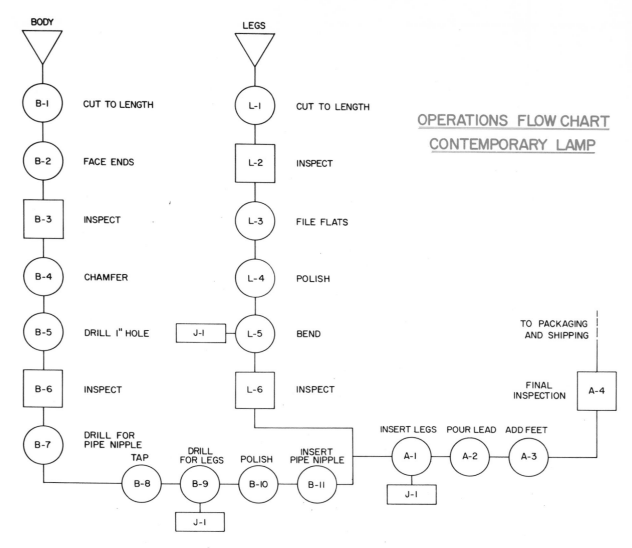

Fig. 17-28. Flow Chart showing manufacturing sequences of the various parts.

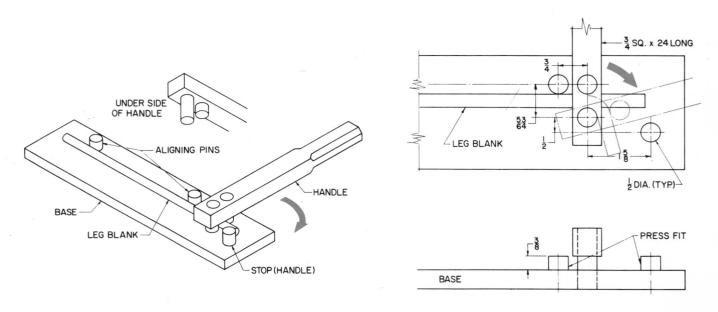

Fig. 17-29. Bending tool used to shape legs.

A bending tool to form the legs is shown in Fig. 17-29, and a drill jig to locate the holes for the legs, Fig. 17-30.

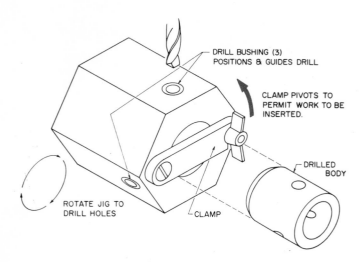

DRILL BUSHING (3)
POSITIONS & GUIDES DRILL

CLAMP PIVOTS TO
PERMIT WORK TO BE
INSERTED.

DRILLED
BODY

ROTATE JIG TO
DRILL HOLES

CLAMP

Fig. 17-30. Drill jig utilized to hold lamp body while it was drilled.

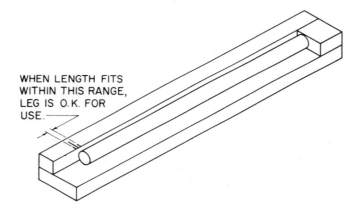

WHEN LENGTH FITS
WITHIN THIS RANGE,
LEG IS O.K. FOR
USE.

Fig. 17-31. Gage to check length of legs.

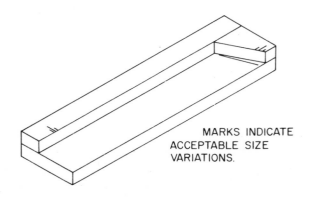

MARKS INDICATE
ACCEPTABLE SIZE
VARIATIONS.

Fig. 17-32. Gage to check bend in leg.

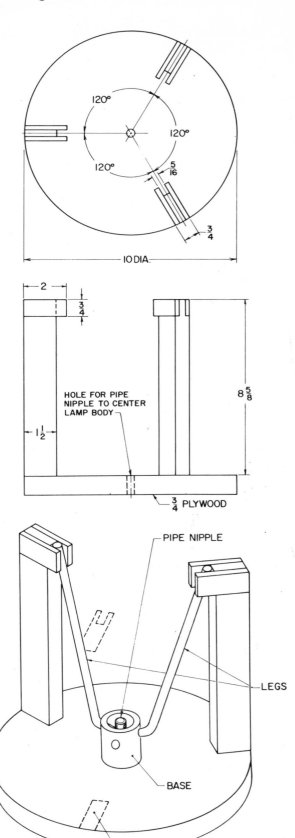

120°
120°
120°
$\frac{5}{16}$
$\frac{3}{4}$
10 DIA.

2
$\frac{3}{4}$
$8\frac{5}{8}$
HOLE FOR PIPE
NIPPLE TO CENTER
LAMP BODY
$1\frac{1}{2}$
$\frac{3}{4}$ PLYWOOD

PIPE NIPPLE
LEGS
BASE
POSITION OF 3rd LEG SUPPORT

Fig. 17-33. Fixture to hold legs while molten lead was poured.

The drawings, Figs. 17-31 and 17-32 show gages designed to assure uniformity in the length of the legs and the angle at which the legs are to be bent. To attach the legs to the body, molten type metal is poured into the body cavity of the base after positioning the pipe nipple and legs, Fig. 17-33. Special training before the handling of molten metals is a "must."

Another solution is to pack plastic steel around the positioned legs.

The rubber or plastic feet, lamp fixtures, wire and plug must be purchased commercially.

Providing shades of appropriate size and shape is important. See Fig. 17-34.

Fig. 17-34. Lamp shade; alternate design suggestion.

Review of Activity

A. What problems were encountered in mass-producing your project? How could they have been avoided?
B. How could the project have been improved?
C. What was the most interesting part of the activity?
D. Why was it interesting?
E. What was the most challenging part of the activity? Why was it challenging?

Special Activities

1. Devise a bulletin board on mass production.
2. Visit a factory that mass-produces a product.
3. Visit a shop that produces objects on a limited production basis.
4. Discuss with a banker how to finance a small business and report to your class.
5. Discuss with an advertising man the steps followed to advertise a product such as the tie rack described in this Unit.

Fig. 17-35. Some examples of metal projects that have been mass-produced in school shops.

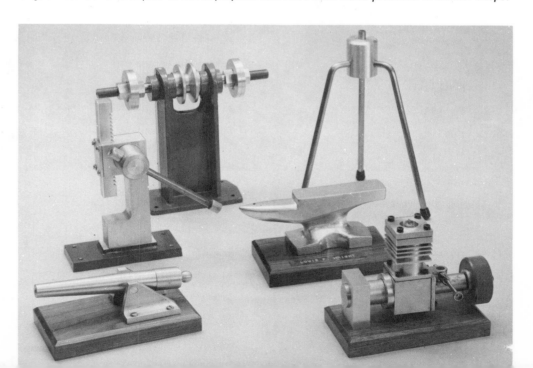

Fig. 18-1. The machine operator is classified as a semiskilled worker.   (Clausing)

Unit 18

METALWORKING CAREERS

Kinds of Jobs in Metalworking

Jobs in the metalworking industry fall into many categories. However, all of the jobs may be classified according to:

Semiskilled.
Skilled.
Technical.
Professional.

Semiskilled Jobs

Most semiskilled workers are employed in manufacturing where they:

1. Operate machines or equipment used to make things, Fig. 18-1.
2. Assemble manufactured parts into complete units.
3. Serve as helpers who assist skilled workers.
4. Work as inspectors or conduct tests to be sure manufactured parts are made to and operate according to specifications, Fig. 18-2.

The majority of semiskilled workers work with their hands and require only a brief on-the-job training program. They are told what to do and how to do it. Frequently, the semiskilled worker does the same job or operation over and over. The work is closely supervised.

Although some semiskilled workers are paid on the number of items they produce, most have annual earnings that are less than skilled workers.

Semiskilled workers are usually the first to lose their jobs when business slows down and are the last to be rehired.

To qualify for better jobs, the semiskilled worker usually enters an apprentice training program or attends classes at a community college or evening school.

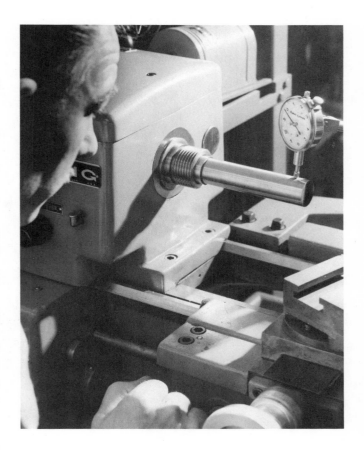

Fig. 18-2. Semiskilled workers work as inspectors or conduct tests to make sure that the manufactured parts will operate according to design specifications.
(Clausing)

183

Fig. 18-3. The tool and die maker is a highly skilled machinist. Here a tool and die maker is machining a mold to make O rings (seals). (H. O. Canfield Co., Inc.)

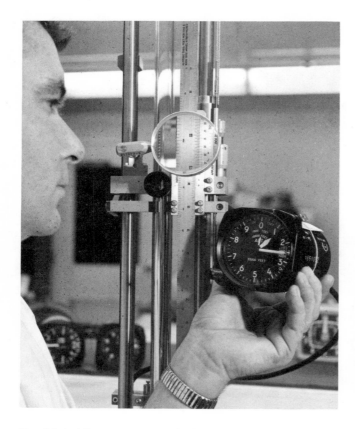

Fig. 18-4. The instrument maker manufactures precise parts that make up the instruments used by industry, medicine, government and science.

Skilled Workers

Skilled workers are considered the backbone of industry. They are the craftsmen who make the tools, machines and equipment that transform raw materials, and the engineer's ideas and designs, into finished products.

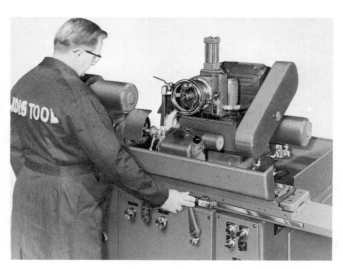

Fig. 18-5. The set up man prepares machines so that the semiskilled worker can operate them. (Landis Tool Co.)

The skilled craftsman may have acquired his skills through a formal apprentice training program, a lengthy on-the-job training program, or while in the armed forces. However, the formal apprentice program is considered the best way to learn a skill. Most of these programs last 4 to 6 years and are carefully planned to give the apprentice broad training in his trade. In addition, the apprentice must have a good math background and be able to read and interpret drawings and blueprints.

machines, grinders, etc. As he must work to very close tolerances (the part must be precisely made), the machinist must be familiar with all types of precision measuring instruments.

The TOOL AND DIE MAKER is a highly skilled machinist who specializes in making tools and dies needed to cut, shape and form metal. He also makes jigs and fixtures used to guide cutting tools and to position the metal while it is being machined. See Fig. 18-3.

Fig. 18-6. Skilled ironworkers place closing pieces of structural steel into position. (Bethlehem Steel Corp.)

The skilled worker must be skillful in working with his hands, and is expected to exercise considerable independent judgment that involves the use of costly tools, machines and raw materials.

He must continually up-date his skills as improvements are made in technical processes. This is often done through company sponsored educational programs.

There are many skilled trades in the metalworking industry. The MACHINIST must be able to operate and set up machine tools such as lathes, drilling machines, milling

The INSTRUMENT MAKER, Fig. 18-4, is another highly skilled craftsman who makes precise parts that make up the instruments used by industry, medicine, government and science. He often assembles and tests instruments.

The SET UP MAN, Fig. 18-5, is a skilled worker who sets up and adjusts machine tools so semiskilled workers can operate them.

If you like working out of doors you may want to be a skilled worker in the steel erection industry, Fig. 18-6. These men have an adventurous job.

Skilled foundry workers like the MOLDER, Fig. 18-7, and COREMAKERS learn their jobs through a formal apprentice program.

Fig. 18-9. Many highly skilled workers are needed to manufacture such complex products as these jet planes. (McDonnell-Douglas)

Fig. 18-7. A molder removing a pattern from a sand mold. He is classified as a skilled worker.

The WELDER is classified as a highly skilled craftsman, Fig. 18-8.

If you are interested in aircraft and rockets, you may want to work in the aerospace industry, Fig. 18-9. Large numbers of highly skilled workers are employed in this area of the economy.

Many skilled craftsmen work in the shipbuilding industry. If you enjoy the sea you may want to work as a metalsmith in the U.S. Navy or Merchant Marine.

Fig. 18-8. A welder fabricating a mammoth, 105-ton tension ring for the roof of the Madison Square Garden Sports and Entertainment Center. (Bethlehem Steel Corp.)

Skilled SHEET METAL WORKERS are always in constand demand, Fig. 18-10.

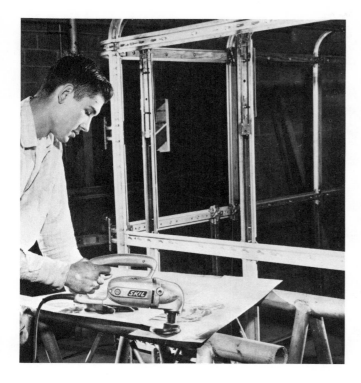

Fig. 18-10. Skilled sheet metal workers are always in constant demand. (Skil)

The skilled artisan produces the hand crafted metal products so sought after today. He usually spends several years learning his trade.

The jobs listed are only a few of the many available in the metalworking industry that require the competence of the skilled worker. Regardless of what you choose to do, if you want to be successful and advance in your job, you will find it to your advantage to complete high school and while there to study mathematics, science, and Industrial Arts.

Technicians

Advances in many areas of industry and science have brought about a demand for persons to do complex work of a highly technical nature. The men and women included in this occupational group are called TECHNICIANS. They work in the realm between the shop and the engineering department. However, the technician usually assists the engineer in research, development and design. He constructs and tests experimental devices and machines, compiles statistics, makes cost estimates and prepares technical reports.

Where do you get training to become a technician? You can start by taking all of the mathematics, science and Industrial Arts that you can fit into your high school schedule.

Upon graduation from high school, you can acquire formal training from many sources. These include the community college, vocational/technical centers, technical institutes and colleges that offer 2-year technical programs. The programs stress mathematics, science, English, engineering and drafting. Instructions are also given to familiarize the student with the tools, machinery and materials related to his area of interest.

The technician belongs to one of the fastest growing occupational group.

The Professions

If you are planning to attend college, you may be interested in one of the professional occupations in metalworking.

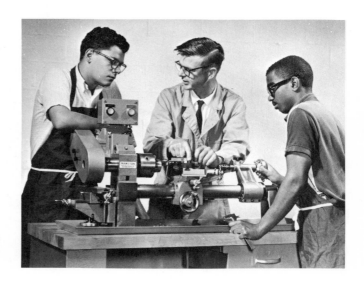

Fig. 18-11. Students should look into the teaching profession. There will be a constant demand for Industrial Education teachers for many years to come. (Hamilton Associates)

There are many excellent jobs in TEACHING, Fig. 18-11. This is a challenging job for those who like to work with people.

ENGINEERING, Fig. 18-12, is one of the largest professional occupations for men. There are also many women engineers and their numbers are growing.

The minimum requirement for entering the engineering profession is a bachelor's degree in engineering. However, some have entered the profession after experience as a foreman or engineering technician.

There are many types of engineers. The INDUSTRIAL ENGINEER is primarily concerned with the safest and most efficient way to use machines, materials and personnel. See Fig. 18-13.

Fig. 18-12. Astronaut decends steps of lunar module ladder as he prepares to walk on the moon. Engineers played a very important role in the design and manufacture of the equipment that made this flight possible. (NASA)

The design and development of new machines and ideas is the responsibility of the MECHANICAL ENGINEER.

The TOOL AND MANUFACTURING ENGINEER devises the methods and means required to manufacture and assemble a product, Fig. 18-14.

AERONAUTICAL ENGINEERS design and plan the manufacture of aerospace products.

The processing of metals and their conversion into commercial products are the concern of the METALLURGICAL ENGINEER.

Where to Get Information About Metalworking Occupations

You can secure more information on jobs in the metalworking industry from many sources. The guidance office and the Industrial Arts teacher in your school are the closest.

Most metalworking occupations are described in the OCCUPATIONAL OUTLOOK HANDBOOK published by the United States Department of Labor. It is usually available in libraries and guidance offices.

Your local community college will be glad to furnish information on the technical programs they offer.

Another excellent source of information is your local State Employment Service. They can inform you of local opportunities in metalworking, as well as the names and local addresses of the trade unions concerned with the metalworking trades.

What an Employer Expects of You

Have you ever given any thought to what the company that employs you will expect in return for the salary they pay you?

They will expect a fair day's work for a fair day's pay. They will look for you to do your assigned work to the best of your ability.

For your part, you should develop a sense of responsibility for the tools and equipment you use. These are very costly. Many employers have more than $100,000 invested in

Fig. 18-13. *The industrial engineer was responsible for planning the safest and most efficient ways to use machines, materials and personnel in the manufacture of these helicopters. (Bell Helicopter Co.)*

tools and equipment for each worker they hire.

You must remember that graduation from school will not be the end of your training. If you want to keep a good job and advance in it you will have to keep up with technical advances. This may be done through in-plant classes and/or advanced studies at community colleges or technical schools.

How to Go About Getting a Job

Securing your first full-time job will be a very important task.

The first thing you must do is to decide what type of work you would like to do. Your guidance office and the local Employment Security Office can give tests that will help determine the area(s) of work where you will have a good chance of succeeding. You can get additional help by answering the following questions:

1. What have I accomplished with some degree of success?
2. What have I done that others have commended me for doing well?
3. What are the things I really like to do?
4. What are the things I DO NOT like to do?
5. What jobs have I held? Why did I leave them?

You will probably find that you have several areas of interest. List them and start gathering information on each one of the areas. This can be done by reading, talking with persons doing this kind of work and visiting industry.

The final step will be to plan your school program to prepare you for entry into the job, or for advanced schooling if that is required.

Let's assume now that you are ready to go out and get that job. How would you go about it?

You must remember that some jobs are always available. Workers get promoted, retire, change jobs, quit, die and are fired. Technological advances create new jobs. YOU must track them down.

Zero in on getting the job. MAKE YOUR JOB APPLICATION IN PERSON. Be specific in the type of job you are after. Don't just ask for a job or inquire of the employment office, "What job openings do you have?"

Preparing a JOB RESUME in advance will speed up the tedious task of filling out job applications. It will also assure uniform information with little chance of confusing responses. The resume should include:

189

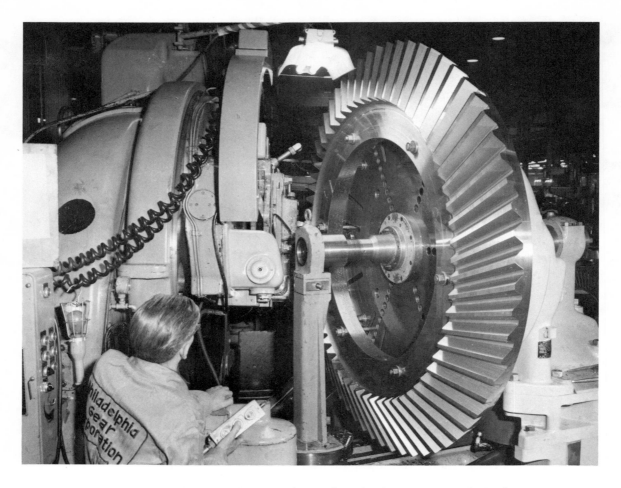

Fig. 18-14. The methods required to produce this large gear were devised
by the tool and manufacturing engineer.   (Philadelphia Gear Corp.)

1. Your FULL name.
2. FULL address and phone number. (Don't forget the zip code.)
3. Place and date of birth. For some jobs, it may be necessary to include a photostat of your birth certificate. Have these available.
4. Your Social Security number.
5. What can you do well?
6. What do you like to do?
7. What do you dislike doing?
8. List the places you have worked with the last place of employment first. Include the following items under each place of employment:
   Name and Address.
   Dates Employed.
   Employer's Name.
   Salary.
   Reason for Leaving Job.
9. Schooling and special training (include dates attending).
10. List of equipment you can operate safely.
11. Names and addresses of references. No relatives. Get permission before using names.

Finally, know where to look for a job. Review the classified section of local newspapers each day. Talk with friends and relatives. They may be aware of job openings at their place of employment before they become official.

New office and factory buildings usually mean new job openings. You may also prepare a list of desirable employers in your community and visit their employment offices.

Remember, in most cases the job will not come to you. YOU must go after it.

What Do You Know About Metalworking Occupations? - Unit 18

1. Metalworking jobs fall into one of the following four classifications:
   A. _____ .
   B. _____ .
   C. _____ .
   D. _____ .

2. If you were a semiskilled worker in metalworking you would probably be employed to do one of the following jobs:
   A. _____ .
   B. _____ .
   C. _____ .
   D. _____ .

3. There are disadvantages that the semi-skilled worker must face on the job. Check the correct answer(s).
   _____ A. He often does the same job or operation over and over for a long period of time.
   _____ B. His job only requires a brief on-the-job training period.
   _____ C. He is the first to lose his job when business slows down.
   _____ D. All of the above reasons.
   _____ E. None of the above reasons.

4. The formal apprentice program usually lasts _____ to _____ years.

The following list is of the matching type. Place the question number on your answer sheet and the letter of the work that describes it correctly, beside it.

5. _____ Machinist.
6. _____ Tool and die maker.
7. _____ Instrument maker.
8. _____ Set up man.
9. _____ Molder.
10. _____ Technician.
11. _____ Industrial engineer.
12. _____ Mechanical engineer.
13. _____ Tool and manufacturing engineer.
14. _____ Aeronautical engineer.

A. Works in the realm between the shop and the engineering department.
B. Primarily interested in the safest and most efficient way to use machines, material and personnel.
C. Design and plan the manufacture of aerospace products.
D. Makes the tools and dies needed to cut, shape and form metal.
E. A skilled foundry worker.
F. Devises the methods and means required to manufacture and assemble a product.
G. Designs and develops new machines and ideas.
H. Makes the parts for the instruments used by industry, medicine, government and science.
I. Adjusts machines and tools so that semi-skilled workers can operate them.
J. Must be able to operate all kinds of machine tools.

15. The _____ engineer is concerned with the processing of metals and their conversion into commercial products.

Special Activities

1. Metals play a very important part in our modern world. How many jobs can YOU name that make use of metal in some shape or form? How many can YOU name that do not make use of metal either directly or indirectly?

JOBS REQUIRING METAL	JOBS NOT REQUIRING METAL

Unit 19
PROJECTS

Designing and constructing metalworking projects will teach you to Think, and to Plan.

Your projects should be items you are interested in making. The projects when completed should compare favorably, in quality, with items available commercially.

NAPKIN RINGS

Material: Aluminum.

Finish: Polished or satin finish.
Remove burrs, sharp edges.

The designs shown are but a few of the many geometric forms that can be used for this project. Use your imagination and design your own.

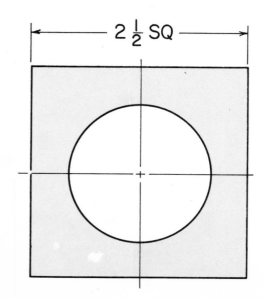

2 ½ SQ

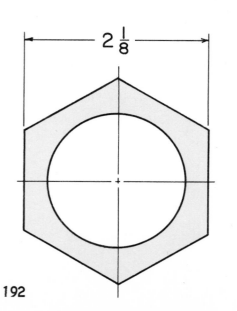

2 ⅛

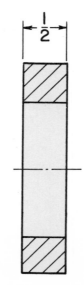

½

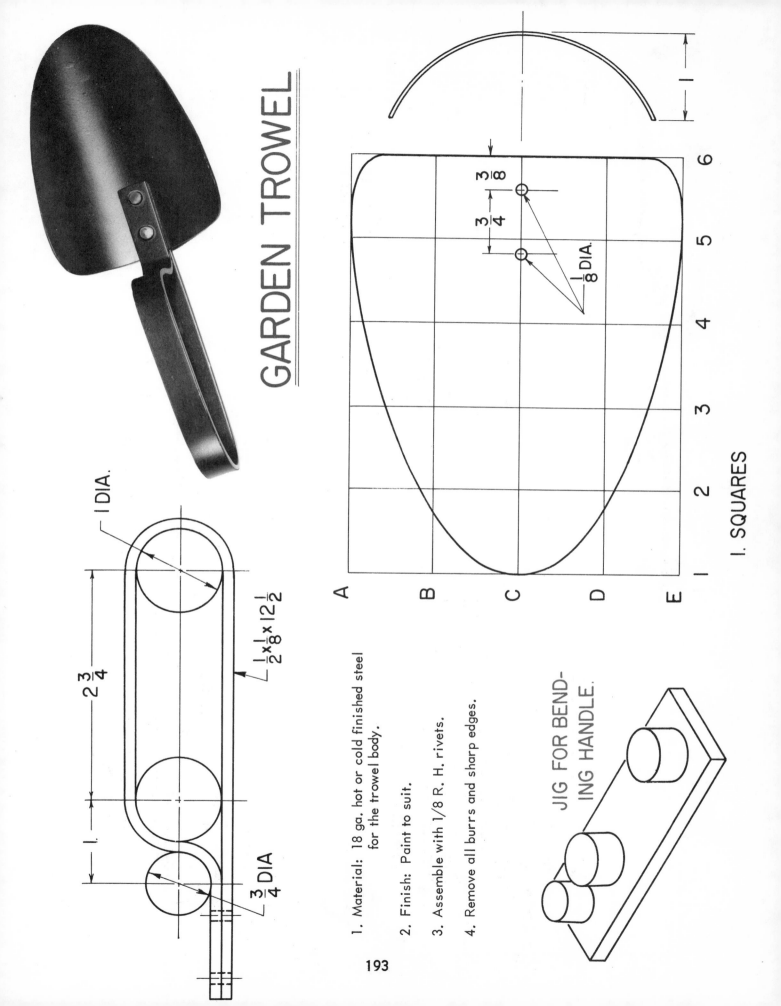

GARDEN TROWEL

I DIA.

$\frac{3}{8}$

$\frac{3}{4}$

$\frac{1}{8}$ DIA.

I. SQUARES

A

B

C

D

E

1 2 3 4 5 6

I DIA.

$2\frac{3}{4}$

$\frac{1}{2} \times \frac{1}{8} \times 12\frac{1}{2}$

I.

$\frac{3}{4}$ DIA

1. Material: 18 ga. hot or cold finished steel for the trowel body.

2. Finish: Paint to suit.

3. Assemble with 1/8 R. H. rivets.

4. Remove all burrs and sharp edges.

JIG FOR BEND-ING HANDLE.

193

SCREWDRIVER

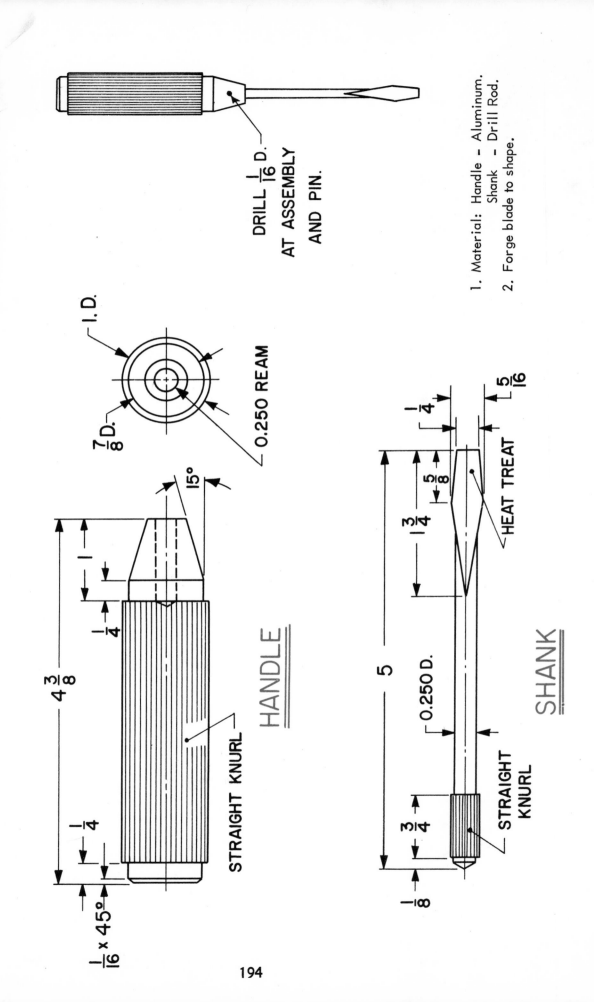

DRILL $\frac{1}{16}$ D.
AT ASSEMBLY
AND PIN.

1. Material: Handle – Aluminum.
   Shank – Drill Rod.
2. Forge blade to shape.

I.D.

$\frac{7}{8}$ D.

0.250 REAM

15°

1

$\frac{1}{4}$

$4\frac{3}{8}$

$\frac{1}{4}$

$\frac{1}{16}$ x 45°

STRAIGHT KNURL

HANDLE

$\frac{1}{4}$

$\frac{5}{8}$

$\frac{5}{16}$

$1\frac{3}{4}$

5

0.250 D.

HEAT TREAT

$\frac{3}{4}$

$\frac{1}{8}$

STRAIGHT KNURL

SHANK

194

WIRY CAT

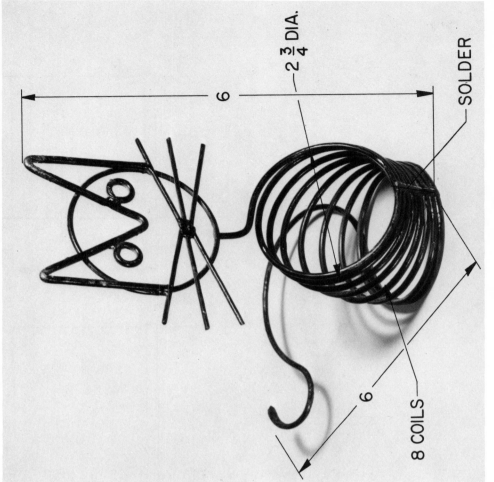

6

2 3/4 DIA.

SOLDER

8 COILS

6

1. Use 1/8 in. diameter wire to form the figure. This may be copper wire, brazing rod or steel coat hangers.

2. Solder all joints.

3. Finish by painting flat black.

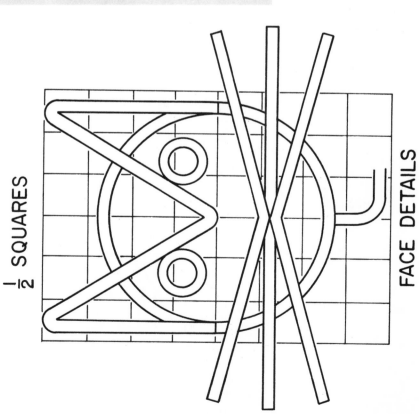

1/2 SQUARES

FACE DETAILS

195

SMALL PLANTER

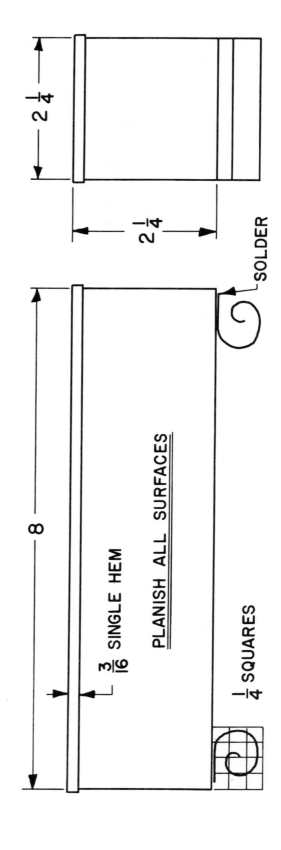

1. Material: 18 ga. copper or brass.

2. Finish: Planish. Buff all exterior surfaces. Apply satin finish to interior surfaces. Protect polished surfaces with clear lacquer spray.

$2\frac{1}{4}$

$2\frac{1}{4}$

SOLDER

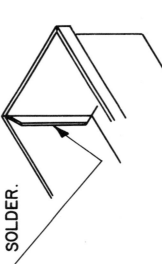

TYPICAL CORNER DETAILS. SOLDER.

8

$\frac{3}{16}$ SINGLE HEM

PLANISH ALL SURFACES

$\frac{1}{4}$ SQUARES

$\frac{5}{16}$ DIA. x $\frac{3}{8}$ LONG TUBING ALTERNATE FEET DESIGN.

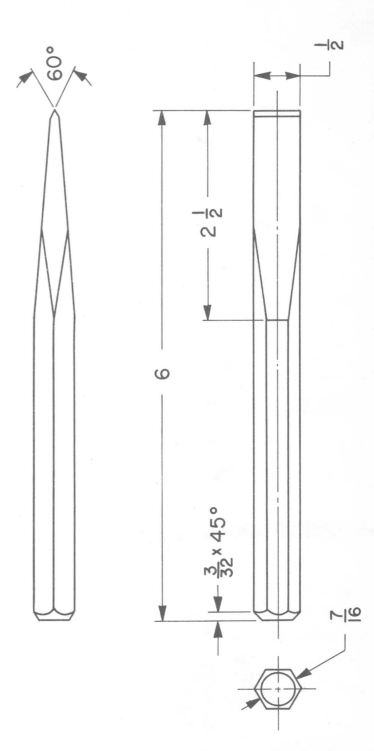

COLD CHISEL

1. Material: 7/16 hexagonal or octagonal tool steel.

2. Heat and forge to shape.

3. File smooth and grind chamfer on chisel head.

4. Heat treat and sharpen.

60°

$2\frac{1}{2}$

$\frac{1}{2}$

6

$\frac{3}{32}$ x 45°

$\frac{7}{16}$

PENCIL HOLDERS

1. Material: Aluminum.

2. Finish: Polished or as machined.

3. Attach felt to bottom.

4. Remove all burrs and sharp edges.

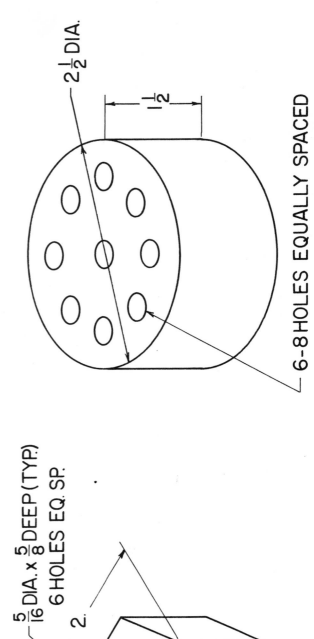

$2\frac{1}{2}$ DIA.

$1\frac{1}{2}$

6-8 HOLES EQUALLY SPACED

$\frac{5}{16}$ DIA. x $\frac{5}{8}$ DEEP (TYP.)
6 HOLES EQ. SP.

2.

$1\frac{1}{2}$

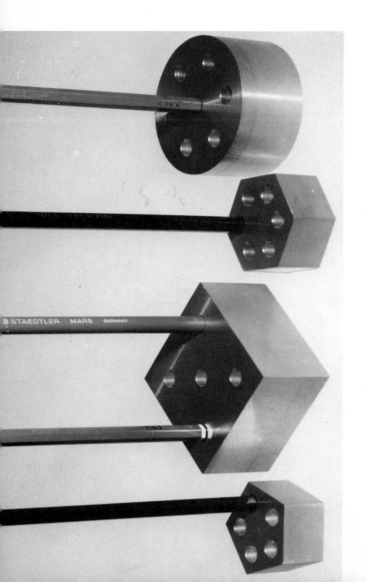

TIC-TAC-TOE GAME

Material: Aluminum and as noted.

Finish: As machined.

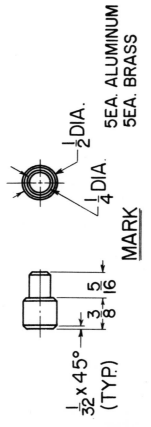

$\frac{1}{2}$ DIA.

$\frac{1}{4}$ DIA.

5EA. ALUMINUM
5EA. BRASS

MARK

$\frac{1}{32} \times 45°$
(TYP.)

$\frac{5}{16}$

$\frac{3}{8}$

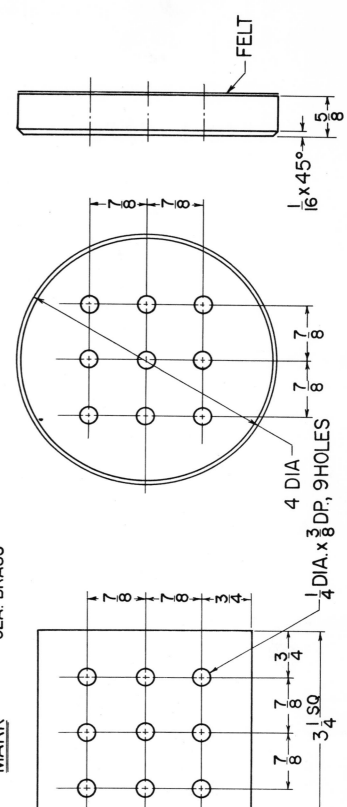

FELT

$\frac{5}{8}$

$\frac{1}{16} \times 45°$

$\frac{7}{8}$ $\frac{7}{8}$

$\frac{7}{8}$

$\frac{7}{8}$

4 DIA

$\frac{1}{4}$ DIA. x $\frac{3}{8}$ DP, 9 HOLES

$\frac{7}{8}$ $\frac{7}{8}$ $\frac{3}{4}$

$\frac{3}{4}$

$\frac{7}{8}$

$3\frac{1}{4}$ SQ

$\frac{7}{8}$

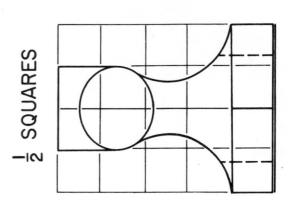

$\frac{1}{2}$ SQUARES

CAST ANVIL

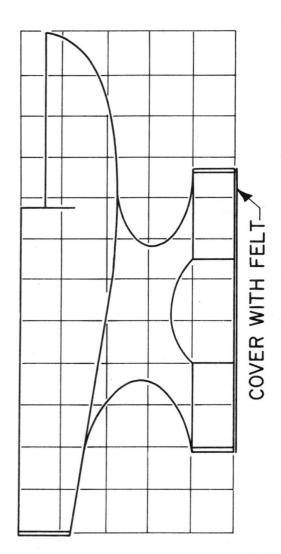

COVER WITH FELT

200

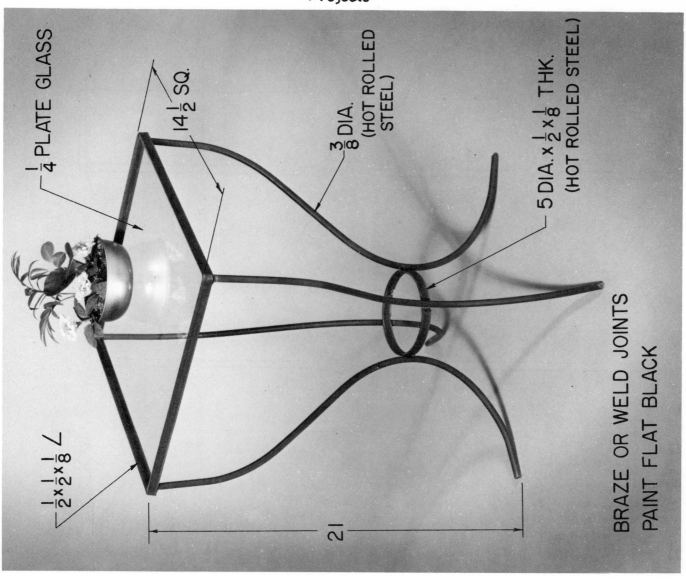

$\frac{1}{4}$ PLATE GLASS

$14\frac{1}{2}$ SQ.

$\frac{3}{8}$ DIA. (HOT ROLLED STEEL)

$\angle \frac{1}{2}\times\frac{1}{2}\times\frac{1}{8}$

21

5 DIA. x $\frac{1}{2}$ x $\frac{1}{8}$ THK. (HOT ROLLED STEEL)

BRAZE OR WELD JOINTS
PAINT FLAT BLACK

PATIO TABLE

LEG BENDING DETAILS

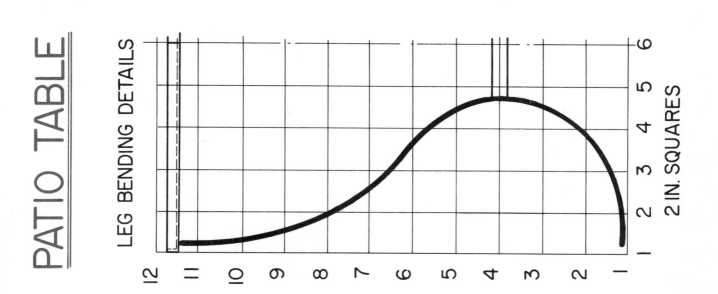

2 IN. SQUARES

MAIL BOX DESIGN PROBLEM

Design, develop the patterns and manufacture a mail box that will meet postal regulations. Get ideas and basic dimensions from mail order catalogs and home planning magazines. Use 26 ga. sheet metal in either a plain or embossed pattern. It may be made from copper, brass or aluminum. Larger mail boxes can be made from galvanized sheet steel. Join seams by spot welding or soldering.

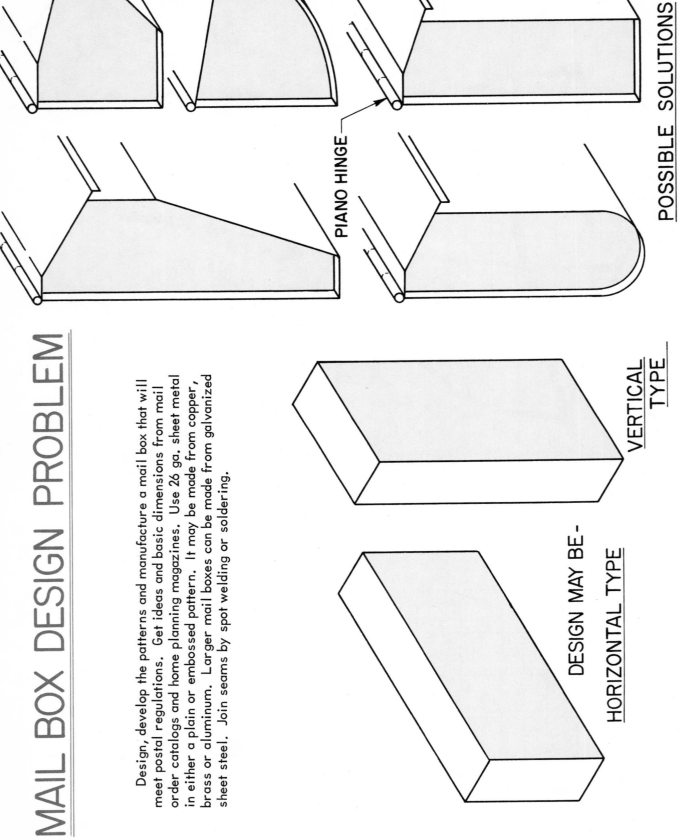

PIANO HINGE

POSSIBLE SOLUTIONS

VERTICAL TYPE

DESIGN MAY BE -
HORIZONTAL TYPE

MACHINED PAPER WEIGHT

Material: Aluminum, brass or cold finished steel.

Finish: As machined or polished.

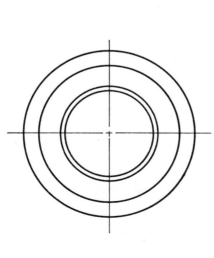

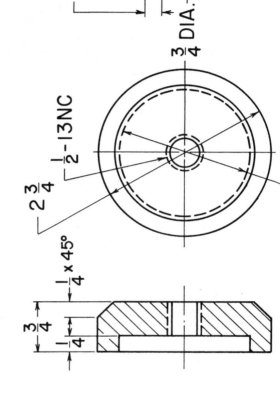

KNOB

BASE

$\frac{3}{4}$ DIA.

$\frac{1}{2}$ -13NC

$1\frac{3}{4}$

$\frac{3}{4}$

$\frac{1}{2}$

$\frac{1}{16} \times 45°$

$\frac{1}{4} \times 45°$

$1\frac{1}{4}$

$2\frac{3}{4}$

$\frac{1}{2}$ -13NC

$\frac{3}{4}$

$\frac{1}{4}$

$\frac{1}{4} \times 45°$

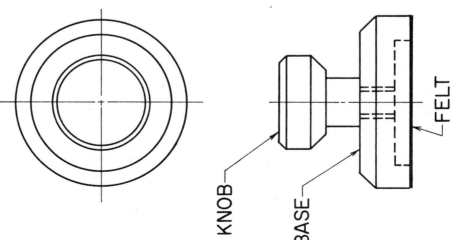

KNOB

BASE

FELT

SCOTTY TABLE LAMP

Material: 3/8 aluminum, or a pattern can be made and the figure cast as shown in photograph. The base may be made from mahogany, walnut or cherry.

Finish: Paint flat black or use a fine abrasive and apply a satin finish.

Design Problem: Provide a way to hold the light socket and shade. It may be made from 3/8 dia. brass tubing.

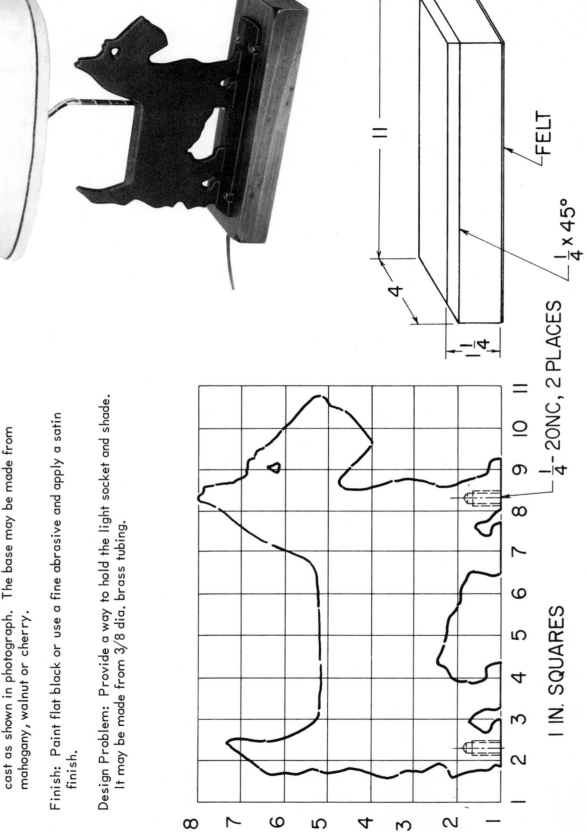

FELT

$\frac{1}{4} \times 45°$

11

4

$1\frac{1}{4}$

$\frac{1}{4}$ - 20NC, 2 PLACES

1 IN. SQUARES

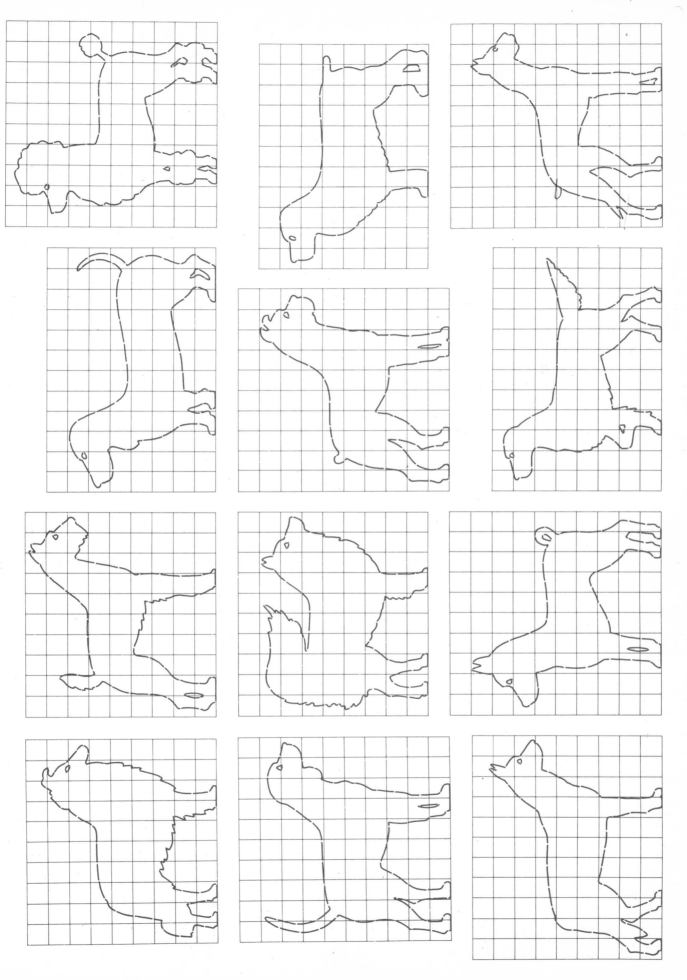

Scotty Table Lamp — Alternate design suggestions.

PENDANTS

Material: 1/8 to 1/4 in. aluminum or brass.

Finish: Buff to a high polish, or use a fine abrasive to produce a satin finish.

Prepare a full size pattern and attach it to the metal with rubber cement. Cut it out and shape and smooth the edges using conventional metalworking tools. The findings used to attach the chain may be purchased commercially.

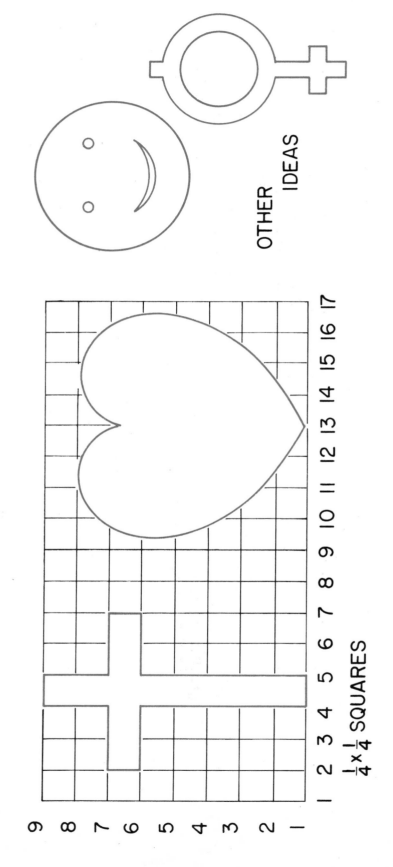

OTHER IDEAS

$\frac{1}{4} \times \frac{1}{4}$ SQUARES

HANDYMAN'S SPECIAL

1. Cold finished steel may be used. However, precision ground tool and die steel is preferred.
2. Saw and file or machine the head to shape. It is recommended that the handle slot be milled.
3. Shape the handle to the size shown. Drill holes for the handle. Fit the handle to the head and drill mounting holes.
4. Heat treat the hammer head and the screwdriver and bottle opener end of the handle. Harden and temper if tool and die steel is used. Case harden if cold finished steel is used.
5. Polish.
6. Mount the wooden handles.

TAPER TO SCREWDRIVER TIP

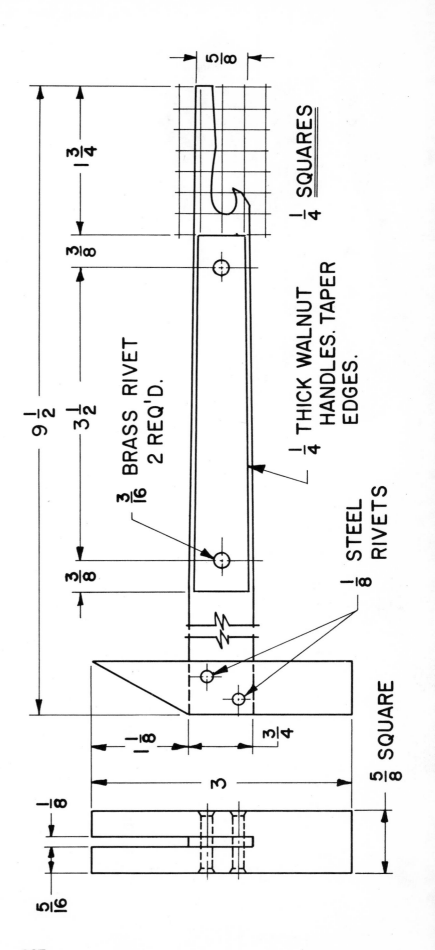

$\frac{1}{4}$ SQUARES

$\frac{1}{4}$ THICK WALNUT HANDLES. TAPER EDGES.

$\frac{3}{16}$ BRASS RIVET 2 REQ'D.

$\frac{1}{8}$ STEEL RIVETS

$1\frac{3}{4}$

$\frac{3}{8}$

$\frac{5}{8}$

$9\frac{1}{2}$

$3\frac{1}{2}$

$\frac{3}{8}$

$\frac{3}{8}$

$1\frac{1}{8}$

$\frac{3}{4}$

3

$\frac{5}{8}$ SQUARE

$\frac{1}{8}$

$\frac{5}{16}$

DESIGN PROBLEM

1. Material: 0.025 aluminum. The roof should be made of 0.025 embossed aluminum.

2. Use round head rivets and sheet metal screws for assembly.

3. Paint the outside surfaces a light green. The roof may be left natural.

4. Design a suitable mount.

5. Remove all sharp edges and burrs.

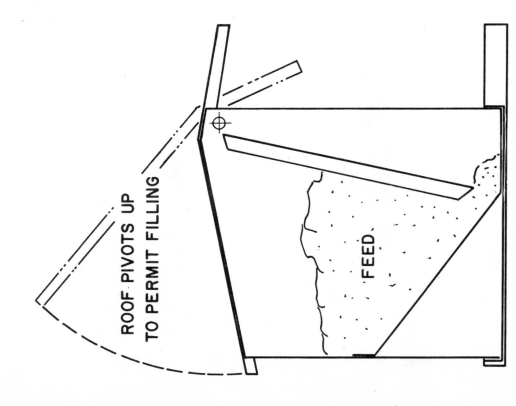

ROOF PIVOTS UP
TO PERMIT FILLING

FEED.

TYPICAL CROSS-SECTION OF BIRD
FEEDER SHOWN

TRIVET

Trivets are used to prevent hot pans and pots from scorching or damaging table tops.

1. Material: Brass or hot finished steel. Walnut handle.

2. Finish: Brass – Polished.
   Steel – Painted flat black.

3. Remove all sharp edges.

4. Smooth all brazed joints.

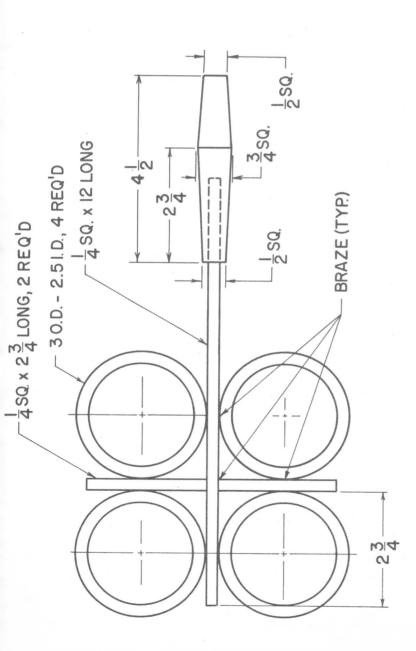

$\frac{1}{4}$ SQ. x 2$\frac{3}{4}$ LONG, 2 REQ'D

3 O.D. – 2.5 I.D., 4 REQ'D

$\frac{1}{4}$ SQ. x 12 LONG

4$\frac{1}{2}$

2$\frac{3}{4}$

$\frac{3}{4}$ SQ.

$\frac{1}{2}$ SQ.

$\frac{1}{2}$ SQ.

BRAZE (TYP.)

2$\frac{3}{4}$

7$\frac{1}{2}$

2

$\frac{5}{8}$

EPOXY HANDLE IN PLACE

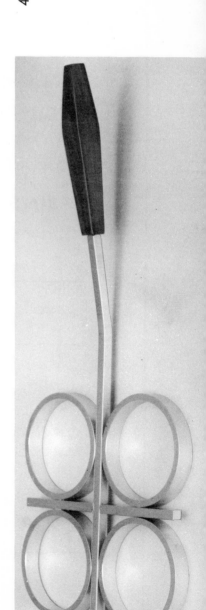

CENTER PUNCH

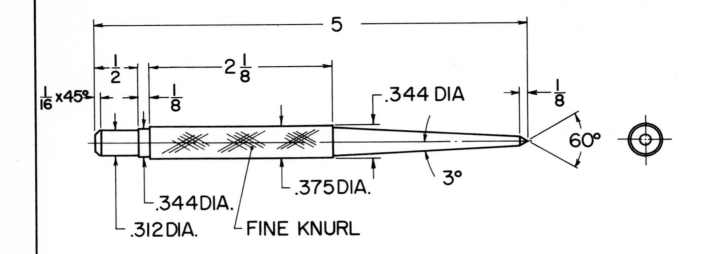

MACHINING SEQUENCE:

1. CUT A PIECE OF DRILL ROD $5\frac{1}{2}$ LONG.
   A. FACE BOTH ENDS.
   B. CENTER DRILL ONE END.

2. MACHINE CENTER DRILLED END AS FOLLOWS:

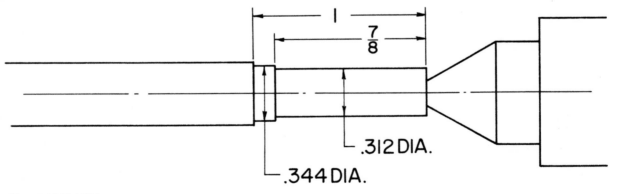

3. KNURL.

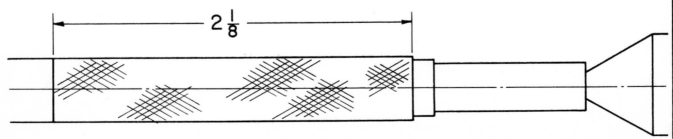

4. REVERSE WORK IN CHUCK.

5. MACHINE TO DIAMETER.

2 ¼

.344 DIA.

6. SET COMPOUND TO CUT 3° TAPER.

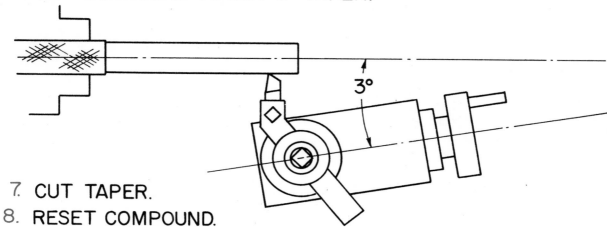

3°

7. CUT TAPER.

8. RESET COMPOUND.

9. MACHINE POINT.

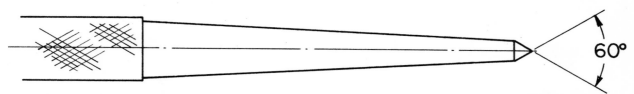

60°

10. REVERSE IN CHUCK AND FINISH MACHINE HEAD TO SIZE.

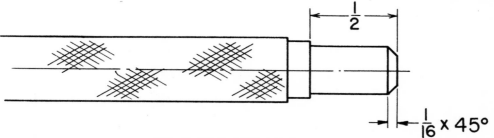

½

$\frac{1}{16}$ × 45°

11. HEAT TREAT COMPLETED PUNCH.

DESIGN PROBLEM

Material: As noted on photo.

Finish: Paint metal figure flat black.

This is a project that can be used as a gift for your father, or a favorite friend who is a golf enthusiast.

Using a little "think power" you can come up with a variation of the spike man that can be used to depict another sport or occupation.

Be careful to remove all burrs and rough edges before applying the finish.

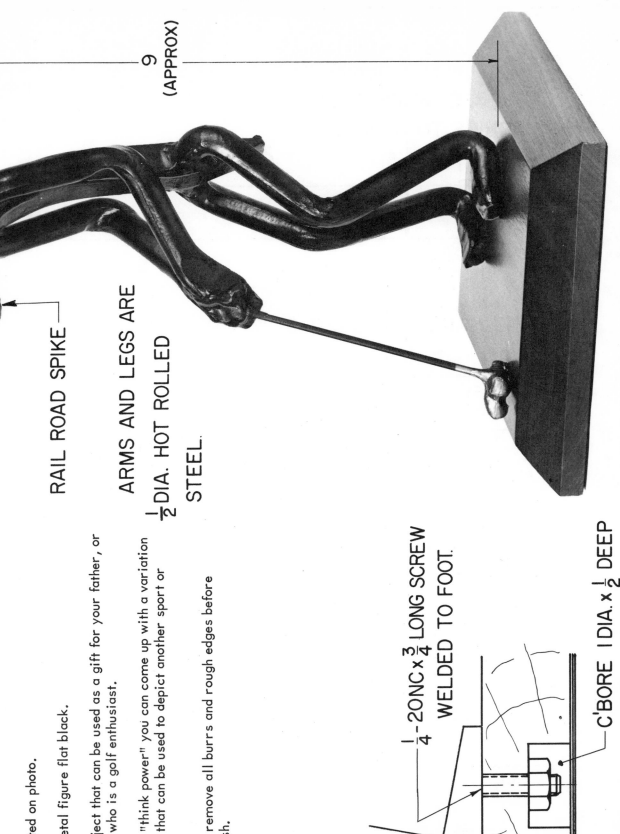

9
(APPROX)

RAIL ROAD SPIKE

ARMS AND LEGS ARE
$\frac{1}{2}$ DIA. HOT ROLLED
STEEL.

$\frac{1}{4}$ – 20NC x $\frac{3}{4}$ LONG SCREW
WELDED TO FOOT.

C'BORE 1 DIA. x $\frac{1}{2}$ DEEP

FELT

RAISED BOWL

1. Material: 14 ga. copper, brass, pewter or aluminum.

2. Finish: Planish all surfaces and buff all exterior surfaces. Apply a satin finish to the interior of the bowl.

3. Solder base to bowl body.

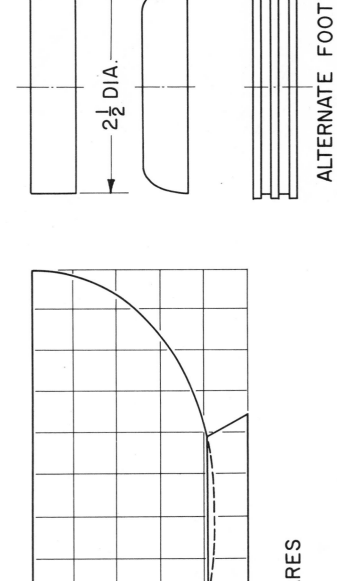

$2\frac{1}{2}$ DIA.

ALTERNATE FOOT DESIGNS

1 IN. OR $\frac{1}{2}$ IN. SQUARES

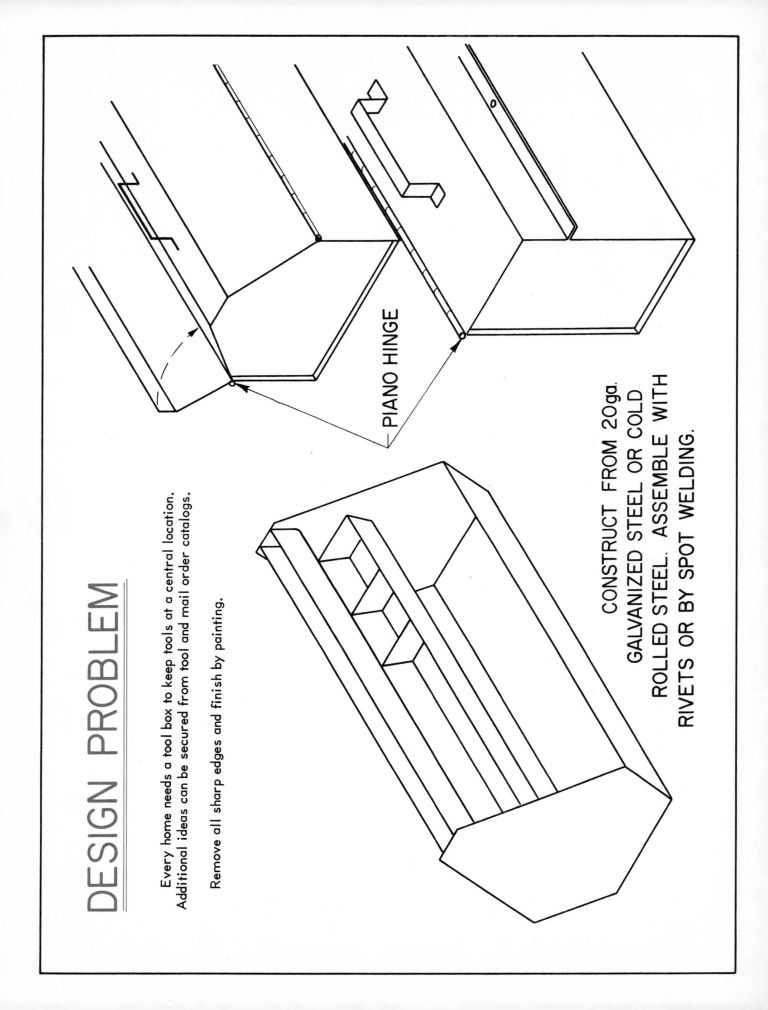

DESIGN PROBLEM

Every home needs a tool box to keep tools at a central location. Additional ideas can be secured from tool and mail order catalogs.

Remove all sharp edges and finish by painting.

PIANO HINGE

CONSTRUCT FROM 20ga. GALVANIZED STEEL OR COLD ROLLED STEEL. ASSEMBLE WITH RIVETS OR BY SPOT WELDING.

CANDLE HOLDER

Material: Cast aluminum.

Finish: Polished or satin finish.

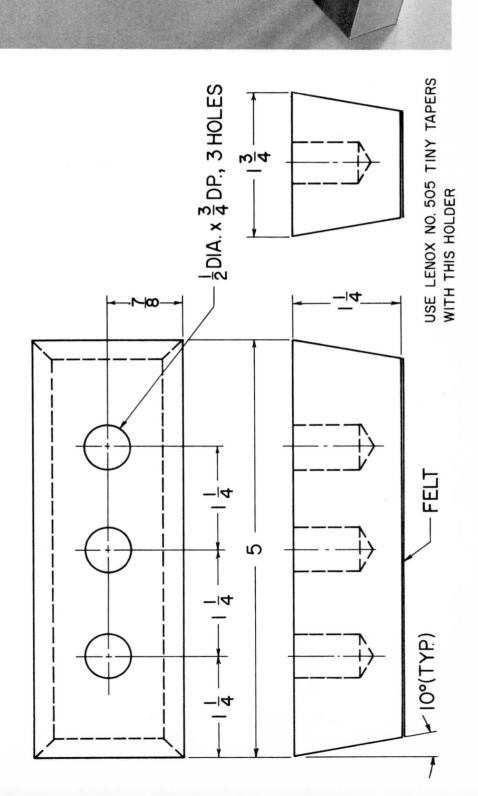

$\frac{1}{2}$ DIA. x $\frac{3}{4}$ DP., 3 HOLES

$1\frac{3}{4}$

$\frac{7}{8}$

$1\frac{1}{4}$

$1\frac{1}{4}$

$1\frac{1}{4}$

5

$1\frac{1}{4}$

FELT

10°(TYP.)

USE LENOX NO. 505 TINY TAPERS WITH THIS HOLDER.

NAPKIN RINGS

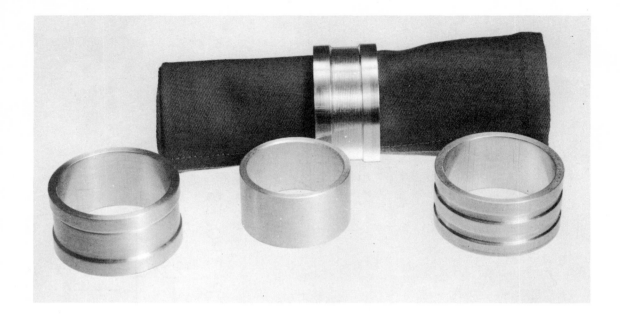

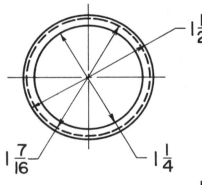

$1\frac{1}{2}$

$1\frac{7}{16}$ $1\frac{1}{4}$

1. Material: Aluminum or brass.

2. Finish: As machined, polished or satin finish.
   Brass may be silver plated.

3. Remove all sharp edges and burrs.

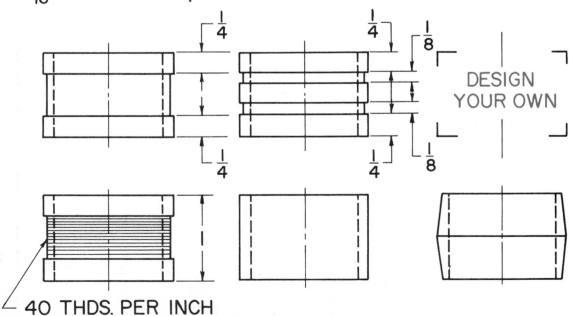

$\frac{1}{4}$ $\frac{1}{4}$ $\frac{1}{8}$

DESIGN
YOUR OWN

$\frac{1}{4}$ $\frac{1}{4}$ $\frac{1}{8}$

40 THDS. PER INCH

CHOW TIME CHIME

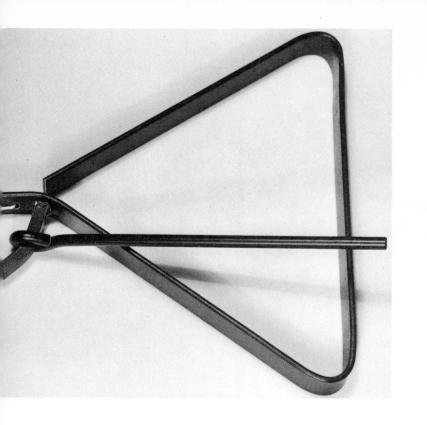

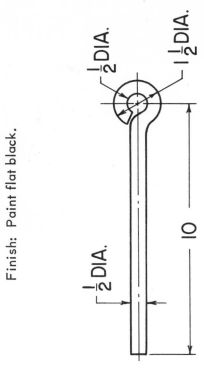

Material: Hot finished mild steel.

Finish: Paint flat black.

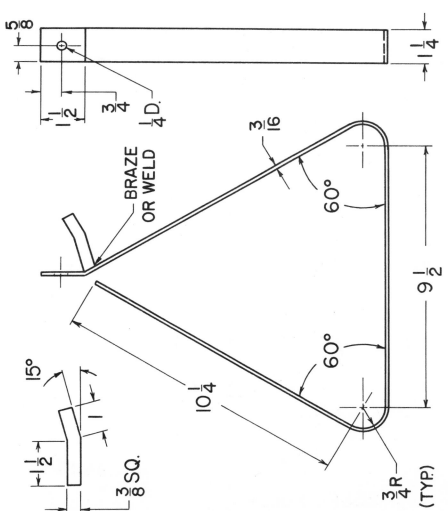

BRAZE OR WELD

$\frac{3}{16}$

60°

60°

$9\frac{1}{2}$

$10\frac{1}{4}$

$\frac{3}{4}$R (TYP.)

$\frac{5}{8}$

$1\frac{1}{4}$

$\frac{1}{2}$

$\frac{3}{4}$

$\frac{1}{4}$D.

15°

1

$1\frac{1}{2}$

$\frac{3}{8}$SQ.

$\frac{1}{2}$DIA.

$1\frac{1}{2}$DIA.

$\frac{1}{2}$DIA.

10

DRAWER PULL

Material: Aluminum.

Finish: Buff to a high polish or use fine abrasive paper for a satin finish.

This project provides a real challenge for the student who likes to operate the metal lathe. It is recommended that the student practice on hard wood before using the more expensive aluminum.

A full size template will make the job easier.

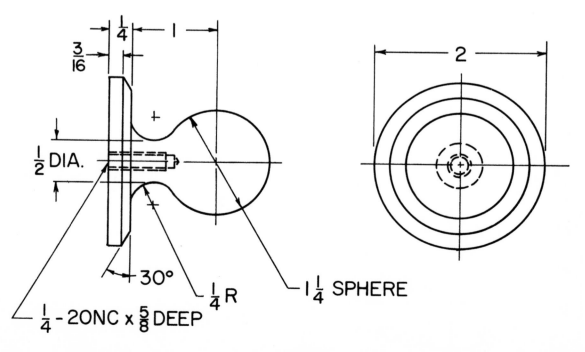

$\frac{3}{16}$
$\frac{1}{4}$ 1
$\frac{1}{2}$ DIA.
30°
$\frac{1}{4}$ R
$1\frac{1}{4}$ SPHERE
$\frac{1}{4}$ - 20NC x $\frac{5}{8}$ DEEP
2

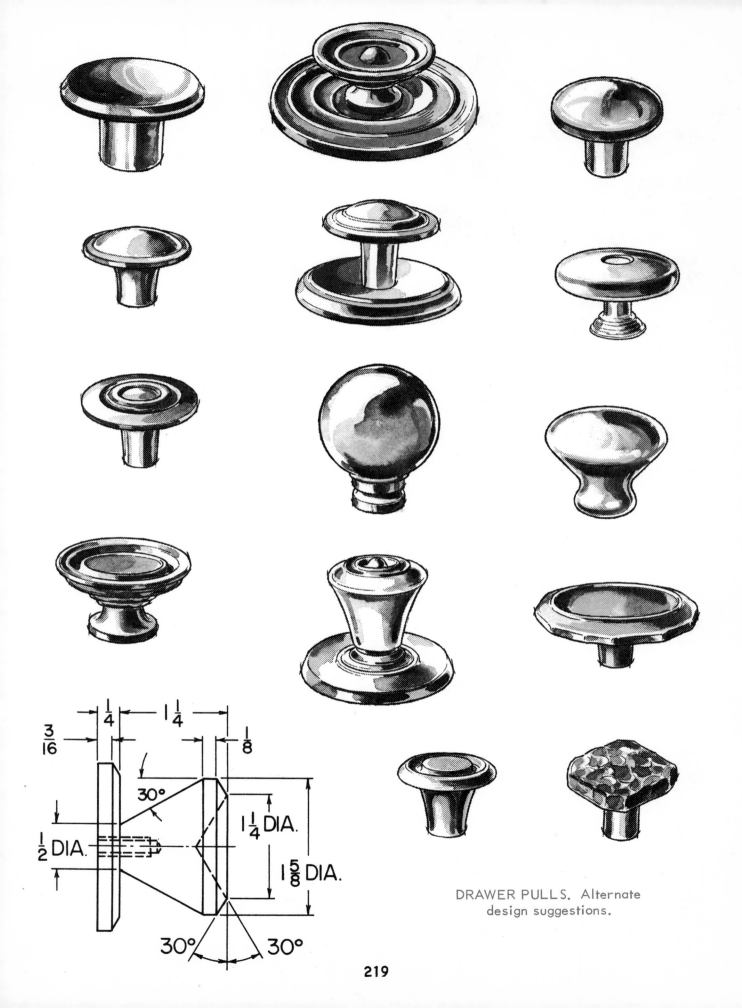

DRAWER PULLS. Alternate
design suggestions.

METAL STRIP SCULPTURE

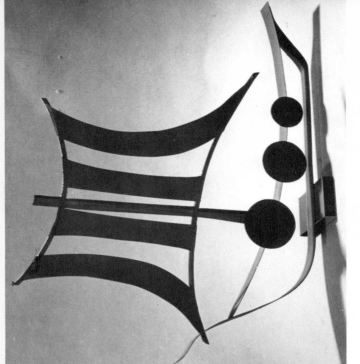

This is a project on which you can really use your imagination. The project illustrated is presented only as a project suggestion.

Metal sculptures may be made of brass, copper or tin plate. Assemble with solder.

Finish by polishing, painting or electroplating.

Remove all burrs and sharp edges and wash away all flux used in soldering.

I IN. SQUARES

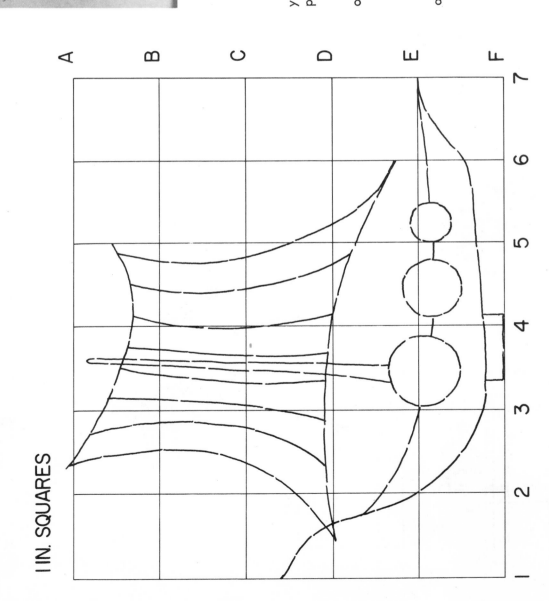

DESIGN PROBLEM

Material: Horseshoe nails and scrap metal.

Finish: Spray paint silver or gold.

These novel figures make fine gifts. Think of the many types of work and play figures you can design — ball players, golfers, swimmers, musicians, etc.

The horseshoe nails are held together by brazing, soldering or epoxy adhesives. Be sure the work is clean before trying to join the parts together and to paint them.

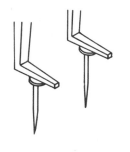

Braze or solder small nails to feet.

$5\frac{1}{2}$

$\frac{1}{2}$ x 2 x 2 HARD WOOD

MODERN GAVEL

Material: Aluminum.

Finish: As machined.

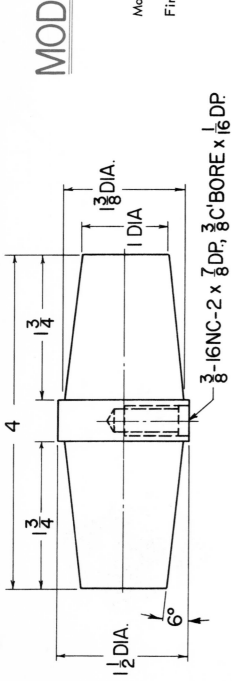

$1\frac{3}{8}$ DIA.

1 DIA

$1\frac{3}{4}$

$1\frac{3}{4}$

4

$1\frac{3}{4}$

6°

$\frac{1}{2}$ DIA.

$\frac{3}{8}$-16NC-2 x $\frac{7}{8}$ DP., $\frac{3}{8}$ C'BORE x $\frac{1}{16}$ DP.

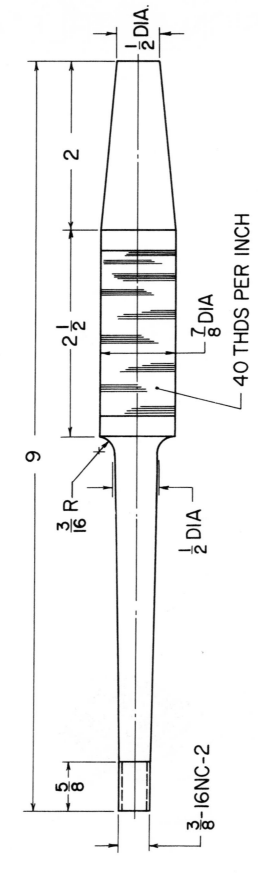

$\frac{1}{2}$ DIA.

2

$2\frac{1}{2}$

$\frac{7}{8}$ DIA

40 THDS PER INCH

9

$\frac{3}{16}$ R

$\frac{1}{2}$ DIA

$\frac{5}{8}$

$\frac{3}{8}$-16NC-2

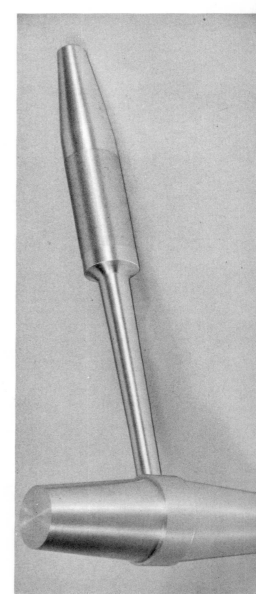

PLAQUE IDEAS

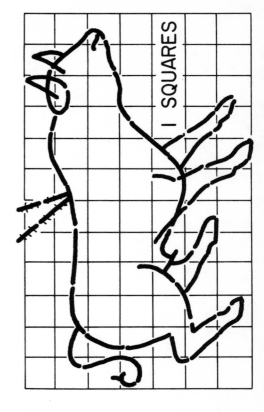

I SQUARES

WIRE WALL PLAQUE

1. Use 1/8 in. diameter wire to form the figures. It may be copper wire, brazing rod or steel coat hangers.

2. Solder all joints.

3. Finish by painting flat black.

BOOK ENDS

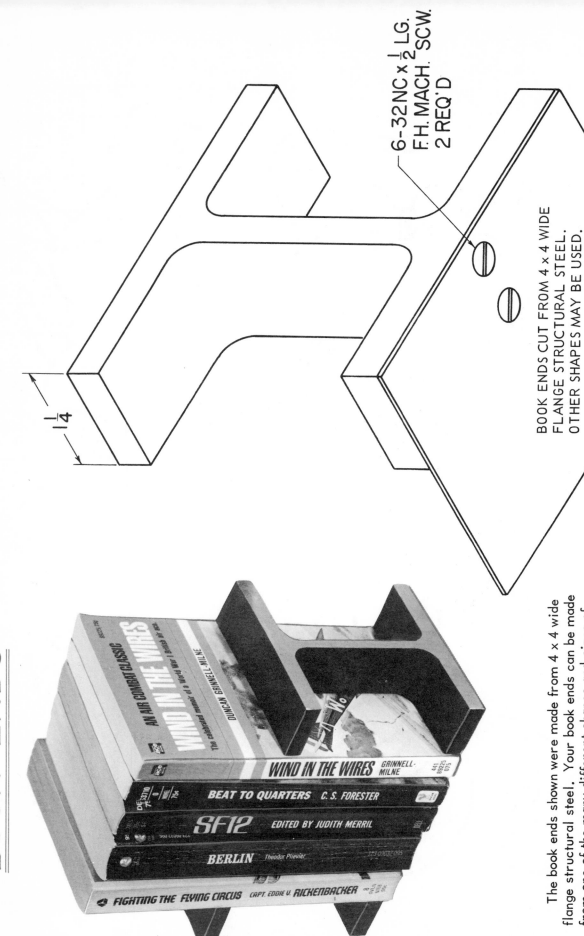

$1\frac{1}{4}$

6-32NC x $\frac{1}{2}$ LG.
F.H. MACH. SCW.
2 REQ'D

BOOK ENDS CUT FROM 4 x 4 WIDE
FLANGE STRUCTURAL STEEL.
OTHER SHAPES MAY BE USED.

The book ends shown were made from 4 x 4 wide flange structural steel. Your book ends can be made from one of the many different shapes and sizes of structural steel and aluminum extrusions available.

Finish by removing all sharp edges and painting with colors of your choice.

BRACELET

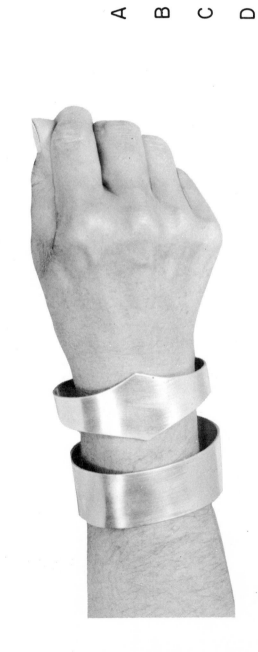

Material: 16 or 18 gauge brass, aluminum, sterling silver or nickel silver.

Finish: Buff to a high polish.

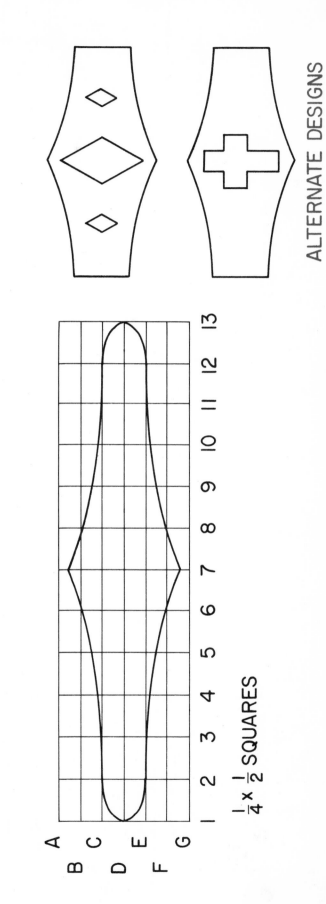

$\frac{3}{4}$ SQUARES

ALTERNATE DESIGNS

$\frac{1}{4} \times \frac{1}{2}$ SQUARES

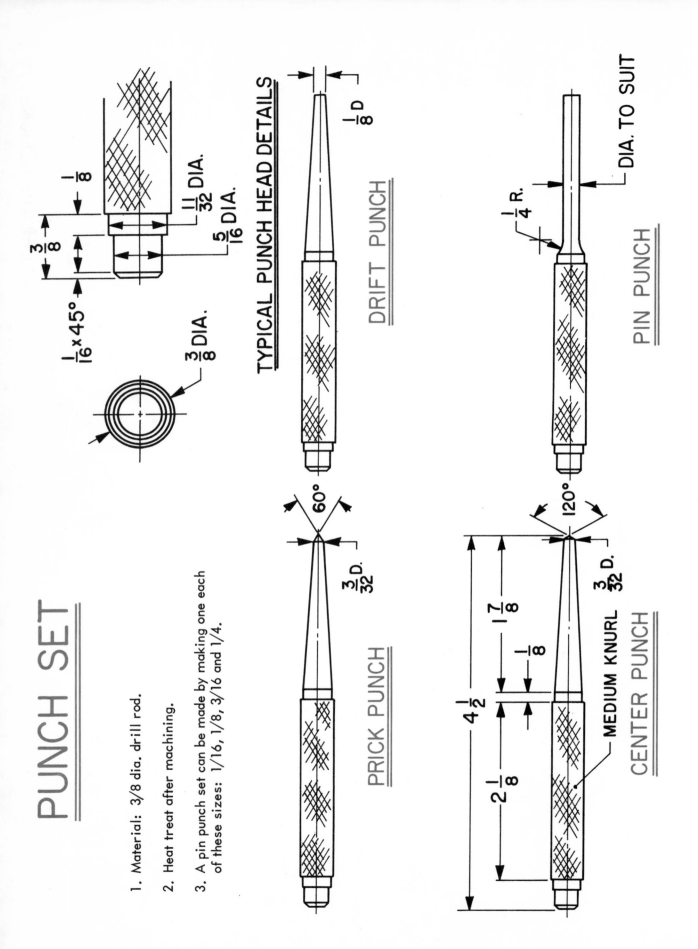

PUNCH SET

1. Material: 3/8 dia. drill rod.

2. Heat treat after machining.

3. A pin punch set can be made by making one each of these sizes: 1/16, 1/8, 3/16 and 1/4.

$\frac{1}{16}$ × 45°

$\frac{3}{8}$

$\frac{1}{8}$

$\frac{11}{32}$ DIA.

$\frac{5}{16}$ DIA.

$\frac{3}{8}$ DIA.

TYPICAL PUNCH HEAD DETAILS

$\frac{1}{8}$ D

DRIFT PUNCH

60°

$\frac{3}{32}$ D.

PRICK PUNCH

$\frac{1}{4}$ R.

DIA. TO SUIT

PIN PUNCH

120°

$\frac{3}{32}$ D.

MEDIUM KNURL

CENTER PUNCH

$4\frac{1}{2}$

$1\frac{7}{8}$

$\frac{1}{8}$

$2\frac{1}{8}$

226

CAST PLAQUE

1. Material: Aluminum or brass.

2. Plaques may be designed to serve as awards by mounting the casting on backing boards.

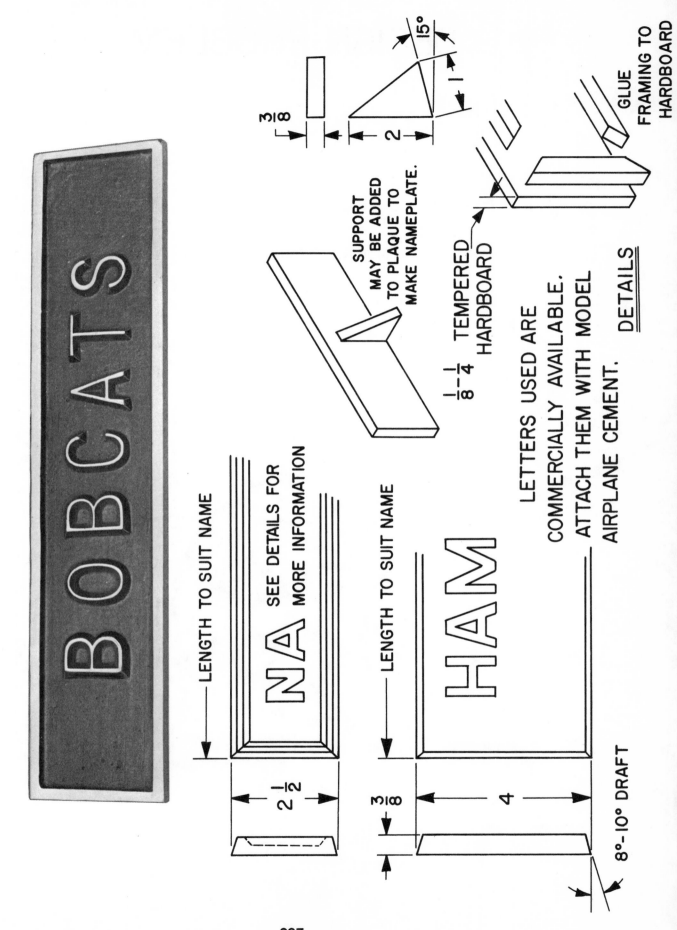

SUPPORT MAY BE ADDED TO PLAQUE TO MAKE NAMEPLATE.

$1-\frac{1}{4}$ TEMPERED HARDBOARD

LETTERS USED ARE COMMERCIALLY AVAILABLE. ATTACH THEM WITH MODEL AIRPLANE CEMENT.

GLUE FRAMING TO HARDBOARD

DETAILS

$\frac{3}{8}$

$\frac{1}{8}$

2

15°

LENGTH TO SUIT NAME

NA SEE DETAILS FOR MORE INFORMATION

$2\frac{1}{2}$

LENGTH TO SUIT NAME

HAM

$\frac{3}{8}$

4

8° - 10° DRAFT

DESIGN PROBLEM

Design a magazine rack using the project shown as a starting point.

This is of Spanish motif which fits in with most room settings and furniture styles.

The dimensions given are approximate but will help you design a rack of suitable size.

Weld or braze all joints. Remove burrs and rough edges before painting.

Small pieces of felt cemented on the bottoms of the feet will prevent rust spots.

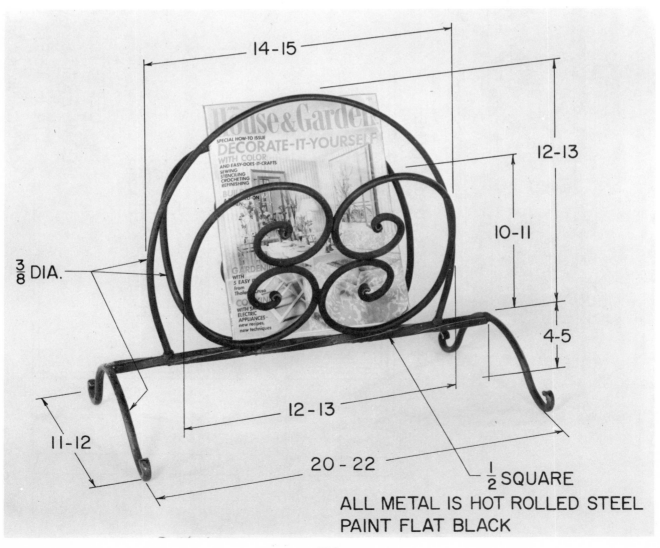

ALL METAL IS HOT ROLLED STEEL
PAINT FLAT BLACK

METAL SCULPTURE

1. Material: Figure – Aluminum or brass.
   Base – Walnut or cherry.

2. The project can be used as a trophy if an appropriate figure is selected. Ideas are available everywhere – the Cougar, Impala, Road Runner, Fire Bird, etc.

3. Use epoxy in figure and base.

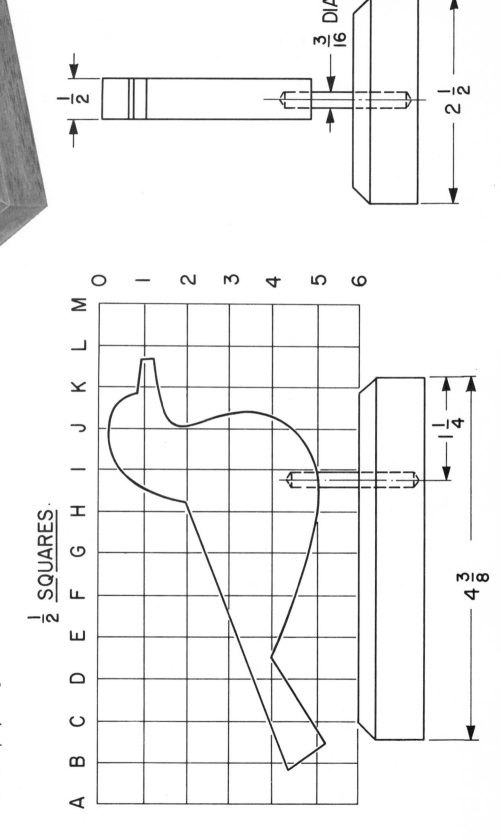

$\frac{1}{2}$ SQUARES.

229

BOTTLE OPENER

Material: 1/8 – 3/16 hard brass or mild steel.

Finish: Polish.

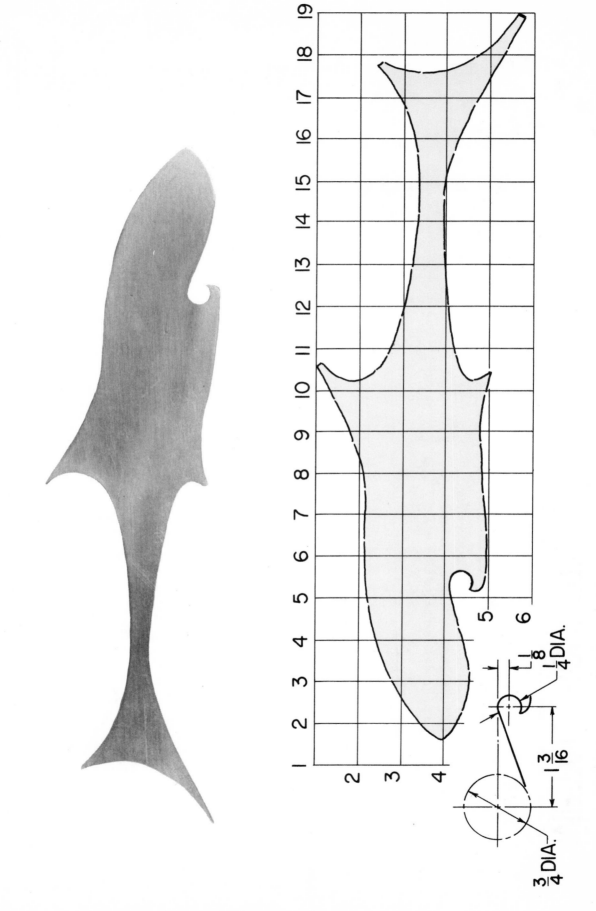

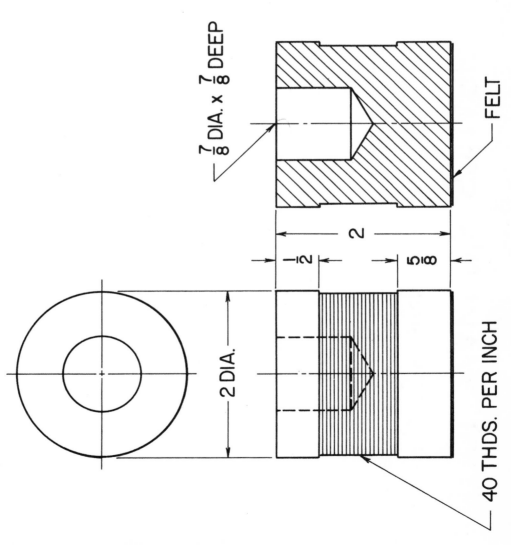

CONTEMPORARY CANDLE HOLDER

1. Material: Aluminum or brass.

2. Finish: As machined.

3. Attach felt to base.

$\frac{7}{8}$ DIA. x $\frac{7}{8}$ DEEP

FELT

2

$\frac{1}{2}$

$\frac{5}{8}$

2 DIA.

40 THDS. PER INCH

TOOL MAKER'S SQUARE

(WITH N/C PROGRAM FOR MACHINING $\frac{1}{16}$ GRADUATIONS ON THE RULE.)

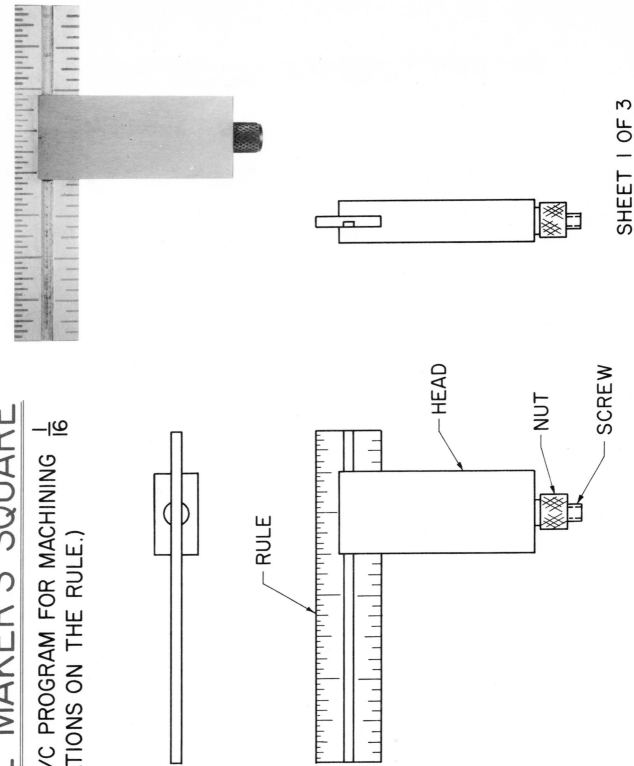

RULE

HEAD

NUT

SCREW

TOOL MAKER'S SQUARE

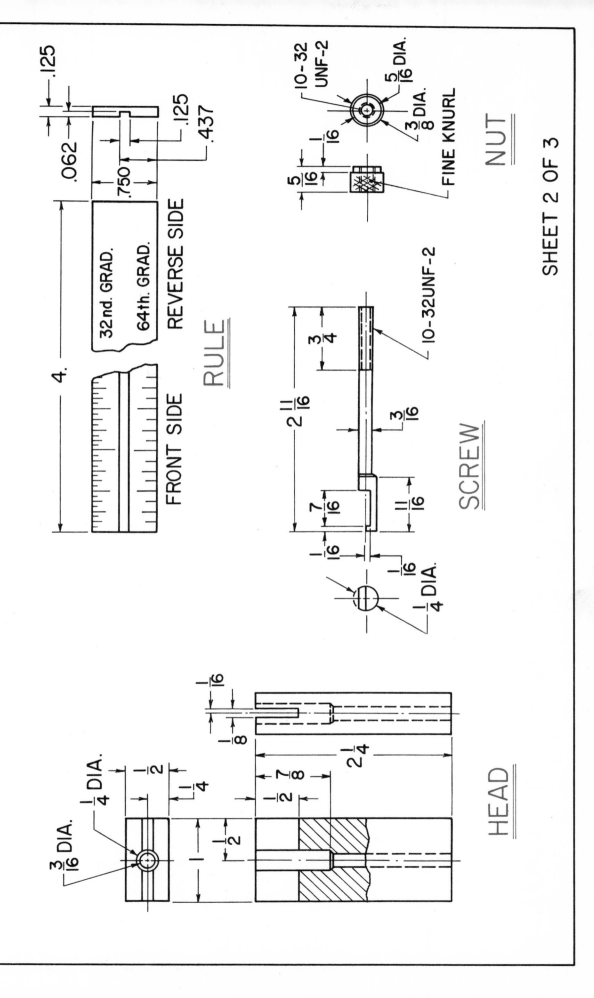

RULE

FRONT SIDE

REVERSE SIDE

32nd. GRAD.

64th. GRAD.

.125

.125

.062

.437

.750

4.

NUT

10-32 UNF-2

5/16 DIA.

3/8 DIA.

FINE KNURL

1/16

5/16

SCREW

10-32UNF-2

3/4

2 11/16

3/16

7/16

11/16

1/16

1/16

1/4 DIA.

HEAD

1/16

1/8

2 1/4

2 7/8

2 1/2

1/2

1/2

1

1/2

1 1/4

3/16 DIA.

1/4 DIA.

Drawing dimensions: .312, .062, .125, .187, .250 — "1"

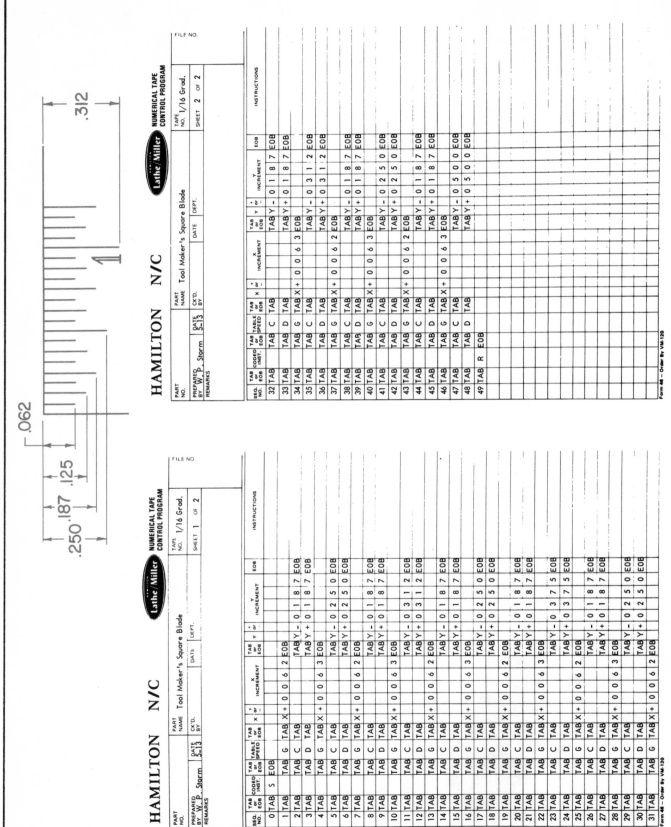

HAMILTON N/C Lathe/Miller — NUMERICAL TAPE CONTROL PROGRAM

PART NAME: Tool Maker's Square Blade
PREPARED BY W. P. Storm **DATE** 5-13
TAPE NO. 1/16 Grad. **SHEET 1 OF 2**
FILE NO.
REMARKS

SEQ. NO.	TAB or EOB	CODED INST.	TAB or EOB	TABLE SPEED	TAB or EOB	+ or − X	X INCREMENT	TAB or Y EOB	+ or − Y	Y INCREMENT	EOB	INSTRUCTIONS
0	TAB	S	EOB									
1	TAB	G	TAB		TAB	X+	0 0 6	2 EOB				
2	TAB	C	TAB					TAB Y−		0 1	8 7	EOB
3	TAB	D	TAB					TAB Y+		0 1	8 7	EOB
4	TAB	G	TAB		TAB	X+	0 0 6	3 EOB				
5	TAB	C	TAB					TAB Y−		0 2	5 0	EOB
6	TAB	D	TAB					TAB Y+		0 2	5 0	EOB
7	TAB	G	TAB		TAB	X+	0 0 6	2 EOB				
8	TAB	C	TAB					TAB Y−		0 1	8 7	EOB
9	TAB	D	TAB					TAB Y+		0 1	8 7	EOB
10	TAB	G	TAB		TAB	X+	0 0 6	3 EOB				
11	TAB	C	TAB					TAB Y−		0 3	1 2	EOB
12	TAB	D	TAB					TAB Y+		0 3	1 2	EOB
13	TAB	G	TAB		TAB	X+	0 0 6	2 EOB				
14	TAB	C	TAB					TAB Y−		0 1	8 7	EOB
15	TAB	D	TAB					TAB Y+		0 1	8 7	EOB
16	TAB	G	TAB		TAB	X+	0 0 6	3 EOB				
17	TAB	C	TAB					TAB Y−		0 2	5 0	EOB
18	TAB	D	TAB					TAB Y+		0 2	5 0	EOB
19	TAB	G	TAB		TAB	X+	0 0 6	2 EOB				
20	TAB	C	TAB					TAB Y−		0 1	8 7	EOB
21	TAB	D	TAB					TAB Y+		0 1	8 7	EOB
22	TAB	G	TAB		TAB	X+	0 0 6	3 EOB				
23	TAB	C	TAB					TAB Y−		0 3	7 5	EOB
24	TAB	D	TAB					TAB Y+		0 3	7 5	EOB
25	TAB	G	TAB		TAB	X+	0 0 6	2 EOB				
26	TAB	C	TAB					TAB Y−		0 1	8 7	EOB
27	TAB	D	TAB					TAB Y+		0 1	8 7	EOB
28	TAB	G	TAB		TAB	X+	0 0 6	3 EOB				
29	TAB	C	TAB					TAB Y−		0 2	5 0	EOB
30	TAB	D	TAB					TAB Y+		0 2	5 0	EOB
31	TAB	G	TAB		TAB	X+	0 0 6	2 EOB				

Form 46 — Order By VM-120

HAMILTON N/C Lathe/Miller — NUMERICAL TAPE CONTROL PROGRAM

PART NAME: Tool Maker's Square Blade
PREPARED BY W. P. Storm **DATE** 5-13
TAPE NO. 1/16 Grad. **SHEET 2 OF 2**
FILE NO.
REMARKS

SEQ. NO.	TAB or EOB	CODED INST.	TAB or EOB	TABLE SPEED	TAB or EOB	+ or − X	X INCREMENT	TAB or Y EOB	+ or − Y	Y INCREMENT	EOB	INSTRUCTIONS
32	TAB	C	TAB					TAB Y−		0 1	8 7	EOB
33	TAB	D	TAB					TAB Y+		0 1	8 7	EOB
34	TAB	G	TAB		TAB	X+	0 0 6	3 EOB				
35	TAB	C	TAB					TAB Y−		0 3	1 2	EOB
36	TAB	D	TAB					TAB Y+		0 3	1 2	EOB
37	TAB	G	TAB		TAB	X+	0 0 6	2 EOB				
38	TAB	C	TAB					TAB Y−		0 1	8 7	EOB
39	TAB	D	TAB					TAB Y+		0 1	8 7	EOB
40	TAB	G	TAB		TAB	X+	0 0 6	3 EOB				
41	TAB	C	TAB					TAB Y−		0 2	5 0	EOB
42	TAB	D	TAB					TAB Y+		0 2	5 0	EOB
43	TAB	G	TAB		TAB	X+	0 0 6	2 EOB				
44	TAB	C	TAB					TAB Y−		0 1	8 7	EOB
45	TAB	D	TAB					TAB Y+		0 1	8 7	EOB
46	TAB	G	TAB		TAB	X+	0 0 6	3 EOB				
47	TAB	C	TAB					TAB Y−		0 5	0 0	EOB
48	TAB	D	TAB					TAB Y+		0 5	0 0	EOB
49	TAB	R	EOB									

Form 46 — Order By VM-120

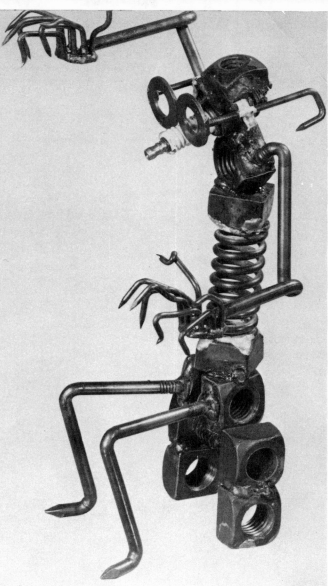

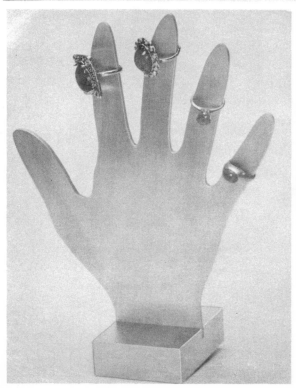

DESIGN PROBLEMS: Above, left. Metal sculptured table lamp.
Right. Welded "monster." Below, left. Finger ring stand. Right.
Quotation mark (metal casting) book ends.

235

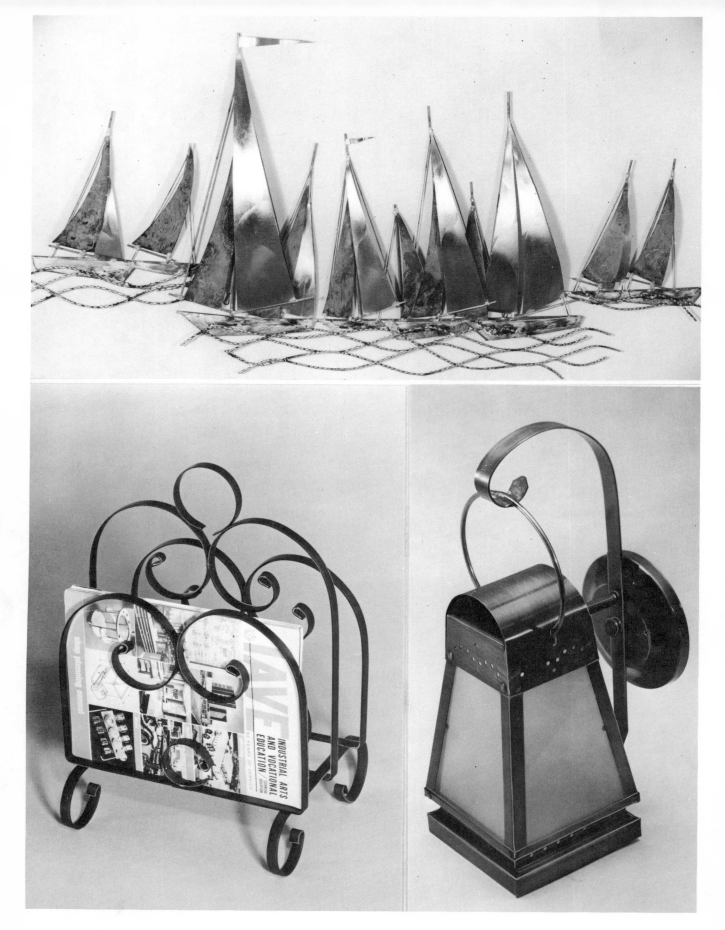

DESIGN PROBLEMS: Above. Wall sculpture, sail-
boat design. Below, left. Magazine rack with scroll.
Right. Porch lantern.

GLOSSARY

ABRASIVE: A material that cuts a material softer than itself.

ACUTE ANGLE: An angle that is less than 90 deg.

ALIGN: Adjusting to given points.

ALLOWANCE: How much larger or smaller a machined surface may be and still have the part work satisfactorily.

ALLOY: A mixture of two or more metals fused or melted together.

ALUMINUM OXIDE: A man-made abrasive. It has largely replaced emery as an abrasive when large quantities of metal must be removed.

ANNEALING: The process of heating metal to a given temperature (the exact temperature and the period of time the tempera- is held depends on the metal) and allowing it to cool slowly to induce softness.

ANNODIZING: A surface finish for aluminum that protects it against corrosion. The process also permits the surface to be dyed a variety of colors.

ANVIL: A block of iron or steel upon which metal is forged.

ASSEMBLY: A unit fitted together from man-ufactured parts.

ASSEMBLY DRAWING: A drawing that shows the machinist how to assemble an object. The component parts in the drawing are usually key-numbered.

AUTOMATION: An industrial technique that substitutes mechanical labor and mechani-cal control for human labor and human con-trol.

AXIS: A center line that passes through an object about which it could rotate. It may also be used as a point of reference.

BERYLLIUM: A metal that weighs about one fourth as much as steel, yet is almost as strong. It is an "exotic metal" and is used extensively in rockets and aircraft where weight is critical, also in nuclear reactors.

BEVEL: An angle that is not at right angles to another line or surface.

BLOWHOLE: A hole produced in a casting when gases are trapped during the pouring operation.

BRASS: An alloy of copper and zinc. It is bright yellow in color.

BRAZING: A process for joining metals by the fusion of nonferrous alloys that have melting temperatures above 800 deg. F. but lower than the metals joined.

BRINELL: A term used to designate the hardness of a piece of metal.

BRITTLENESS: Characteristics that cause a material to break easily.

BRONZE: An alloy of copper and tin. It is reddish-gold in color.

BUFFING: The technique of bringing out the luster of metal. Polishing.

BURR: The sharp edge remaining on the metal after cutting or machining.

BUSHING: A bearing or a guide for a cutting tool in a fixture.

CARBON STEEL: Steel in which the physical and mechanical properties depend primarily on the carbon content of the metal.

CASE HARDENING: A process of surface hardening iron-base metals so the surface layer or "case" of the metal is made hard-er than the interior or core.

CASTING: An object made by pouring molten metal into a mold.

CENTER, DEAD: A stationary or non-rotating center.

CENTER, LIVE: A rotating center.

237

CHAMFER: To bevel a sharp external edge.

CHASING THREADS: Cutting threads on a lathe.

CHATTER: Vibrations caused by the cutting tool springing away from the work. This produces small ridges on the machine surface.

CHIP: To cut with a chisel.

CHUCK: A device on a machine tool which holds work or cutting tools.

CLEARANCE: The distance by which one part clears another part.

CLOCKWISE: From left to right in a circular motion. The direction clock hands move.

COINING: A metalworking technique that impresses the image or characters that are on a die and punch onto a plain metal surface.

COLOR CODING: A method used to identify steel. Each type of commonly used steel is identified by a different color.

COLOR TEMPER: Using the color range steel passes through when heated to determine the proper degree of hardness.

CONCAVE SURFACE: A curved depression in the surface of an object.

CONCENTRIC: Having a common center.

CONTOUR: The outline of an object or figure; particularly curved or irregular outline.

CONVENTIONAL: Not original; customary, or traditional.

CONVEX SURFACE: Rounded surface raised on an object.

COOLANT: A fluid or gas used to cool the cutting edge of a tool to prevent it from burning up during the machining operation.

COPPER: A base metal that is reddish brown in color.

CORE: A body of sand or other material that is formed to the desired shape and placed in a mold to produce a cavity or opening in a casting.

COUNTERBORE: Enlarging a hole to a given depth and diameter.

COUNTERCLOCKWISE: From right to left in a circular motion. The opposite direction clock hands move.

COUNTERSINK: Chamfering a hole to receive a flat-head screw.

CUTTING FLUID: A liquid used to cool and lubricate a cutting tool and to remove chips.

DIE: A tool used to cut external threads. Also, a tool used to impart a desired shape to a piece of metal.

DIE CASTING: A method of casting metal under pressure by injecting it into the metal dies of a die casting machine.

DIVIDING HEAD: An attachment for machine tools that is used to accurately space holes, slots, gear teeth and flutes on round metal stock.

DOG, LATHE: A device for clamping work so that it can be machined between centers.

DRAFT: The clearance on a pattern that allows easy withdrawal of the pattern from the mold.

DRIFT: A tapered piece of flat steel used to separate tapered shank tools (like drills) from sleeves, sockets and machine spindles.

DRILLING: Cutting round holes by use of a cutting tool with a sharpened point.

DRILL ROD: A carbon steel rod accurately and smoothly ground to size. Available in a large range of sizes.

DROP FORGING: Shaping metal by heating and hammering it into impressions in dies.

ECCENTRIC: Not on a common center. A device that converts rotary motion into a reciprocating (back and forth) motion.

ECM: Abbreviation for the metal removal process, Electro Chemical Machining.

EDM: Abbreviation for the metal removal process, Electrical Discharge Machining.

EMERY: A natural (not man-made) abrasive for grinding and polishing.

EMERY CLOTH: Cloth with emery abrasive cemented to its surface. Used to clean and polish metal.

EXTRUDE: To force metal through a die to produce a desired shape.

EZY-OUT: A tool used to remove broken bolts and studs from tapped holes. It is made in several sizes.

FACE: To make a flat surface by machining.

FACEPLATE: A circular plate that fits on to the headstock spindle and drives or carries work to be machined.

FERROUS: Denotes a family of metals in which iron is major ingredient.

FILLET: The curved surface that connects two intersecting surfaces that form an angle.

FIXTURE: A device used to hold metal while

it is being machined.

FLASK: A wooden or metal form consisting of a cope (the top portion) and a drag (the bottom portion) used to hold the sand that forms the mold in metal casting.

FLUTE: A groove machined in a cutting tool to help in the removal of chips. Permits coolant to reach the cutting point of the tool.

FLUX: Chemicals used in soldering, brazing and welding to prevent oxidation and promote better fusion of the metals.

FORGE: To form metal with heat and/or pressure.

GATE: The point where molten metal enters the mold cavity.

GALVANIZE: To coat steel with zinc.

GAUGE: A tool used for checking the size of metal parts.

GEARS: Toothed wheels that are employed to transmit rotary motion from one shaft to another shaft without slippage.

GREEN SAND: Foundry sand moistened with water.

HARDENING: The process whereby certain iron-base alloys are heated and quenched (cooled) to produce a hardness superior to that of the untreated metal.

HEAT TREATMENT: The careful application of a combination of heating and cooling cycles to a metal or an alloy in the solid state to bring about certain desirable conditions such as hardness and toughness.

HERF: Abbreviation for the metal forming process High Energy Rate Forming.

I.D.: Abbreviation for inside diameter.

INDEPENDENT CHUCK: A chuck in which each jaw can be moved independently of the other jaws.

INSPECTION: The measuring and checking of finished parts to determine whether they have been made according to specifications.

INTERCHANGEABLE: Refers to a part that has been made to specific dimensions and tolerances and is capable of being fitted in a mechanism in place of a similarly made part.

JIG: A device that holds work in position, and positions and guides the cutting tool.

KEY: A small piece of metal fitted in a shaft and in the hub to prevent a gear or pulley from rotating on a shaft.

KEYWAY: The slot or recess cut in a shaft that holds the key.

KNURLING: Operation that presses grooves into the surface of cylindrical work while it rotates in the lathe.

LAPPING: Technique of producing a smooth, accurate surface to a bearing or other mating part by using fine abrasives.

LAY OUT: To locate and scribe points for machining and forming operations.

MACHINABILITY: How easily the metal can be machined.

MACHINIST: A person who is skilled in the use of machine tools and is capable of making complex machine setups.

MAJOR DIAMETER: The largest diameter of a thread.

MANDREL: A cylindrical piece of steel used to support work for machining operations.

MILL: To remove metal with a rotating cutter on a milling machine.

MILLING MACHINE: A machine that removes metal by means of a rotary cutter.

MINOR DIAMETER: The smallest diameter of a screw thread. Also known as the "root diameter."

NC: Abbreviation for the National Coarse series of screw threads.

NF: Abbreviation for the National Fine series of screw threads.

NONFERROUS: Metals containing no iron.

O.D.: Abbreviation for outside diameter.

OFF CENTER: Eccentric, not accurate.

PEENING: Using the peen (rounded) end of a hammer to decorate the surface of metal.

PEWTER: An alloy of tin (91 percent), copper (1 1/2 percent) and antimony (7 1/2 percent). Modern pewter does not contain lead.

PICKLING: Chemical treatment to remove scale from metal.

PIN PUNCH: A tool made of carbon steel with a long cylindrical end that is used to remove pins and rivets. It can also be employed to punch holes in sheet metal.

PITCH: The distance from a point on one thread to a similar point on the next thread.

PLANISH: To finish or smooth the surface of sheet metal by hammering it lightly with a hammer having a mirror smooth face.

POLISH: To produce a smooth or glossy surface by friction.

PYROMETER: A device for measuring high temperatures. Temperatures are determined by measuring the electric current generated in a thermocouple (two dissimilar metals welded together) as it heats up.

QUENCHING: Rapid cooling by contact with fluids or gases.

REAMER: A cutting tool used to finish a drilled hole to exact size.

RELIEF: An undercut or offset surface which provides clearance.

RISER: A reservoir of molten metal provided to compensate for the contraction of cast metals as they solidify.

ROCKWELL HARDNESS: A method of measuring the hardness of a piece of material using a Rockwell hardness testing machine.

ROOT DIAMETER: The smallest or "minor diameter" of a screw thread.

RUNNER: Channel through which molten metal flows from the sprue to the casting and risers.

SAE: Abbreviation for the Society of Automotive Engineers.

SAFE EDGE: Edge of a file which has no teeth cut in it.

SANDBLAST: To clean surfaces of castings by using sand blown at high pressure.

SCALE: Oxidation caused on metal surfaces by heating them.

SCRIBE: To draw a line with a scriber or other sharp pointed tool.

SCROLL: A curved section widely used for decorative purposes.

SETUP: The term used to describe the positioning of the work, cutting tools and machine attachments on a machine tool.

SHEAR: To cut sheet metal between two blades.

SHIMS: Pieces of sheet metal, available in various thicknesses, used between mating parts to provide proper clearances.

SILICON CARBIDE: The hardest and sharpest of the man-made abrasives.

SLUG: Small piece of metal used as spacing material.

SOLDERING: A method of joining metals by means of a nonferrous filler metal, without fusion of the base metals. Normally carried out at temperatures lower than 800 deg. F.

SPOTFACE: To machine a round spot on a rough surface, usually around drilled hole; to provide seat for screw or bolt head.

SPRUE HOLE: The opening in a mold into which the molten metal is poured.

STANDARD: An accepted base for a uniform system of measurement and quality.

STRAIGHTEDGE: A precision tool used to check the accuracy of flat surfaces.

SURFACE PLATE: A plate of cast iron, cast steel or granite that has one or more surfaces finished to a smooth, flat surface. It is used as a base for layout measurements and inspection.

TAP: Tool used to cut internal threads.

TAP DRILL: The drill used to make a hole prior to tapping.

TAPPING: The operation that produces internal threads with a tap. It may be done by hand or machine. Tapping also refers to the operation of removing molten metal from a furnace.

TEMPLATE: A pattern or guide.

THREAD: The act of cutting a screw thread.

TIN: A soft, shiny metal. It is nontoxic and when used as plating provides excellent protection against corrosion.

TOLERANCE: The permissible deviation from a basic dimension.

TOOL CRIB: A room or area in a machine shop where tools and supplies are stored and dispensed as needed.

TOOLROOM: The area or department where tools, jigs, fixtures and the like are manufactured.

TRAIN: A series of meshed gears.

TRUE: On center.

TURN: To machine on a lathe.

UNIVERSAL CHUCK: A chuck on which all jaws move simultaneously at a uniform rate to automatically center round or hexagonal stock.

VENTS: Narrow openings in molds that permit gases generated during pouring to escape.

WHEEL DRESSER: A device utilized to true the face of a grinding wheel.

WORKING DRAWING: A drawing that gives the machinist the information on how to make and assemble a mechanism.

WROUGHT IRON: Iron with most of the carbon removed. It is tough; easy to bend, and to weld.

X-RAY: An inspection technique used to find flaws in manufactured parts. The part is not damaged by the inspection process.

TABLES

FRACTIONAL INCHES
INTO DECIMAL AND MILLIMETERS

INCH	DECIMAL INCH	MILLIMETER	INCH	DECIMAL INCH	MILLIMETER
1/64	0.0156	0.3967	33/64	0.5162	13.0968
1/32	0.0312	0.7937	17/32	0.5312	13.4937
3/64	0.0468	1.1906	35/64	0.5468	13.8906
1/16	0.0625	1.5875	9/16	0.5625	14.2875
5/64	0.0781	1.9843	37/64	0.5781	14.6843
3/32	0.0937	2.3812	19/32	0.5937	15.0812
7/64	0.1093	2.7781	39/64	0.6093	15.4781
1/8	0.125	3.175	5/8	0.625	15.875
9/64	0.1406	3.5718	41/64	0.6406	16.2718
5/32	0.1562	3.9687	21/32	0.6562	16.6687
11/64	0.1718	4.3656	43/64	0.6718	17.0656
3/16	0.1875	4.7625	11/16	0.6875	17.4625
13/64	0.2031	5.1593	45/64	0.7031	17.8593
7/32	0.2187	5.5562	23/32	0.7187	18.2562
15/64	0.2343	5.9531	47/64	0.7343	18.6531
1/4	0.25	6.5	3/4	0.75	19.05
17/64	0.2656	6.7468	49/64	0.7656	19.4468
9/32	0.2812	7.1437	25/32	0.7812	19.8437
19/64	0.2968	7.5406	51/64	0.7968	20.2406
5/16	0.3125	7.9375	13/16	0.8125	20.6375
21/64	0.3281	8.3343	53/64	0.8281	21.0343
11/32	0.3437	8.7312	27/32	0.8437	21.4312
23/64	0.3593	9.1281	55/64	0.8593	21.8281
3/8	0.375	9.525	7/8	0.875	22.225
25/64	0.3906	9.9218	57/64	0.8906	22.6218
13/32	0.4062	10.3187	29/32	0.9062	23.0187
27/64	0.4218	10.7156	59/64	0.9218	23.4156
7/16	0.4375	11.1125	15/16	0.9375	23.8125
29/64	0.4531	11.5093	61/64	0.9531	24.2093
15/32	0.4687	11.9062	31/32	0.9687	24.6062
31/64	0.4843	12.3031	63/64	0.9843	25.0031
1/2	0.50	12.7	1	1.0000	25.4

Exploring Metalworking

MEASUREMENT SYSTEMS

ENGLISH SYSTEM

MEASURES OF TIME
60 sec. = 1 min.
60 min. = 1 hr.
24 hr. = 1 day
365 dy. = 1 common yr.
366 dy. = 1 leap yr.

DRY MEASURES
2 pt. = 1 qt.
8 qt. = 1 pk.
4 pk. = 1 bu.
2150.42 cu. in. = 1 bu.

MEASURES OF LENGTH
12 in. = 1 ft.
3 ft. = 1 yd.
5 1/2 yd. = 1 rod
320 rods = 1 mile
5,280 ft. = 1 mile
1,760 yd. = 1 mile
6,080 ft. = 1 knot

LIQUID MEASURES
16 fluid oz. = 1 pt.
2 pt. = 1 qt.
32 fl. oz. = 1 qt.
4 qt. = 1 gal.
31 1/2 gal. = 1 bbl.
231 cu. in. = 1 gal.
7 1/2 gal. = 1 cu. ft.

MEASURES OF AREA

144 sq. in. = 1 sq. ft.
9 sq. ft. = 1 sq. yd.
30 1/4 sq. yd. = 1 sq. rod
160 sq. rods = 1 acre
640 acres = 1 sq. mile

MEASURES OF WEIGHT (Avoirdupois)
7,000 grains (gr.) = 1 lb.
16 oz. = 1 lb.
100 lb. = 1 cwt.
2,000 lb. = 1 short ton
2,240 lb. = 1 long ton

MEASURES OF VOLUME
1,728 cu. in. = 1 cu. ft.
27 cu. ft. = 1 cu. yd.
128 cu. ft. = 1 cord

METRIC SYSTEM

The basic unit of the metric system is the meter (m). The meter is exactly 39.37 in. long. This is 3.37 in. longer than the English yard. Units that are multiples or fractional parts of the meter are designated as such by prefixes to the word "meter". For example:

1 millimeter (mm.) = 0.001 meter or 1/1000 meter
1 centimeter (cm.) = 0.01 meter or 1/100 meter
1 decimeter (dm.) = 0.1 meter or 1/10 meter
1 meter (m.)
1 decameter (dkm.) = 10 meters
1 hectometer (hm.) = 100 meters
1 kilometer (km.) = 1000 meters

These prefixes may be applied to any unit of length, weight, volume, etc. The meter is adopted as the basic unit of length, the gram for mass, and the liter for volume.

In the metric system, area is measured in square kilometers (sq. km. or km.²), square centimeters (sq. cm. or cm.²), etc. Volume is commonly measured in cubic centimeters, etc. One liter (1) is equal to 1,000 cubic centimeters.

The metric measurements in most common use are shown in the following tables:

MEASURES OF LENGTH
10 millimeters = 1 centimeter
10 centimeters = 1 decimeter
10 decimeters = 1 meter
1000 meters = 1 kilometer

MEASURES OF WEIGHT
100 milligrams = 1 gram
1000 grams = 1 kilogram
1000 kilograms = 1 metric ton

MEASURES OF VOLUME
1000 cubic centimeters = 1 liter
100 liters = 1 hectoliter

Tables

CONVERSION TABLES

TO REDUCE	MULTIPLY BY	TO REDUCE	MULTIPLY BY
LENGTH			
miles to km.	1.61	km. to miles	0.62
miles to m.	1609.35	m. to miles	0.00062
yd. to m.	0.9144	m. to yd.	1.0936
in. to cm.	2.54	cm. to in.	0.3937
in. to mm.	25.4	mm. to in.	0.03937
VOLUME			
cu. in. to cc. or ml.	16.387	cc. to cu. in.	0.061
cu. in. to l.	0.0164	l to cu. in.	61.024
gal. to l.	3.785	l to gal.	0.264
WEIGHT			
lb. to kg.	0.4536	kg. to lb.	2.2
oz. to gm.	28.35	gm. to oz.	0.0353
gr. to gm.	0.0648	gm. to gr.	15.432

DECIMAL EQUIVALENTS NUMBER SIZE DRILLS

NO.	SIZE OF DRILL IN INCHES	NO.	SIZE OF DRILL IN INCHES	NO.	SIZE OF DRILL IN INCHES	NO.	SIZE OF DRILL IN INCHES
1	.2280	21	.1590	41	.0960	61	.0390
2	.2210	22	.1570	42	.0935	62	.0380
3	.2130	23	.1540	43	.0890	63	.0370
4	.2090	24	.1520	44	.0860	64	.0360
5	.2055	25	.1495	45	.0820	65	.0350
6	.2040	26	.1470	46	.0810	66	.0330
7	.2010	27	.1440	47	.0785	67	.0320
8	.1990	28	.1405	48	.0760	68	.0310
9	.1960	29	.1360	49	.0730	69	.0292
10	.1935	30	.1285	50	.0700	70	.0280
11	.1910	31	.1200	51	.0670	71	.0260
12	.1890	32	.1160	52	.0635	72	.0250
13	.1850	33	.1130	53	.0595	73	.0240
14	.1820	34	.1110	54	.0550	74	.0225
15	.1800	35	.1100	55	.0520	75	.0210
16	.1770	36	.1065	56	.0465	76	.0200
17	.1730	37	.1040	57	.0430	77	.0180
18	.1695	38	.1015	58	.0420	78	.0160
19	.1660	39	.0995	59	.0410	79	.0145
20	.1610	40	.0980	60	.0400	80	.0135

NATIONAL COARSE AND NATIONAL FINE THREADS AND TAP DRILLS

SIZE	THREADS PER INCH	MAJOR DIA.	MINOR DIA.	PITCH DIA.	TAP DRILL 75 PERCENT THREAD	DECIMAL EQUIVALENT	CLEARANCE DRILL	DECIMAL EQUIVALENT
2	56	.0860	.0628	.0744	50	.0700	42	.0935
	64	.0860	.0657	.0759	50	.0700	42	.0935
3	48	.099	.0719	.0855	47	.0785	36	.1065
	56	.099	.0758	.0874	45	.0820	36	.1065
4	40	.112	.0795	.0958	43	.0890	31	.1200
	48	.112	.0849	.0985	42	.0935	31	.1200
6	32	.138	.0974	.1177	36	.1065	26	.1470
	40	.138	.1055	.1218	33	.1130	26	.1470
8	32	.164	.1234	.1437	29	.1360	17	.1730
	36	.164	.1279	.1460	29	.1360	17	.1730
10	24	.190	.1359	.1629	25	.1495	8	.1990
	32	.190	.1494	.1697	21	.1590	8	.1990
12	24	.216	.1619	.1889	16	.1770	1	.2280
	28	.216	.1696	.1928	14	.1820	2	.2210
1/4	20	.250	.1850	.2175	7	.2010	G	.2610
	28	.250	.2036	.2268	3	.2130	G	.2610
5/16	18	.3125	.2403	.2764	F	.2570	21/64	.3281
	24	.3125	.2584	.2854	I	.2720	21/64	.3281
3/8	16	.3750	.2938	.3344	5/16	.3125	25/64	.3906
	24	.3750	.3209	.3479	Q	.3320	25/64	.3906
7/16	14	.4375	.3447	.3911	U	.3680	15/32	.4687
	20	.4375	.3725	.4050	25/64	.3906	29/64	.4531
1/2	13	.5000	.4001	.4500	27/64	.4219	17/32	.5312
	20	.5000	.4350	.4675	29/64	.4531	33/64	.5156
9/16	12	.5625	.4542	.5084	31/64	.4844	19/32	.5937
	18	.5625	.4903	.5264	33/64	.5156	37/64	.5781
5/8	11	.6250	.5069	.5660	17/32	.5312	21/32	.6562
	18	.6250	.5528	.5889	37/64	.5781	41/64	.6406
3/4	10	.7500	.6201	.6850	21/32	.6562	25/32	.7812
	16	.7500	.6688	.7094	11/16	.6875	49/64	.7656
7/8	9	.8750	.7307	.8028	49/64	.7656	29/32	.9062
	14	.8750	.7822	.8286	13/16	.8125	57/64	.8906
1	8	1.0000	.8376	.9188	7/8	.8750	1-1/32	1.0312
	14	1.0000	.9072	.9536	15/16	.9375	1-1/64	1.0156
1-1/8	7	1.1250	.9394	1.0322	63/64	.9844	1-5/32	1.1562
	12	1.1250	1.0167	1.0709	1-3/64	1.0469	1-5/32	1.1562
1-1/4	7	1.2500	1.0644	1.1572	1-7/64	1.1094	1-9/32	1.2812
	12	1.2500	1.1417	1.1959	1-11/64	1.1719	1-9/32	1.2812
1-1/2	6	1.5000	1.2835	1.3917	1-11/32	1.3437	1-17/32	1.5312
	12	1.5000	1.3917	1.4459	1-27/64	1.4219	1-17/32	1.5312

LETTER SIZE DRILLS

A	0.234	J	0.277	S	0.348
B	0.238	K	0.281	T	0.358
C	0.242	L	0.290	U	0.368
D	0.246	M	0.295	V	0.377
E	0.250	N	0.302	W	0.386
F	0.257	O	0.316	X	0.397
G	0.261	P	0.323	Y	0.404
H	0.266	Q	0.332	Z	0.413
I	0.272	R	0.339		

Tables

SCREW THREAD ELEMENTS FOR UNIFIED AND NATIONAL FORM OF THREAD

THREADS PER INCH (n)	PITCH (p) $p = \frac{1}{n}$	SINGLE HEIGHT SUBTRACT FROM BASIC MAJOR DIAMETER TO GET BASIC PITCH DIAMETER	DOUBLE HEIGHT SUBTRACT FROM BASIC MAJOR DIAMETER TO GET BASIC MINOR DIAMETER	83 1/3 PERCENT DOUBLE HEIGHT SUBTRACT FROM BASIC MAJOR DIAMETER TO GET MINOR DIAMETER OF RING GAGE	BASIC WIDTH OF CREST AND ROOT FLAT $\frac{p}{8}$	CONSTANT FOR BEST SIZE WIRE ALSO SINGLE HEIGHT OF 60 DEG. V–THREAD	DIAMETER OF BEST SIZE WIRE
3	.333333	.216506	.43301	.36084	.0417	.28868	.19245
3 1/4	.307692	.199852	.39970	.33309	.0385	.26647	.17765
3 1/2	.285714	.185577	.37115	.30929	.0357	.24744	.16496
4	.250000	.162379	.32476	.27063	.0312	.21651	.14434
4 1/2	.222222	.144337	.28867	.24056	.0278	.19245	.12830
5	.200000	.129903	.25981	.21650	.0250	.17321	.11547
5 1/2	.181818	.118093	.23619	.19682	.0227	.15746	.10497
6	.166666	.108253	.21651	.18042	.0208	.14434	.09623
7	.142857	.092788	.18558	.15465	.0179	.12372	.08248
8	.125000	.081189	.16238	.13531	.0156	.10825	.07217
9	.111111	.072168	.14434	.12028	.0139	.09623	.06415
10	.100000	.064952	.12990	.10825	.0125	.08660	.05774
11	.090909	.059046	.11809	.09841	.0114	.07873	.05249
11 1/2	.086956	.056480	.11296	.09413	.0109	.07531	.05020
12	.083333	.054127	.10826	.09021	.0104	.07217	.04811
13	.076923	.049963	.09993	.08327	.0096	.06662	.04441
14	.071428	.046394	.09279	.07732	.0089	.06186	.04124
16	.062500	.040595	.08119	.06766	.0078	.05413	.03608
18	.055555	.036086	.07217	.06014	.0069	.04811	.03208
20	.050000	.032475	.06495	.05412	.0062	.04330	.02887
22	.045454	.029523	.05905	.04920	.0057	.03936	.02624
24	.041666	.027063	.05413	.04510	.0052	.03608	.02406
27	.037037	.024056	.04811	.04009	.0046	.03208	.02138
28	.035714	.023197	.04639	.03866	.0045	.03093	.02062
30	.033333	.021651	.04330	.03608	.0042	.02887	.01925
32	.031250	.020297	.04059	.03383	.0039	.02706	.01804
36	.027777	.018042	.03608	.03007	.0035	.02406	.01604
40	.025000	.016237	.03247	.02706	.0031	.02165	.01443
44	.022727	.014761	.02952	.02460	.0028	.01968	.01312
48	.020833	.013531	.02706	.02255	.0026	.01804	.01203
50	.020000	.012990	.02598	.02165	.0025	.01732	.01155
56	.017857	.011598	.02320	.01933	.0022	.01546	.01031
60	.016666	.010825	.02165	.01804	.0021	.01443	.00962
64	.015625	.010148	.02030	.01691	.0020	.01353	.00902
72	.013888	.009021	.01804	.01503	.0017	.01203	.00802
80	.012500	.008118	.01624	.01353	.0016	.01083	.00722
90	.011111	.007217	.01443	.01202	.0014	.00962	.00642
96	.010417	.006766	.01353	.01127	.0013	.00902	.00601
100	.010000	.006495	.01299	.01082	.0012	.00866	.00577
120	.008333	.005413	.01083	.00902	.0010	.00722	.00481

Using the Best Size Wires, the measurement over three wires minus the Constant for Best Size Wire equals the Pitch Diameter.

MACHINE SCREW AND CAP SCREW HEADS

FILLISTER HEAD

SIZE	A	B	C	D
#8	.260	.141	.042	.060
#10	.302	.164	.048	.072
1/4	3/8	.205	.064	.087
5/16	7/16	.242	.077	.102
3/8	9/16	.300	.086	.125
1/2	3/4	.394	.102	.168
5/8	7/8	.500	.128	.215
3/4	1	.590	.144	.258
1	1 5/16	.774	.182	.352

FLAT HEAD

SIZE	A	B	C	D
#8	.320	.092	.043	.037
#10	.372	.107	.048	.044
1/4	1/2	.146	.064	.063
5/16	5/8	.183	.072	.078
3/8	3/4	.220	.081	.095
1/2	7/8	.220	.102	.090
5/8	1 1/8	.293	.128	.125
3/4	1 3/8	.366	.144	.153

ROUND HEAD

SIZE	A	B	C	D
#8	.297	.113	.044	.067
#10	.346	.130	.048	.073
1/4	7/16	.1831	.064	.107
5/16	9/16	.236	.072	.150
3/8	5/8	.262	.081	.160
1/2	13/16	.340	.102	.200
5/8	1	.422	.128	.255
3/4	1 1/4	.526	.144	.320

HEXAGON HEAD

SIZE	A	B	C
1/4	.494	.170	7/16
5/16	.564	.215	1/2
3/8	.635	.246	9/16
1/2	.846	.333	3/4
5/8	1.058	.411	15/16
3/4	1.270	.490	1 1/8
7/8	1.482	.566	1 5/16
1	1.693	.640	1 1/2

SOCKET HEAD

SIZE	A	B	C
#8	.265	.164	1/8
#10	5/16	.190	5/32
1/4	3/8	1/4	3/16
5/16	7/16	5/16	7/32
3/8	9/16	3/8	5/16
7/16	5/8	7/16	5/16
1/2	3/4	1/2	3/8
5/8	7/8	5/8	1/2
3/4	1	3/4	9/16
7/8	1 1/8	7/8	9/16
1	1 5/16	1	5/8

Tables

PHYSICAL PROPERTIES OF METALS

METAL	SYMBOL	SPECIFIC GRAVITY	SPECIFIC HEAT	MELTING POINT*		LBS. PER CUBIC INCH
				DEG. C	DEG. F.	
Aluminum (Cast)	Al	2.56	.2185	658	1217	.0924
Aluminum (Rolled).	Al	2.71	–	–	–	.0978
Antimony	Sb	6.71	.051	630	1166	.2424
Bismuth	Bi	9.80	.031	271	520	.3540
Boron.	B	2.30	.3091	2300	4172	.0831
Brass.	–	8.51	.094	–	–	.3075
Cadmium.	Cd	8.60	.057	321	610	.3107
Calcium	Ca	1.57	.170	810	1490	.0567
Carbon	C	2.22	.165	–	–	.0802
Chromium	Cr	6.80	.120	1510	2750	.2457
Cobalt	Co	8.50	.110	1490	2714	.3071
Copper.	Cu	8.89	.094	1083	1982	.3212
Columbium . . .	Cb	8.57	–	1950	3542	.3096
Gold	Au	19.32	.032	1063	1945	.6979
Iridium	Ir	22.42	.033	2300	4170	.8099
Iron	Fe	7.86	.110	1520	2768	.2634
Iron (Cast) . . .	Fe	7.218	.1298	1375	2507	.2605
Iron (Wrought) .	Fe	7.70	.1138	1500–1600	2732–2912	.2779
Lead	Pb	11.37	.031	327	621	.4108
Lithium	Li	.057	.941	186	367	.0213
Magnesium . . .	Mg	1.74	.250	651	1204	.0629
Manganese . . .	Mn	8.00	.120	1225	2237	.2890
Mercury	Hg	13.59	.032	38.7	37.7	.4909
Molybdenum. . .	Mo	10.2	.0647	2620	4748	.368
Monel Metal. . .	–	8.87	.127	1360	2480	.320
Nickel	Ni	8.80	.130	1452	2646	.319
Phosphorus . . .	P	1.82	.177	43	111.4	.0657
Platinum.	Pt	21.50	.033	1755	3191	.7767
Potassium. . . .	K	0.87	.170	62	144	.0314
Selenium.	Se	4.81	.084	220	428	.174
Silicon.	Si	2.40	.1762	1427	2600	.087
Silver.	Ag	10.53	.056	961	1761	.3805
Sodium	Na	0.97	.290	97	207	.0350
Steel	–	7.858	.1175	1330–1378	2372–2532	.2839
Strontium	Sr	2.54	.074	–	–	.0918
Sulphur.	S	2.07	.175	115	235.4	.075
Tantalum	Ta	10.80	–	2850	5160	.3902
Tin	Sn	7.29	.056	232	450	.2634
Titanium.	Ti	5.3	.130	1900	3450	.1915
Tungsten	W	19.10	.033	3000	5432	.6900
Uranium	U	18.70	–	–	–	.6755
Vanadium	V	5.50	–	1730	3146	.1987
Zinc	Zn	7.19	.094	419	786	.2598

* Circular of the Bureau of Standards No. 35, Department of Commerce and Labor.

CONVERSION TABLE
METRIC TO ENGLISH

WHEN YOU KNOW: ⬇	MULTIPLY BY: * = Exact		TO FIND: ⬇
	VERY ACCURATE	APPROXIMATE	
LENGTH			
millimeters	0.0393701	0.04	inches
centimeters	0.3937008	0.4	inches
meters	3.280840	3.3	feet
meters	1.093613	1.1	yards
kilometers	0.621371	0.6	miles
WEIGHT			
grains	0.00228571	0.0023	ounces
grams	0.03527396	0.035	ounces
kilograms	2.204623	2.2	pounds
tonnes	1.1023113	1.1	short tons
VOLUME			
milliliters		0.2	teaspoons
milliliters	0.06667	0.067	tablespoon
milliliters	0.03381402	0.03	fluid ounces
liters	61.02374	61.024	cubic inches
liters	2.113376	2.1	pints
liters	1.056688	1.06	quarts
liters	0.26417205	0.26	gallons
liters	0.03531467	0.35	cubic feet
cubic meters	61023.74	61023.7	cubic inches
cubic meters	35.31467	35.0	cubic feet
cubic meters	1.3079506	1.3	cubic yards
cubic meters	264.17205	264.0	gallons
AREA			
square centimeters	0.1550003	0.16	square inches
square centimeters	0.00107639	0.001	square feet
square meters	10.76391	10.8	square feet
square meters	1.195990	1.2	square yards
square kilometers		0.4	square miles
hectares	2.471054	2.5	acres
TEMPERATURE			
Celsius	*9/5 (then add 32)		Fahrenheit

Tables

CONVERSION TABLE
ENGLISH TO METRIC

WHEN YOU KNOW:	MULTIPLY BY: * = Exact		TO FIND:
	VERY ACCURATE	APPROXIMATE	
LENGTH			
inches	* 25.4		millimeters
inches	* 2.54		centimeters
feet	* 0.3048		meters
feet	* 30.48		centimeters
yards	* 0.9144	0.9	meters
miles	* 1.609344	1.6	kilometers
WEIGHT			
grains	15.43236	15.4	grams
ounces	* 28.349523125	28.0	grams
ounces	* 0.028349523125	.028	kilograms
pounds	* 0.45359237	0.45	kilograms
short ton	* 0.90718474	0.9	tonnes
VOLUME			
teaspoon		5.0	milliliters
tablespoon		15.0	milliliters
fluid ounces	29.57353	30.0	milliliters
cups		0.24	liters
pints	* 0.473176473	0.47	liters
quarts	* 0.946352946	0.95	liters
gallons	* 3.785411784	3.8	liters
cubic inches	* 0.016387064	0.02	liters
cubic feet	* 0.028316846592	0.03	cubic meters
cubic yards	* 0.764554857984	0.76	cubic meters
AREA			
square inches	* 6.4516	6.5	square centimeter
square feet	* 0.09290304	0.09	square meters
square yards	* 0.83612736	0.8	square meters
square miles		2.6	square kilometer
acres	* 0.40468564224	0.4	hectares
TEMPERATURE			
Fahrenheit	* 5/9 (after subtracting 32)		Celsius

A. D. Althouse, C. H. Turnquist, and W. A. Bowditch: MODERN WELDING, Goodheart-Willcox Co., Inc., South Holland, Illinois.

Arthur D. Anderson: A DESIGNER'S NOTEBOOK, McKnight and McKnight Publishing Co., Bloomington, Illinois.

T. Gardner Boyd: METALWORKING, Goodheart-Willcox Co., Inc., South Holland, Ill.

Leroy F. Bruce: SHEET METAL SHOP PRACTICES, American Technical Society, Chicago, Illinois.

John L. Feirer: GENERAL METALS, McGraw-Hill Book Co., New York, New York.

John L. Feirer and John R. Lindbeck: INDUSTRIAL ARTS METALWORK, Chas. A. Bennett Co., Inc., Peoria, Illinois.

Carl Gerbacht and Frank E. Robinson: UNDERSTANDING AMERICA'S INDUSTRIES, McKnight and McKnight Publishing Co., Bloomington, Illinois.

Henry J. Kauffman: MACHINE SHOP AND FOUNDRY PROJECTS, McKnight and McKnight Publishing Co., Bloomington, Illinois.

Charles F. Kettering and Allen Orth: AMERICAN BATTLE FOR ABUNDANCE, General Motors Corp., Detroit, Michigan.

Roy E. Knight: MACHINE SHOP PROJECTS, McKnight and McKnight Publishing Co., Bloomington, Illinois.

John R. Lindbeck: DESIGNING TODAY'S MANUFACTURED PRODUCTS, McKnight and McKnight Publishing Co., Bloomington, Ill.

O. A. Ludwig and W. J. McCarthy: METALWORKING TECHNOLOGY AND PRACTICE, McKnight and McKnight Publishing Co., Bloomington, Illinois.

Delmar W. Olson: INDUSTRIAL ARTS FOR THE GENERAL SHOP, Prentice-Hall, Inc., Englewood Cliffs, New Jersey.

PROCEDURE HANDBOOK OF ARC WELDING DESIGN AND PRACTICE, The Lincoln Electric Co., Cleveland, Ohio.

C. Vernon Siegner: ART METALS, Goodheart-Willcox Co., Inc., South Holland, Ill.

Robert E. Smith: FORGING AND WELDING, McKnight and McKnight Publishing Co., Bloomington, Illinois.

Robert E. Smith: UNITS IN ETCHING, SPINNING, RAISING AND TOOLING METAL, McKnight and McKnight Publishing Co., Bloomington, Illinois.

F. E. Tustison, R. F. Kranzusch and D. C. Blide: METALWORK ESSENTIALS, The MacMillan Company, Riverside, New Jersey.

John R. Walker: MACHINING FUNDAMENTALS, Goodheart-Willcox Co., Inc., South Holland, Illinois.

John R. Walker: METAL PROJECTS - BOOK 1, Goodheart-Willcox Co., Inc., South Holland, Illinois.

John R. Walker: MODERN METALWORKING, Goodheart-Willcox Co., Inc., South Holland, Illinois.

Acknowledgments

While it would be a most pleasant task, it would be impossible for one person to develop the material included in this text by visiting the various industries represented and observing, studying and taking the photos first hand.

My sincere thanks to those who helped in the gathering of the necessary material, information and photographs. Their cooperation was most appreciated.

John R. Walker
Bel Air, Maryland

INDEX

Index

Index